Local Subsidies for Industry

Local Subsidies for Industry

BY

JOHN E. MOES

Chapel Hill

THE UNIVERSITY OF NORTH CAROLINA PRESS

Preface

At the December 1959 meeting of the American Economic Association, Professor Machlup spoke the following words of wisdom: "The charges of 'unrealism' which politicians level against economic theory stem less from its technical language or from its esoteric assumptions than, I submit, from its concern with total strangers, somewhere, sometime, and its disregard of 'my good friends' here and now."[1] Economists, therefore, to be more effective, might more often than has hitherto been the case deviate from their habit of tendering advice to legislators at the national level and seek for means of implementing desirable policies at the state level or that of local governmental units. For at these levels there may exist greater sympathy, because of greater direct concern, with certain propositions an economist may make inspired by his personal concern for the national good or that of the world and means of implementation as well. Frequently this may have to take the form of measures designed to offset impositions by the national government that are harmful to the economy at large and particularly so to the regions in question. The inhabitants of these regions may be "total strangers" to the national government with respect to a particular issue because of unfavorable power relations in a given political reality; as long as this situation persists the economist's remonstrances addressed to the legislators at the national level, while certainly not totally useless, are not likely to be heeded. The economist may then find a more rewarding task in advising regional and local governments regarding what it may be within their power to do in order to create conditions desired by these governments and that are also in the national interest. This type of regional economics may be sharply distinguished from the regional economics which seeks how

1. "Relations between Economic Theory and Economic Policy: A Discussion," *American Economic Review,* L (May, 1960), 52.

an area may benefit at the expense of the greater whole through the enactment of measures at the national level; to a large extent the need to develop the former arises because the latter *is*, in practice, well developed. Regionalism, just as nationalism, may be constructive or destructive. Examples of the latter type we shall encounter in this work; the intention of this book is to make a contribution toward the development of the former type of regional economics.

However, this work is not conceived merely as a study of a particular region's problems, although at times, because of its emphasis on the Southern United States, it may give that impression. As far as empirical material regarding organized local effort to attract industry by means of financial inducements—the subject it is dealing with—is concerned, it draws upon sources and presents evidence pertaining to other parts of the United States as well. In that sense its scope is nationwide, but the basic underlying problem, that of un- and underemployment, is universal and occurs in its most pressing form in the underdeveloped countries. The utilization of their labor force to the fullest possible extent is of obvious importance to countries engaged in an effort to raise their standard of living, and accordingly in the literature on economic development much thought has been given to the possibilities of effectively absorbing the underemployed in the production process. The analysis applied in this book reflects my interest in and previous work on underdeveloped countries and consists in part of an application to an American setting of an apparatus familiar to specialists in development problems.

But to bring out the possibilities for a practical solution which the American environment offers, certain aspects of the theory had to be further developed and elaborated. This was particularly so because of the stress on *local* self-help in the present treatise: concern with decentralized action has given rise to a model of competitive subsidization contained in abstract outline in Chapter VI and further discussed in subsequent chapters. While each environment has its own possibilities and limitations, the theory of decentralized subsidization of industry as well as certain practical considerations relating to the local approach may contain elements that are of interest to those concerned with economic development and the problem of un- and underemployment in general. It may further be pointed out that, contrary to the writings of many authors who draw a sharp distinction between the type of unemployment that is endemic in most underdeveloped countries and that which occasionally plagues the more advanced industrialized nations, the present work takes a unified view of the unemployment problem.

Since my opinion on the subsidization of industry by local communities in the United States—due to the background of this study sketched above no doubt—is squarely opposed to the opinion prevailing among authors who have specifically expressed themselves on the subject, this work is very critical of the existing literature. This can unfortunately not be helped; one cannot in a work which it is hoped will have some practical impact, simply state one's position without making any attempt to deal with the extensive body of literature on the subject and the various objections raised against the subsidization practice therein—and still make a convincing case. The only reaction to such a procedure, if it would evoke any reaction at all, would probably be a reiteration of these various objections. Thus I have made an effort to state my position as clearly as possible in its philosophical foundation and as it is anchored in economic theory, without neglecting the more humdrum task of taking up the opponents of the subsidization practice on every practical detail they have raised.

While writing this book I received financial support from the Inter-University Committee for Economic Research on the South during the academic year 1959-60 and the summer of 1960 and from the Institute for Research in the Social Sciences at the University of Virginia during the summer of 1959. This aid is hereby gratefully acknowledged.

For his support and encouragement of my work in every possible way and for his stimulating intellectual impact, my greatest debt is to Professor James M. Buchanan of the University of Virginia. Professors Irma Adelman of Stanford University, James A. Morris of the University of South Carolina, and Gordon Tullock of the University of South Carolina read the entire manuscript and made many suggestions for improvement. I am also grateful to Professors Anthony Downs of the University of Chicago, Ernst W. Swanson of North Carolina State College, Lorin A. Thompson of the University of Virginia, and Leland B. Yeager of the University of Virginia for helpful comments and discussions. Professor Thompson in his capacity of director of the Bureau of Population and Economic Research at the University of Virginia also provided aid in the person of William Craig Stubblebine, my research assistant, whose efficiency and organizational ability probably prevented the foundering of the project in administrative chaos. Without Mr. Stubblebine's help and initiative I certainly could not have mustered anywhere near the amount of source material that underlies this study. Miss Ruth Richie was an ideal typist who also corrected my English. As anyone can see, I did not always listen to her. Last but not least, thanks are due to Professor Charles L. Quittmeyer of the University of Virginia, with whom I roamed the southern Appalachians in the summer of 1959 in pursuit of first-hand information for our diverse projects and who showed me how to get it, and to Glynn Williams, who assisted me during subsequent field work throughout the South. Finally, I am grateful to all those—correspondents, librarians, and those interviewed—who were good enough to answer questions and to provide me with material.

Addis Ababa
March, 1961

JOHN E. MOES

Contents

Contents

Local Subsidies for Industry

CHAPTER I

Theoretical Justification of Subsidies

Local subsidies and rigidities in the labor market. There is in the United States, especially in the South, a widespread practice of attracting industry to a certain locality or state by means of special inducements or subsidies. The word "subsidy" in this context should be interpreted broadly, for often the methods used do not involve outright payments (although this is not unknown), but rather the leasing of sites or plants at a low rental, tax exemption, and other devices, all of which have in common that the enterprise is not required to pay the full value of property transferred to it or services rendered. These practices are generally condemned for various reasons that will be examined in this treatise. It will be shown that the lines of reasoning leading to this prevailing adverse opinion are fallacious, and a general case will be made in favor of local subsidies to industry. In broad outline, the argument is to the effect that when circumstances make the subsidization of industry attractive to a local community, conditions are also such that this type of action will bring the economy as a whole closer to the social welfare optimum as usually defined. Thus the case is analogous to that in favor of competition between individuals and enterprises, and it will in fact be demonstrated that competition between local groups or municipalities arises as a result of imperfections in the labor market and tends to mitigate the effect of wage rigidities.

Among the undesirable effects of wage rigidity are unemployment, underemployment, and geographic displacement of people who would prefer to stay in their own locality if they could find a job at a wage equal to or lower than what they can earn elsewhere, but who are forced to migrate in the absence of such an opportunity. This latter observation points to a factor that weighs heavily with the population of regions that have experienced a good deal of out-migration and which is one of the main considerations in local attempts to attract industry. Of course conditions in localities that do not offer sufficient employment opportunity would be worse if those in need of jobs could not migrate to other places, but what we should strive for is that people be given a free choice between accepting employment at home at a relatively low wage and migrating to another locality where they can earn more.

At this point it is well to remember that the concept of "pure competition" is not only an abstract analytical device but also describes a state of affairs which is ideal in many respects. For its social implications the most serious deviation from this condition in our present-day society is found in the labor market. If wages were completely flexible, a wage would always be established that clears the market and unemployment would be absent.[1] The local impact of a change in the demand for labor would be distributed between all, and adaptation would be accomplished without any serious disruptions. Existing industries could be retained or new ones promptly attracted on the basis of wage competition, and a fall in the local wage level would be reflected in a fall in the price of locally produced goods and rentals. Thus real wages would fall less than money wages, property owners sharing in the decline. Migration would be induced by wage differentials between localities, but those desirous to remain in their old surroundings would be under no compulsion to leave as employment opportunity would exist throughout the economy. Similarly, wage differentials between occupations would be reduced to a minimum consistent with differences in skills and preferences of the labor force, since transfer from one occupation to another would always be possible for those possessing the required qualifications. There would be both social security and opportunity.

The fact that we have come to accept the unemployment of some 4 to 5 percent of the labor force as normal indicates to what extent this country has allowed itself to drift away from these ideal conditions. In addition, a sizeable proportion of our labor force, especially in the South, is forced to remain in farming and other occupations where labor productivity is extremely low; there are depressed areas which suffer from perpetual unemployment; and last but not least, each year a large number of people is forced to seek employment away from home. In this book I hope to convince the reader that competition

1. Except in very poor and overpopulated regions where the marginal productivity of labor may be zero or very close to it. Also, there might still be some fractional unemployment, but this would be reduced to insignificant proportions.

between localities in attracting industry by means of subsidies may go a long way in rectifying these conditions, which are in no small part the result of labor policies pursued at the federal level.

The dual function of wages. To state the case in favor of subsidies in a general fashion, it is necessary to discuss the essential nature of wage rigidity and the forms which unemployment may assume. First, we must recognize that wage rigidity in the downward direction also occurs in the total absence of collusion among workers and government wage-fixing. If this were not true there would in such markets either be full employment, or the wage level would fall to the point where the wage would be just sufficient to compensate the worker for the physical energy expended on the job. We know of course from experience that in competitive labor markets unemployment may be widespread at wages well above this level. In advanced societies this is observed during depressions and in depressed areas, while in low-income countries unemployment is a perennial problem, inherent in the low marginal productivity of labor.

That wages under these circumstances do not either clear the market or fall to near-zero stems from the fact, pointed out by Gitlow, that wages have two functions: (1) to allocate productive resources; and (2) to provide the incentive to work which is necessary in a free society.[2] A question then immediately arises as to the involuntary nature of unemployment that is the result of inability or unwillingness of the employer to pay wages that will give the worker this incentive. This question has been discussed by Rees, who suggests the possibility that the unemployed workers are willing to accept wages below the prevailing rate but that employers refuse to exercise their power to lower wages.[3] I think that this is correct but it does not imply, as Rees concludes, that employers by and large do not maximize profits in the short run. Wages and labor cost are not the same thing: to labor cost there is another dimension, namely the amount of work the employee will do for the money he is being paid. When the worker feels that the pay is satisfactory he will cooperate, labor turnover tends to be reduced, the employer may be able to attract and keep superior workers and will meet with public approval. All this increases productivity and thus tends to reduce labor cost. But high rates of themselves work in the opposite direction, and the employer, therefore, must weigh two offsetting effects of any change in the wage rate.

2. A. L. Gitlow, "Wages and the Allocation of Employment," *Southern Economic Journal,* XXI (July, 1954), 62.

3. Albert Rees, "Wage Determination and Unvoluntary Unemployment," *Journal of Political Economy,* LIX (April, 1951), 143-53.

During periods of rapidly changing price level the money illusion enters into the picture, and this helps explain why even in a competitive labor market depressions may be quite severe and prolonged (the expected wage being the wage earned in the past) while inflation may help alleviate unemployment.[4]

It may be objected that such unemployment should still be considered voluntary, for the theory implies that while the workers may be willing to come to the premises and stay a certain number of hours at wages lower than those prevailing, they refuse to do a normal day's work.[5] Be this as it may, the situation is entirely different from one in which the employer would be unable to hire a number of laborers sufficient to accomplish the task at hand. The crucial point is not that at these low rates the labor force would be lacking in quantity, but that paying wages lower than the prevailing ones increases labor cost. Moreover, in such a situation there would undoubtedly be many individuals, perhaps even the great majority of the unemployed, who would be keen to put in their best efforts at the lower wage level, since they would become better off when hired. However, the wage decrease would certainly be resented by those who were already employed at the time it came into effect, a general spirit of discontent would come to prevail, and the result would be bad for the employer.

In the low-income countries a physical factor may in addition be involved. At wages below the going norm the worker may simply become physically incapable of performing his task in a satisfactory manner. In other words, it may be physiologically impossible to reduce labor cost by lowering real wages. The involuntary nature of unemployment can then, of course, not be questioned. In none of these cases can paying lower wages solve the unemployment problem, for this would not reduce but increase labor cost.[6]

4. It should be realized that this psychological factor in the presence of unemployment is necessary to explain any "lagging behind" of money wages under inflationary conditions (except for sheer inertia). As soon as full employment is reached real wages are more likely to rise under the impact of inflation than to decline. This effect would result from the prevailing bookkeeping practice under which profits are computed on the basis of historical cost rather than replacement cost—a practice which in times of inflation tends to exaggerate profits and therefore also profit expectations. Hence employers bid against each other in the market for labor on the basis of an exaggerated notion regarding labor's marginal product value. Then, when the inflation ceases, real wages have reached a level inconsistent with full employment and which it is hard to reduce, and unemployment results.

5. This point was raised by Gordon Tullock.

6. The fact that wages may be rigid in the downward direction for good reasons unconnected with wage fixing by government or labor organizations is sometimes

Since the labor force in each enterprise tends to be expanded to the point where labor cost is equal to the marginal revenue product of the "last" employee, the elimination of unemployment requires that labor cost and the marginal revenue product of the "last" worker in the labor force (the size of which is of course itself a function of the wage rate) be brought in line with each other. It does not follow, however, that the remedy in concrete terms is the same in all cases. Where deflation aggravates the problem, a necessary part of a sensible solution is to cause the price level to return to the pre-deflation level by means of an expansion of the money supply. This is the Keynesian case, which needs no further elaboration. Whether beyond that monetary policy, notably a policy of inflation, can do any good is very doubtful. If inflation is adopted as a deliberate policy to cope with problems of unemployment, the money veil is likely to wear so thin that it can no longer hide anything, least of all the loss in real wages workers may be suffering. As a result entrepreneurs have to adjust money wages promptly in order to avoid widespread dissatisfaction and the fall in productivity to which this leads. When a certain rate of change in the price level comes to be the expected thing, then the advantages proponents of an easy money policy claim can materialize only when this rate of change is itself continuously increased. (And, if we can conceive of this going on for some time, this would also come to be expected, so that successively higher derivatives of the price level with respect to time become relevant.) Thus, ultimately nothing may be gained, the net effect being the disruption of income distribution which inflation causes.

In poverty-stricken areas the effect may be even more serious. There, as we have seen, prevailing wages may be so low that it is

overlooked. Thus Henry C. Simons, in an essay (*Economic Policy for a Free Society* [Chicago: University of Chicago Press, 1948], p. 141) with which otherwise I find myself in profound agreement (also with respect to the spirit of the quoted passage), says: "We imply that any wage is excessive if more qualified workers are obtainable at that wage than are employed—provided only that the industry is reasonably competitive as among firms. Reduction of rates would permit workers to enter who otherwise would be compelled to accept employment less attractive to them and less productive for the community or to accept involuntary unemployment. This amounts to saying that any relative wage may be presumed to be too high if it requires the support of force (organization) or law." However, to take a simple case, when the marginal productivity of labor in the economy as a whole is zero one cannot reasonably argue that any wage above zero is "excessive." It is excessive only in the sense that it interferes with the allocation function of the market, but this cannot be improved by reducing wages that already minimize labor cost. The fact that wages must also serve to keep the workers at least reasonably satisfied (and capable of functioning biologically) should not be played down in any discussion of this subject, if only because it will always prevail in the considerations of the employer that determine his wage policy.

biologically impossible to reduce labor cost by lowering real wages. In that case any loss in real wages that workers may sustain under the cover of the money illusion (which also blinds the eyes of the employer) or through mere inertia will lead to an *increase* in labor cost and a fall in total output[7]—the exact opposite of its effect in the high-income countries. This is perhaps a case in which minimum wages geared to an escalator would be justifiable in principle! Needless to say that it is better to avoid the inflation, at least on this score.

From these considerations it may be seen that an approach to unemployment problems consisting of an attempt to reduce the real wage level is not very promising. The perennial problem of unemployment in a free exchange economy may be seriously aggravated by a failure of the monetary authorities to maintain price stability or in the presence of conditions that permit labor unions to push up real wages through the exercise of monopoly power, but beyond this there remains the fact that a perfect functioning of the labor market such as we usually associate with "perfect competition" can never come about spontaneously. We have seen that the basic problem arises because of the dual purpose that wages serve: to allocate labor and to induce the worker to apply himself. The inducement function may interfere with the allocation function. The former requires that the worker be paid a certain amount for his services, which, for psychological and sometimes also physiological reasons, it is especially difficult if not impossible to reduce. But the allocation function requires that entrepreneurial labor cost be perfectly flexible. The only solution, then, is to drive a wedge between what the entrepreneur must pay and what the laborer receives. This is where subsidies may play a role.

Forms of unemployment. Unemployment may be open or "disguised." Disguised unemployment exists where no specific members of the labor force can be singled out as being idle, but where, most often in family enterprise, workers could be withdrawn without any marked effect on production. All or most members of the labor force may be actually idle part of the time or they may busy themselves with all sorts of activities that are hardly productive at all.[8] Disguised

7. The effect upon employment is uncertain. Since the cost of labor increases, less labor will be demanded. But the cost of labor increases because the amount of labor performed per man-hour decreases (in greater proportion than the wage rate), and therefore, if employment is measured in man-hours, it may go either up or down. Even if it goes up this merely means, of course, that more people toil longer hours while producing less.

8. A striking example of the latter appeared some time ago in a newspaper account of the great labor mobilization in communist China. Obviously impressed, the reporter described how nowadays in China six people do jobs that used to be done by two and

unemployment may be institutionalized to the extent that entrepreneurs, for reasons of social prestige, are obligated to employ a
partly redundant labor force. A society in which it prevails is usually
characterized by an abundance of domestic servants, petty trade, and
frequent religious holidays.

In the United States disguised unemployment is mostly found in
the South on a large number of small-scale farms. The reason for its
occurrence, as elsewhere, is the lack of employment opportunity in
other occupations. On the family farm everyone contributes his share
in the work and lives, but labor productivity, especially at the margin,
is extremely low in many rural areas. This frequently leads to idleness because further effort applied to the farm is so unrewarding that
it is not worthwhile. Where it does not—people working what may
be considered a regular working day, or even more—there is of
course no underemployment in the common sense connotation of the
term. However, from the point of view of economic analysis there
are good reasons to classify workers in an occupation where the
marginal productivity of labor is low compared to what it is in other
occupations as underemployed, provided that at least some of these
workers are willing to transfer and have the necessary qualifications.
For neither in this case nor in that characterized by outright idleness
is the labor force effectively used,[9] while the cause of the waste is also
the same: lack of employment opportunity in the high-productivity
occupations, resulting from wage rigidity. Accordingly, in the literature on underdeveloped countries the term "disguised unemployment"
has long been extended to areas of relatively low labor productivity.
In this view open unemployment may be seen as a "low-wage" occupation in which the marginal productivity of labor is zero (but for which
the worker nevertheless may receive payment in the form of a dole)—
the extreme case in a spectrum ranging from idleness to full employment in the sense that every qualified worker can find a job in the
occupation of his choosing.

*Labor productivity in agriculture, industrial wages, and the transfer
of workers.* In a primarily agrarian society, such as the South was not
so long ago, a worker's wage expectation may be closely related to
average labor productivity on the "typical" farm from which he is

how in the cities youthful pioneers are posted on street corners to tell the people not
to spit.

9. This similarity has been stressed by Joan Robinson in "Disguised Unemployment,"
Economic Journal, XLVI (June, 1936), 225-37.

recruited.[10] For it is average rather than marginal productivity that determines the level of living to which the worker is accustomed, and which therefore he comes to consider as a reasonable standard of remuneration for effort. It may be possible to attract workers at wages below that level when the marginal productivity of labor on the farm is very low, but as we have seen it is in the employer's interest to meet the standards of the society. Moreover, if accepting industrial employment means that the worker ceases to be part of the farm household it may not even be possible to find a sufficient number of workers willing to take a job at less than average farm income, for the transfer would then mean a reduction in the worker's level of living. For these reasons wages in industry in a society in which labor is in the process of transferring from agriculture to industry are usually well above the marginal productivity of labor in agriculture and may be above average productivity in that occupation.

There must of course be an incentive for workers to make the change, and therefore in a dynamic sense (because adjustment to a new equilibrium cannot be instantaneous) a limited differential is necessary or the transfer would not be implemented at all. Here one is thinking of the usual differential in wages between an expanding and a contracting industry. The factors analyzed above, however, are of a different nature. They do not merely point to a limited differential in marginal labor productivity between agriculture and industry necessary to further a smooth transfer of workers from the former to the latter, but to the establishment of an effective wage minimum in industry that impedes further expansion long before the marginal productivity of labor has fallen to anywhere near that in agriculture. This then may well cause a situation in which the bottleneck to the transfer of labor from agriculture to industry is lack of employment opportunity, not a lack of capable workers willing to transfer at the existing differential. That in the South this is true in reality is well-known, but this is also due to other factors that keep industrial wages high.

Given the fact that industrial wages cannot fall below a certain level, whether and how soon underemployment in agriculture will be eliminated depends entirely on the dynamics of the situation. The level of investment determines the rate at which new jobs are created

10. This may change in the course of time under the impact of minimum wage legislation and union activity. At present we still abstract from these factors, but they are introduced in the following sections. Due to their existence we cannot expect any simple correlations between farm incomes and industrial wages.

in industry, while technological change in agriculture and natural growth of the rural population continuously reinforce the number of potential applicants. This may eventually pull up farm incomes (and the marginal productivity of labor in farming) to the level of wages paid in industry (which of course themselves may be boosted as the process goes on) or it may not. Data presented in Chapter II indicate that lately the gap has been widening. Such a situation is completely different from one in which, at any given time, relative wages tend to adjust so as to bring about a full employment equilibrium in which, given worker preferences, all labor is effectively used and nobody has an incentive to change.

Minimum wage legislation and unions. The factors so far discussed are inherent in the market mechanism under the conditions visualized. But in America today the problem is seriously aggravated by the imposition of a federal minimum wage and especially by the action of labor unions, which in some occupations has resulted in preposterous wage boosts considering labor market conditions in general. In either case the effect on the wage level extends far beyond the individuals immediately affected. Firms have to maintain certain wage differentials, corresponding to skill, seniority, etc., in order to keep their labor force contented, and when the wages of their lowest-paid employees are raised due to the imposition of a nation-wide federal minimum wage, they must also raise the wages of the others.[11] In a good many instances this has led to immediately visible unemployment, but in an expanding economy like that of the South the harm done often escapes direct observation. When the tendency is toward expansion of the labor force in industry, then minimum wages may merely counteract this tendency, condemning workers who would otherwise have found employment at wages attractive to them to remain in farming and other low-income occupations. And it cannot be emphasized enough that a nation-wide minimum wage discriminates against those regions most directly affected by it, to wit, the low-income

11. For instance, when the $1.00 wage minimum went into effect, average earnings in many Southern industries (e.g. work clothing, lumbering, furniture, and electronics components) were $1.00 per hour or less, including piecework incentives. When the base rates had to be increased to $1.00, earnings throughout the plants were also forced to rise since the piecework incentive program still demanded a bonus for fast workers. As a result average earnings in many apparel plants were inflated from about $1.00 per hour to $1.10 to $1.15. See L. Clinton Hoch, "The Location Decision," a paper presented before the Semi-Annual Conference, Production Executives Division, The National Association of Shirt, Pajama and Sportswear Manufacturers, New York, June 20, 1957, pp. 5-6 (mimeographed).

regions in the country, notably the South.[12] Within these regions,
the lowest-income groups (small-scale farmers, etc.) are the immediate
victims. A minimum wage tends to increase the gap likely to exist
already, for fundamental reasons analyzed above, between the incomes
of those lucky enough to find industrial employment and those in the
low-income occupations not covered. While enacted in the name of
social justice and equality (although not necessarily for that reason),
the effect is to perpetuate inequality at the expense of the poorest in
our society and to interfere with the country's industrial expansion.[13]
In this context may also be mentioned the Walsh-Healey Public Contracts Act and the Davis-Bacon Act under which minimum wages are
determined in various industries which do work for the government,
so that only firms that meet these standards are awarded government
contracts.

The effect of union activity throughout the nation is largely
similar.[14] For a number of well-known reasons, union bargaining
power differs considerably between industries.[15] Where it is greatest,
wages are driven up more than elsewhere. This then causes discrepancies in the marginal productivity of transferable labor between
the unionized industries themselves as well as between unionized and
non-unionized sectors of the labor market. The effect also exists
when, as in the important southern textile industry, a majority of
enterprises manages to remain unorganized by voluntarily meeting

12. Thus in April 1954, just prior to the increase of the federal minimum wage
from 75 cents to 90 cents an hour, the proportion of factory workers earning less than
90 cents was 1.1 percent in the Far West, 2.3 percent in the Middle West, 4.1 percent
in the Northeast, and 20.2 *percent in the South* (U.S. Department of Labor, *Factory
Workers' Earnings,* Bulletin No. 1179 [Washington, 1955], pp. 1-3).

13. I am aware that this view is not popular and that economic arguments have
been advanced in defense of minimum wage legislation and collective bargaining. A
discussion of the controversy about the "North-South" wage differential has been
relegated to Appendix I, p. 199.

14. The following should not be interpreted as an indictment against labor unions
per se. For some constructive proposals to limit union activity to a possibly useful role
within the company, see John V. Van Sickle, *Planning for the South* (Nashville: Vanderbilt University Press, 1943), pp. 194-95, and H. Gregg Lewis, "The Labor-monopoly
Problem: a Positive Program," *Journal of Political Economy,* LIX (August, 1951),
277-87.

15. From the point of view of economic development it is especially important to
realize that union power is strengthened when an industry has a great expansion
potential. Under unionism, profits that would otherwise guide this expansion and
provide the means for it tend to be diverted to the wage earners in that particular
industry. This counteracts the rise in the *general* wage level that would otherwise
occur as a result of the expansion. For a listing of a number of other factors
that determine union bargaining strength see Lewis, "The Labor-monopoly Problem,"
p. 285.

union scales. The resulting distortion of resource allocation subtracts from national income and causes income inequalities between workers in the so-called "high-wage" and "low-wage" industries. Thus the problem of unequal labor productivity arises not only between agriculture on the one hand and industry in general on the other, but between all sectors of the economy. To the extent that the workers prevented from entering "high-wage" industries by means of the union-maintained wage level are absorbed in other occupations, this does not lead to open unemployment but gives rise to the widespread condition which falls under our definition of "disguised unemployment." Disguised unemployment or underemployment in this sense is thus not only a characteristic of underdeveloped countries but, perhaps to an equal extent, of advanced nations such as the United States.

From this it should not be inferred that union activity may not also be a cause of open unemployment. Although wages can never be sufficiently flexible to avoid this contingency in a changing economy, wage fixing, whether by the state or by the unions, contributes to the problem in large measure. There are, of course, instances of union-approved wage cuts in order to avoid the unemployment of members, and conceivably the prestige of union leadership could be used to overcome the natural reluctance of wage earners to accept even temporary or merely monetary wage reductions. But experience does not indicate that such is the rule, rather, the opposite is true. Even where local unions have indicated their willingness to allow a reduced wage scale, this has often been thwarted by the central union, which may be in a position to exercise pressure upon the employer by threatening to strike plants located elsewhere. The establishment of uniform wage scales throughout the country (in disregard of local differences in supply and demand of labor)[16] being one of the primary avowed objectives of the union movement,[17] it is clear that there cannot be much hope

16. This objective of the unions, which has been accomplished in some industries, also ignores differences in the cost of living between areas. This is not merely a matter of price levels, but also of climate, size of cities, etc. The purchasing power of wages may be the same between two places, but if in one of them heavy outlays for clothing, heating, and commuting to work are necessary which may be avoided in the other, the cost of living in a welfare sense is higher in the former. The implication of this observation with respect to the "equal pay for equal work" argument as between the North and the South should be obvious.

17. See for instance Jules Backman, *Wage Determination: An Analysis of Wage Criteria* (Princeton, N.J.: D. Van Nostrand Company, Inc., 1959), pp. 36 ff; also Richard A. Lester, "Southern Wage Differentials: Developments, Analysis, and Implications," *Southern Economic Journal*, XIII (April, 1947), 389.

for a reasonable attitude on the part of its leadership in dealing with the special problems of regions and local communities. Bowing to this attitude of the unions, several large corporations operating on a nation-wide scale have adopted a policy of equal wage and fringe benefits in all their plants,[18] and some have even come to believe, or at least frequently state in public, that fair treatment of the labor force requires such a policy. Naturally, in the case of the footloose industries, this takes away some of their incentive to expand operations in surplus labor areas, where in spite of everything the general wage level may still be relatively low as compared to other regions. Such a benevolent policy toward prospective employees may therefore in the long run do more harm than good to the low-income regions. The union, however, the majority of its members residing in the more industrialized high-wage regions of the nation, fears the attraction of low wages to industry, and attempts to overcome this competitive advantage of the low-wage regions by compelling industry to adopt the same wage scale everywhere. For the same reason unions (as well as entrepreneurs with a stake in the profitability of plants located in high-wage areas) are among the most fervent proponents of federal minimum wage legislation.[19]

Labor cost in surplus labor areas. Such policies, however, can never be completely successful. Here we must again remember that wages and labor cost are two distinct things. When wages are well above locally prevailing standards, and when, in a labor surplus area, every job in industry is considered a boon by an underemployed population, the labor force will tend to give its fullest cooperation to the employer, and this leads to greater productivity at given wages than elsewhere.[20]

18. Lester (*ibid.*, p. 387) lists glass, rayon, autos, aircraft, and federal civil service employees; James A. Morris, in a more recent paper ("A Reappraisal of Regional Wage Differentials," a paper read before the meeting of the Southern Economic Association, Jacksonville, Florida, November 20, 1959) includes basic steel and major meat-packing concerns among industries in which wage differentials have been eliminated or substantially narrowed, but emphasizes that in the major industries of the South (textiles, lumber, apparel, and food-processing) unions have not been generally strong enough to force northern wage patterns on southern plants. As a result, substantial wage differentials have continued to exist between the South and other regions and within the South.

19. On the international plane the same tendency can be observed. Textile manufacturers in Lancashire, England, espoused with vigor the cause of minimum wages for the exploited Indian worker.

20. This is true because the worker is satisfied with what he is paid and also because he is aware of the fact that when he loses his job it may not be easy to find another. Clinton Hoch (*op. cit.*, p. 8) emphasizes the latter factor: "Fundamentally, of course, the best assurance against absenteeism and high turnover rates is a basic surplus of applicants. When the worker is aware that her [his] replacement is easily accomplished, work attitudes and productivity are excellent."

Moreover, employers in labor surplus areas find it possible to hire superior workers at their going wage and thus "cream" the market. These factors undoubtedly explain in large measure a fact generally observed by entrepreneurs newly locating in the South: that southern labor, after a short training period, is at least as efficient as labor in the North and often surpasses the latter, in spite of the greater experience of the northern workers.[21] This is generally true whether or not the southern plant is unionized, the absence of a union often being quoted as an additional advantage. It has nothing to do with the alleged innate superior ability of the "pure" Anglo-Saxon stock of the workers in the South, but is the direct result of conditions in the southern labor market.

The above also explains why in the literature on plant location and in statements of entrepreneurs so much emphasis is placed upon the distinction between cheap labor (by which is meant a low wage level) and the *availability of labor,* the entrepreneur presumably attaching more importance to the latter. To the economist it is obvious that,

21. Typical in this respect are the findings of Wofford and Kelly in their study of three industrial plants established in Mississippi after World War II (B. M. Wofford and T. A. Kelly, *Mississippi Workers* [University, Alabama: The University of Alabama Press, 1955]). Absentee-rate and labor-turnover were below the national average, while productiveness on the job was about the same as that of workers elsewhere with similar equipment. This favorable conclusion was equally true of Negroes. In general the workers with most schooling did not represent the "cream of the crop" among vocational and mechanical workers (except for technical training), and those with rural background made a better showing than workers from the city. In all three plants management found that not only unskilled and semi-skilled labor, but also skilled operators, maintenance men, and craftsmen (including tool and die makers) were available in the local labor market and could be recruited with a minimum of expense and effort, even at times characterized by high-level business activity.

Maurice Fulton also mentions the superiority of workers drawn from the farm in occupations requiring technical aptitude, which he explains on the ground that farm boys nowadays are quite familiar with mechanical equipment (Maurice Fulton, "Plant Location—1965," *Harvard Business Review,* XXXIII [March-April, 1955], 42). These observations regarding the southern labor force have an important bearing on the main argument to be developed in this treatise, namely that it is feasible to create local employment opportunity in labor surplus areas by means of modest financial inducements to industry. In this connection it may further be observed that the possibility of recruiting workers at all skill levels in small southern towns and cities is enhanced by the fact that often workers who have migrated to distant manufacturing centers are willing to return as soon as an opportunity to find work nearer to home occurs, even if this means a considerable wage reduction. See Gerald C. Somers, "Labor Supply for Manufacturing in a Coal Area," *Monthly Labor Review,* LXXVII (December, 1954), 1327-30; Gerald C. Somers, "Labor Recruitment in a Depressed Rural Area," *Monthly Labor Review,* LXXXI (October, 1958), 1113-20; George T. Starnes, William M. Wilkins, and Paul P. Wissman, *The Labor Force of Two Rural Industrial Plants* (Charlottesville, Va.: Bureau of Population and Economic Research of the University of Virginia, 1951).

as long as there is no ceiling to the wage level, labor is always available to the individual entrepreneur, so that what he is in fact interested in is labor cost. But that does not mean that these statements lack substance, for wages and labor cost are *not* identical. Apart from the "political" expediency of expressing things that way, they should be interpreted to mean that where labor is said to be "available" the enterpreneur usually receives more in return for the wages he pays than in a tight labor market, and that this may be more important than possible wage differentials. In this sense, and given the confusing terminology, there even is some rationale in the often-heard contention that the South need not rely upon the attraction of cheap labor to implement its industrial ambitions.

But having said this, it is necessary to point out the obvious limitations to this way of thinking. To bring forth such cooperation of the southern labor force as would minimize entrepreneurial labor cost, all that is needed, in the general case, is that entrepreneurs meet prevailing local standards. If the reader recalls the factors that determine wages in a free market characterized by a labor surplus, he will realize that saying this practically amounts to a tautology, *for local wages are set with a view to minimizing labor cost.* Thus, whereas it is true that a region such as the South might at first retain a labor cost advantage over other regions at equal wages, the advantage is greatest when entrepreneurs establishing branch plants are free and uninhibited so as to set wages conforming to the local pattern. Moreover, the establishment of a high-wage plant in a labor surplus region may have the effect of creating dissatisfaction with scales in other enterprises that previously were deemed perfectly acceptable. This could lead to the eventual loss of established firms and might impair the chances of the region to attract industry in the future.[22] At the local level, this danger is keenly realized and was repeatedly pointed out to me by spokesmen of industrial development corporations and similar groups. Industrial prospects may, if necessary, be persuaded that it is in the best interest of all concerned that they adjust their wage scale to that prevailing locally, and the establishment of a plant unable to comply with such a request may be discouraged.[23] For similar reasons there

22. There can of course be no reasonable objection to the bidding up of wages as a result of competition for labor between enterprises in a full employment situation, even if this means that certain firms are eliminated in the process. On the contrary, this is a normal and desirable course of events that leads to higher living standards. But here we are discussing a situation in which there is a labor surplus.

23. Compare also Glenn E. McLaughlin and Stefan Robock, *Why Industry Moves South,* Report No. 3, National Planning Association (Washington: Committee on the South, N.P.A., June, 1949), p. 71.

often is a tendency to discourage industries that would bring a union into a town.[24] In such cases a community is faced with a choice between losing an industry with its contingent immediate benefits and the prospect of impeding its future development.

It follows, then, that in the best interest of southern economic development all efforts to force up the wage level in southern surplus labor areas to that of other regions should be resisted with determination. Such efforts can only serve to prolong unduly the existing cleavage between the real low-income occupations (primarily agriculture) and the relatively high incomes prevailing in other sectors of the southern economy and will also have the effect of forcing people to leave the area in search of employment opportunity elsewhere. These should be matters of genuine concern, while the North-South wage comparison as an argument per se is irrelevant in every respect. There is no economic or moral principle which dictates that wages everywhere within a nation should be the same any more than between nations. There are presumably few economists who would argue that Mexico or Canada should decree industrial wages comparable to those prevailing in this country, or that attempts of Mexican or Canadian unions to force employers to pay such wages would be in the best interest of these nations. Yet there are many economists who will argue that within the United States this kind of thing is all right. I must confess that the difference escapes me. While a relatively low-income area such as the South derives great benefits from being part of a wealthy nation (unimpeded flow of capital, free migration), it is hardly an unmixed blessing as long as national policy permits the pressures for prematurely establishing wage-equality between the parts to continue.

The general case in favor of subsidization. Having discussed the factors which cause, in the labor market, the deviations from the ideal pattern that would permit the absorption of all labor (assuming that marginal productivity of labor is above zero), we can proceed to state the general case in favor of subsidizing the wage bill. It exists whenever: one, there is a discrepancy between the marginal productivity of transferable labor in different occupations as a result of restricted employment opportunity in the relatively highly-paid occupations at

24. The establishment of a unionized plant may lead to the unionization of hitherto unorganized establishments. Thus in Front Royal, Virginia, "the arrival of the Viscose Corporation speeded unionization. Before long, most but not all other industrial enterprises had been unionized" (Wesley C. Calef and Charles Daoust, *What Will New Industry Mean to My Town?* [Washington: U.S. Department of Commerce, 1955], p. 13).

the there prevailing wage level; and two, whenever there is involuntary idleness as a result of restricted employment opportunity at the prevailing wage level in any occupation that qualified un- or underemployed workers are desirous to enter. If we take the wage scales throughout the economy as unalterable in the downward direction, then only a system of wage subsidies can, theoretically at least, simulate a purely competitive market and bring about the social optimum, which requires that the conditions listed above be eliminated.[25]

A theoretically simple solution would be to give each employer in the high-wage industries a sum of money (or a tax reduction) for every wage payment he makes. This sum should be sufficient to induce him to expand his labor force to a point where the marginal productivity of labor throughout these industries would have become equal to the marginal productivity in the low-wage industries, where it would rise as a result of the transfer of workers to the high-wage industries.[26] Thus the national income would increase as workers transferred from occupations in which their marginal productivity was low to others in which it would be higher,[27] until this was no longer possible. To perpetuate this condition, the subsidies might have to be continued indefinitely, but the amount paid each employer would have to be varied in accordance with changing circumstances. The marginal productivity of labor in each industry would be measured by that part of the wage bill paid by the employer, and this would guide the subsidizing agent in making the necessary adjustments. Since actual wages would continue to differ between industries,[28] there would be no equilibrium in the sense that no worker would have an incentive to change occupations. As before, lack of employment op-

25. It may be noted that the absence of these conditions defines full employment in the broadest sense.

26. For convenience of exposition, we assume a homogeneous labor force made up of workers who have no preference for working in one industry over another except that they prefer a high wage over a low wage.

27. Note that our farm program, which subsidizes an industry where labor productivity is low, is the exact opposite of this. However, in many regions this may in practice have little direct effect upon the transfer of labor to other industries because the differential that remains is large enough to induce a sufficient number of workers (and in the South generally many times more than that) to seek employment elsewhere when the opportunity exists. As I have argued above, the bottleneck lies in the limited absorption capacity of industry at prevailing wage scales, not in a lack of availability of qualified workers at the prevailing differential.

28. By assumption, wages in the high-wage industries would remain at least at their previous level, while the wage-level in the low-wage industries would rise to the level of the marginal productivity of labor that would be established in every industry.

portunity in high-wage industries would prevent further absorption of labor in these industries, but from the point of view of maximizing national income additional transfers would not be desirable. And the scheme would lead to a narrowing of wage differentials between industries. There is no need to elaborate on this aspect of the matter, for at this stage we are not formally concerned with the problem of income distribution, which, of course, would have to be considered at a less abstract level, along with practical matters of administration. A scheme such as that outlined above could never be carried out in practice, or, if it were attempted, would only make matters worse for reasons the reader can undoubtedly supply himself. The model does, however, serve an analytical purpose in that it demonstrates in principle how subsidization of the wage bill can be used to simulate a competitive labor market, at least in its efficiency aspect. In this respect it can be compared with a more complicated model to be developed later which has practical possibilities. The above may now be illustrated with a numerical example.

There are two kinds of occupation: farming and truck driving. Truck drivers are organized in a teamsters union and receive a wage of $600 a month.[29] The marginal productivity of labor in farming is $100, but most farms are family enterprises with a monthly net income of about $200, depending very little on hired labor. As our homogeneity assumption implies, farmers are perfectly capable of driving trucks (and in fact most of them do so every day in their own enterprise), but transfer to the lucrative truck driving business is impossible because at the high wage level prevailing there no further employment opportunity exists. A further expansion of trucking could, however, greatly increase national income since it would permit more specialization between farms.

We postulate that at first there are 100 truck drivers and 1,100 farmers, and that introduction of the subsidization scheme outlined above would lead to the absorption of 500 farmers in trucking. This causes the marginal productivity of labor in farming to rise to $300 per month and that in trucking to fall to the same level. Since truck drivers continue to receive $600, the employers receive $300 per month for each man in their employ—a total of $180,000 in subsidies. The farm sector alone may not be able to bear this burden, but this is not necessary. Part of the burden could be imposed upon the trucking sector itself. Unfair as this may seem, it should be remembered that

29. I am willing to change this example against an appropriate fee to be paid by the teamsters' union.

farmers must live so truck drivers can eat. Besides, we are not here dealing with questions of equity. If it is realized that all may share in the burden of taxation, it becomes clear that no matter what figures we choose (i.e. no matter how high wages in the privileged sector are assumed to be), our scheme can always be carried out.[30] And since it would increase national income, it is in principle possible to carry it out in such a way that everyone's real income after taxes would go up. The essence of the scheme is to reduce entrepreneurial labor cost in the high-wage industries to a level commensurate with an optimal allocation of labor. The manner in which the subsidies are raised does not affect the principle.

In practice the problem of raising the necessary funds in an acceptable manner of course looms large. Furthermore, so far the formal part of the argument has been purely static, especially in that wages in the various high-wage occupations have been taken as "given" or exogenous variables. Any realistic approach to the problem must take into consideration the possible effect of the adoption of a subsidization scheme on these wages. Union demands, for instance, may be stepped up in the absence of the penalty of unemployment under a system of adjustable subsidies until the transfer problem becomes so great, and the distribution of income so inequitable, that the system would topple of its own weight. Therefore one would be hesitant to recommend such a system other than in a milieu that has the power and determination to cope with this possible contingency. This is only one of the many difficulties one can think of. All depends, therefore, upon the way in which the scheme is executed, by whom, and under what circumstances—for instance to what extent the forces that cause localized unemployment originate within the community itself or whether the community is the victim of policy decisions at a higher level. Because

30. Harrod, in discussing the possibility of subsidizing wages in order to eliminate unemployment, appears to differ on this point, when he writes: "*Provided that the 'living wages' do not exceed the average net product of labour* . . . it will certainly be possible to make the wages up out of the pool of total national output, while still leaving enough over for the profit incentive, etc. In principle, then, this solution is possible, and the difficulty is to devise the machinery for implementing it" (italics mine) (R. F. Harrod, "Full Employment and Security of Livelihood," *Economic Journal,* LIII [December, 1943], 324). However, this difference does not exist in reality, for Harrod's argument implies that there exists an ethical judgment that prohibits subtraction from the "living wage" by means of taxation. Harrod then goes on to discuss a concrete proposal for implementing a subsidization scheme that may perhaps have merit for Britain but the application of which in the United States is inconceivable.

of this it is necessary, before any policy suggestions can be attempted, to study the milieu in which the unemployment problem arises, the forms that it takes, and its magnitude. In this we shall mostly, although not exclusively, be concerned with the occurrence of "disguised" unemployment in the South.

CHAPTER II

Aspects of the Underemployment Problem in the South

The purpose of this chapter is to present a global picture of the underemployment problem in the South as a background against which existing policies as well as further proposals to provide enterprises with special incentives to locate in a certain area should be evaluated. Unfortunately the results of the 1960 census were not available at the time of writing, but there did exist a sufficient amount of reasonably up-to-date material that could be used to gain an impression.

The low-income farm problem. In a statement before the Subcommittee on Low-Income Families of the Joint Committee on the Economic Report, in November 1955, Charles E. Bishop, Professor of Agricultural Economics, North Carolina State College, made some pertinent observations which very adequately sum up the nature of the low-income farm problem in the South. He indicated that in 1949 the mean net income from agriculture per white farm family in the Southeast was approximately 32 percent less than the mean income of white nonfarm families in the Southeast, and 40 percent less than that of nonfarm families in the non-Southeast. The net income derived from agriculture per farm family in the Southeast in 1949 was $1,611 compared with $3,675 per farm family in the non-Southeast.[1] Comparison of these figures shows that by and large farm incomes in the Southeast, but not in the rest of the country, were far below average incomes in other occupations and that the differential between farm incomes in the Southeast and the rest of the country was very much greater than that between nonfarm incomes. In fact, it has been argued that the latter may be entirely accounted for by differences in the average size of cities between the two regions—life in large cities

1. U.S. Congress, Subcommittee on Low-Income Families, Joint Committee on the Economic Report, *Hearings, Low-Income Families,* 84th Cong., 1st Sess. (Washington: U.S. Government Printing Office, 1955), p. 394.

entailing certain expenses that are much less in smaller places—and probably does not indicate a lower level of living.[2] It appears that during the last decade this picture has not changed markedly, except for a relative decline in mean farm incomes throughout the nation.[3]

The South, therefore, exhibits a pattern akin to that commonly found in the so-called underdeveloped countries and which goes under the name of "economic dualism": a relatively highly developed industrial sector and an agrarian sector somewhat bypassed by modern developments and lagging behind in prosperity. Of course the analogy should not be carried too far, one important difference being that the "developed" sector in the South has by now absorbed the great majority of the labor force, while southern agriculture is by no means stagnant. Yet, as Bishop indicates: "Many farmers in low-productivity areas currently use essentially the same methods of hand tillage as were used a generation ago. Using the same methods of production as were previously used, these farmers have been unable to increase their productivity to a level enjoyed by farmers employing more advanced technology."[4] It may certainly be said without exaggeration that improvements in farm technology have been much greater in other parts of the country, and the resulting fall in prices has adversely affected the southern farmer.

An analysis of the causes of this divergent development falls beyond the scope of this work. Imperfect knowledge of advanced techniques is one reason and imperfections in the capital market are often indicated as another, but for our purpose it is necessary to emphasize that the availability of surplus labor on the farm is itself a main cause of the failure to introduce technological innovations at a rate comparable to other areas. For many of these innovations—although by no means all—are of a labor saving nature, and when there is idle labor and/or labor cost is low it may be more economical to continue in the old manner. And to the extent that in such a situation mechanization takes place anyway, it may well aggravate the rural employment situation. Workers, even in farming, must earn a certain living wage that may exceed the marginal productivity of labor, and thus landlords may find it to their advantage to replace their

2. See for instance D. Gale Johnson, "Some Effects of Region, Community Size, Color and Occupation on Family and Individual Income," Conference on Research in Income and Wealth, National Bureau of Economic Research, *Studies in Income and Wealth*, XV (1952), pp. 49-60. See also vol. VI (1943), p. 226.

3. See John M. Brewster, "Long Run Prospects of Southern Agriculture," *Southern Economic Journal*, XXVI (October, 1959), 134-40.

4. Joint Committee on the Economic Report, *Hearings, Low-Income Families*, p. 397.

tenants or sharecroppers by new machinery, operated with hired labor at lower cost. A case in point, both with respect to the delay caused by low labor cost and the possibly disturbing impact of mechanization in the presence of surplus labor, is the lagging but nevertheless proceeding introduction of cotton-picking machinery in the Southeast.

Thus there is an intimate interdependence between the pace of development in industry and that in agriculture. By opening up employment opportunity for surplus labor on the farm, industrial development tends to raise labor productivity in agriculture, and that in turn makes it possible and profitable to introduce labor saving techniques on the farm. This also holds for changes in farming toward activities that inherently require less labor throughout the year or in the busy seasons. Moore quotes an example: "A fairly large landowner in Columbus, Georgia, has recently gone out of cotton entirely in favor of beef cattle, simply because his sharecroppers had left in such large numbers for jobs in town. He is better off and so are his former croppers. Note the sequence—the sharecroppers left first, and the change in farming methods followed."[5] The raising of crops in this country by methods that require a heavy labor input during a relatively short period and keep the workers idle the rest of the time is part of the whole underemployment picture, and frantic activity during the height of the season can certainly not be pointed to as a justification for the idleness at other times. The establishment of full employment—that is, of true alternatives in other occupations at the there prevailing wage rate for workers now engaged in these agrarian pursuits—would lead to mechanization or else to the abandonment of the crops in question in favor of other countries where labor productivity is generally low. As Hoover and Ratchford point out: "A further change which would represent economic progress is a shift towards the type of agriculture which permits more continuous use of the labor supply on the farm and avoids the underemployment which has characterized southern agriculture. Thus in Mississippi in 1944, farmers worked 567 per cent more during the month in which they were busiest than in the month in which they worked least. In Iowa the figure was only 167 percent."[6]

Average and marginal productivity of labor on low-income farms. The fact that labor productivity on a great many southern farms is

5. Arthur Moore, *Underemployment in American Agriculture,* Planning Pamphlets No. 77 (Washington: National Planning Association, 1952), p. 58.

6. Calvin B. Hoover and B. U. Ratchford, *Economic Resources and Policies of the South* (New York: The Macmillan Company, 1951), p. 299.

very low, and that therefore, with but few exceptions, the region as a whole may be characterized as a labor surplus area, has been established by numerous studies and surveys. Thus Bishop states:

The productivity of labor is low and underemployment of labor is high in the South. A high proportion of the labor on low-production farms is not employed in income-generating uses. For example, on low-production farms in the southern Piedmont of North Carolina approximately 40 percent of the farm family labor resources (excluding those in non-agricultural work) is not productively employed. . . .

. . . .

On the average, farms in the Southeast use about 77 percent as much labor per rural farm male resident 14 years old and over as farms in the rest of the United States. The average return per hour of labor on southeastern farms, however, is only about 65 percent of the average return from labor on farms in other regions. Furthermore, given the kinds of farm commodities now produced and the methods of production currently employed, the use of additional labor on farms in the Southeast will add very little to the incomes of farm families. . . .

. . . .

A study in the Southern Piedmont of North Carolina indicates that, on the average, labor on low-production farms is used up to the point that it yields a return of only about $1.20 per 9½ hour day of additional labor, and that the rate of return decreases as the amount of labor used increases.[7]

If similar relations hold elsewhere—and there is no reason to question this, for diminishing returns in agriculture is a universal phenomenon —it is obvious that a low average productivity of farm labor is accompanied by an even much lower marginal productivity.[8] It is im-

7. Joint Committee on the Economic Report, *Hearings, Low-Income Families,* p. 394. Bishop refers to: J. G. Sutherland and C. E. Bishop, *Possibilities for Increasing Production and Incomes on Small Commercial Farms, Southern Piedmont Area, North Carolina,* North Carolina Agricultural Experiment Station Technical Bulletin No. 117 (Raleigh, 1955).

8. This is also indicated in Earl O. Heady and C. B. Baker, "Resource Adjustments to Equate Productivities in Agriculture," *Southern Economic Journal,* XXI (July, 1954), 36-52. Computations carried out by these authors on the basis of four random samples covering the 1950 production year in the Alabama Piedmont, northern Iowa, southern Iowa, and a dry-farming area in Montana gave the following results:

	Montana	North Iowa	South Iowa	Alabama
marginal product ($ / month)	61.80	68.04	48.05	40.57
average product ($ / month)	1559	905	547	127

From this it can be seen that even in prosperous farm areas, where average labor productivity (and hence average farm income) is high, marginal labor productivity tends to be much below prevailing wage rates in nonfarm occupations. This does

portant to note this, for it is easy to register average productivity in a global fashion from readily available income data, while the quantitative determination of marginal productivity requires a detailed production study in each case. Marginal productivity of labor on the farm, however, is the crucial variable that should be compared with the wage rates prevailing in nonfarm occupations (which may be taken to measure marginal productivity of labor in these occupations). It is the relation between the marginal productivities which indicates the material gain that may be obtained when workers should transfer from the farm to nonfarm jobs, and which in many cases (especially when no change of residence is necessary) also determines the willingness of workers to do so. As the quantitative data presented suggest, the ratio may be in the neighborhood of 1:10. But this is not all for, as Bishop also points out,[9] the existence of idleness on the farm is the direct result of the very low returns to additional effort. Even if one is as poor—by American standards—as these low-income farm families are and has time to spare, it is hardly worth while to work some more if this will yield but $1.20 a day. Idleness in such circumstances is certainly not indicative of unwillingness to work when this is more remunerative. For all practical purposes, therefore, the marginal productivity of farm labor in the presence of widespread idleness may be taken to be in the vicinity of zero. We conclude that idleness and/or low average productivity of farm labor are indicative of extremely low marginal productivity, and therefore that these conditions establish the existence of unvoluntary underemployment in the sense specified in Chapter I. This lends validity to studies which base their conclusions regarding the expendability of labor in southern agriculture largely upon the low-income level prevailing in this sector of the economy. Estimates have been made of the size of the "reserve army of underemployed," to paraphrase a Marxian term, upon the basis of income classifications, which also give us an idea of the geographical spread of the underemployment condition. But before we look into these, we may briefly survey the condition of hired farm laborers, a large number of which must also definitely be classified as underemployed in the productivity sense.

not necessarily mean that farm labor is willing to transfer to these occupations (compare *supra*, p. 10), but when, as in the Alabama case, average productivity of labor in farming falls far below the industrial wage level, there can be no doubt about the existence of surplus labor in agriculture that is ready to transfer to industry. That this condition exists in rural areas throughout the South we know of course also directly.

9. Joint Committee on the Economic Report, *Hearings, Low-Income Families*, p. 395.

Farm wages and nonfarm wages. Another way of assessing differentials in labor productivity in much of agriculture and other occupations (primarily manufacturing) is afforded by a comparison of farm wages and nonfarm wages. Since these are wages paid on the job, such a comparison does not take into consideration idleness among certain categories of farm workers, which is quite extensive in off-seasons. Rather, they indicate the marginal productivity of farm labor during active seasons when help is needed, and as such they vary from year to year with the size of the harvest and expected crop returns. However, they are in general much below the rates for unskilled workers in industry, even at the peak of the busy season, and invariably also much below the federal minimum wage, which thus impedes the transfer of these laborers to more remunerative occupations outside agriculture. In July 1955 farm wages per hour without board or room averaged 61 cents in the South Atlantic region and 54 cents in the East South Central region as compared to an average wage of $1.29 per hour for production workers in manufacturing industry in South Carolina. Similar differentials existed throughout the southern states and, to a somewhat lesser extent, also elsewhere in the nation. At that time the average daily farm wage rate without board and room was $4.00 in the East South Central division and $4.75 in the South Atlantic region.[10] Thus farm wages were about 50 percent of the wages of the lowest-paid workers in manufacturing and most other occupations and somewhere in the neighborhood of 40 percent of average earnings of factory workers in the Southeast, which for 1955 was estimated at $1.41 (or about 75 percent of the national average).[11] As compared to earlier periods, it would appear as if on the whole the gap has widened; that a widening of the gap took place during the pre-war period is without any doubt. Data gathered by Ducoff on a state by state basis show that in 1942 in the southern area the ratio between average daily farm wages (without board) and industrial wages in industry (common laborers) ranged from 37 percent in Kentucky to 60 percent in Virginia.[12] From 1914 to 1939 wages of unskilled factory workers increased 193 percent on

10. U.S. Congress, Subcommittee on Low-Income Families, Joint Committee on the Economic Report, *Characteristics of the Low-Income Population and Related Federal Programs*, 84th Cong., 1st Sess. (Washington: U.S. Government Printing Office, 1955), pp. 205, 235.

11. U.S. Senate, Committee on Banking and Currency, *Selected Materials on the Economy of the South*, 84th Cong., 2nd Sess. (Washington: U.S. Government Printing Office, 1956), p. 26.

12. Herman Jay Braunhut, "Farm Labor Wage Rates in the South," *Southern Economic Journal*, XVI (October, 1949), 190.

the average, those of farm laborers hired by the day without board only 9 percent.[13]

In addition to earning low wages when they work, the income of farm workers is depressed as a result of widespread seasonal unemployment of long duration among them. It is true that not all of the people who work for wages on farms primarily depend upon these wages: many of them are farm operators themselves, often sharecroppers or tenants who occasionally work as hired laborers. Others are migratory workers or regular hired hands, living permanently on the farm where they are employed. Still, there is a category of people living in rural areas whose income is mostly derived from seasonal employment as wage earners on farms in the vicinity. A recent survey[14] comprising communities in Arkansas, Louisiana, Georgia, and New Mexico indicated that the male heads of such households in Arkansas and Louisiana averaged less than 36 weeks of employment from a combination of farm and nonfarm jobs. In Georgia, where nonfarm opportunities were relatively good at the time of the survey, the corresponding figure was 42 weeks. Annual earnings for male heads of households were as follows: Arkansas, $827; Georgia, $1,157; Louisiana, $703; New Mexico, $1,256. The higher average for New Mexico was associated with the fact that many workers there were migrants, who were more fully employed than nonmigrants, and also was affected by the circumstance that some of those surveyed were skilled workers.

We speak of the "lost potential" to indicate the production foregone during downturns of the business cycle, but here we have a lost potential that has persisted throughout cycles. Now that our economic system is on challenge before the world and our economy is burdened with unprecedented armament expenditures, we may well ask ourselves whether we can still afford this waste of our labor resources. And those who think that it is "fair" to demand equal pay for equal work throughout the nation and that further boosts of the minimum wages covering those lucky enough to be employed in manufacturing, communications, and mining are in order would do well to contemplate data such as those presented here and ponder whether we

13. *Ibid.*, citing Daniel J. Ahearn, *The Wages of Farm and Factory Laborers, 1914-1944.*

14. U.S. Department of Agriculture, Bureau of Agricultural Economics, and Department of Labor, Bureau of Employment Security, *Unemployment and Partial Unemployment of Hired Farm Workers in Four Areas* (Washington, April, 1953), cited in Joint Committee on the Economic Report, *Hearings, Low-Income Families*, pp. 216-17.

should not be concerned first and foremost about the inequalities they reveal. For the worst inequalities are inequalities of opportunity, and, as Professor Nicholls stated a few years ago: "At the present minimum wage of $1, most low-income farm people would be glad to work in a local industry as an alternative (or perhaps in combination with) the 25 to 30 cents an hour they are now earning in agriculture. Insofar as a still higher minimum wage might limit the creation of additional nonfarm job opportunity, I believe that the losses of low-income farm people would far more than outweigh any possible gains for those Southern people already employed in covered industries."[15] It is also evident that, *given the labor surplus in agriculture,* our farm program has not done and cannot do much, if anything, for the low-income groups in agriculture who are primarily dependent upon their labor, to wit, the large category comprising hired farm laborers, tenants, sharecroppers, and small-scale subsistence farmers. The spoils practically all go to the large landowners and commercial farmers who have crops to sell, land to put in the soil-bank, and to whom, in short, the property rent accrues.

Extent of the low-income farm problem. How large is in fact the group of low-income rural workers willing and capable to transfer to more remunerative occupations and in what areas are they concentrated? Of the studies that give some indications, few are primarily directed to answering it and all are based upon inadequate data. It is of course inherently difficult to make such estimates. As Levitan says after discussing the intricate problems encountered in estimating the number of jobs needed to eliminate unemployment in urban labor surplus areas: "It is even more difficult to make any estimates of the number of additional jobs needed in the rural areas because of the lack of appropriate statistics of unemployment in these areas and the difficulty of translating underemployment into labor surplus data. With the currently available data, the assumptions would have to be more heroic than in the case of previous calculations in connection with industrial areas. The margin of error in such a case may be too great to be useful even as a rough guide for policy decisions."[16] This may be true if the policy is to be a centralized one, but of course in each locality a sufficiently accurate picture of the underemployment situation exists at any time or may be easily obtained. For our purpose

15. *Ibid.,* p. 444.

16. Sar A. Levitan, *Federal Assistance to Labor Surplus Areas,* a report prepared at the request of the chairman of the Committee on Banking and Currency, U.S. House of Representatives, 85th Cong., 1st Sess. (Washington: U.S. Government Printing Office, 1957), pp. 34-35.

such estimates as have been made may be quoted for the impression they convey, even though at best they only indicate the general magnitude of the problem at the time they were made in a rapidly changing situation.

In 1949 experts on low-income families for the Joint Committee on the Economic Report estimated that in the nation as a whole there were approximately one million full-time farm operators, able-bodied, of working age, and with little outside employment or income, whose annual production in the preceding year had been worth under $1,500 per year. The income level of the great majority of their families was comparable to an urban income of between $1,200 and $1,500. The income-level of an additional 600,000 similar families was estimated between $1,200 and $1,800. And finally there were some 400,000 part-time farmers, able-bodied and of working age, whose combined farm and nonfarm income was $2,000 or less. Thus, if the line is drawn at $2,000, there were at least two million full- and part-time farmers whose productivity was low. This does not include an estimated one million hired farm workers and an additional 500,000 others living in the open country or in towns of less than 2,500 inhabitants with incomes below the $2,000 mark. Average factory pay, at that time, was about $60 per week.[17] It was felt that if the productivity of the workers in the categories mentioned could be raised to the level of the average rural nonfarm worker or person employed on a medium-sized commercial family farm, the effect would be that of adding 2,500,000 workers to the labor force. The great majority of these underemployed families lived in the Southeast, with heavy concentrations in the southern Appalachians and in the cotton belt.[18]

Some later estimates are less inclusive. Thus in 1954 there were about 1.4 million farm families with money incomes under $1,000. Of these, nearly one million lived in the South.[19] In a large number of cases, however, these families did not include able-bodied persons

17. In the South, however, it was less. Brewster, in his recent article (*op. cit.*, p. 136), mentions that the average annual wage of factory workers in the eight-state area comprised in his study (the Carolinas, Alabama, Georgia, Tennessee, Mississippi, Arkansas, and Louisiana) rose from about $2,300 in 1950 to more than $3,200 in 1955, while there is no reason to suppose that incomes derived from farming in this area increased in that period.

18. See Arthur Moore, *op. cit.*, pp. 9-12; also U.S. Congress, Joint Committee on the Economic Report, *Underemployment of Rural Families*, 82d Cong., 1st Sess. (Washington: U.S. Government Printing Office, 1951), pp. 4-6. The latter document features a map showing the areas having the highest concentration of underemployed farm families (p. 6).

19. Joint Committee on the Economic Report, *Characteristics of the Low-Income Population and Related Federal Programs*, p. 11.

of working age, capable of accepting remunerative employment, but rather were comprised of aged or retired persons, widows with young children, etc.[20] On the other hand, nonfarm rural low-income families were not considered, while undoubtedly a large number of farm workers belonging to families in higher income brackets were available for off-farm employment. In 1952 the total number of farm workers available was estimated at about one million in seven southern states (Alabama, Georgia, Kentucky, Mississippi, North Carolina, Tennessee, and Virginia). This, again, did not include an undoubtedly large number of other low-income rural residents desirous to obtain a manufacturing job should the occasion present itself.

Diminution of the farm labor force, "forced" migration, and farm income. As matters now stand, the most hopeful aspect of the underemployment problem in farming is the continuation of a long trend toward fairly rapid diminution of the farm labor force. In the lowest income groups this has as yet had little effect, but, as mentioned above, a large percentage of these families do not comprise members suitable to engage in off-farm employment. To that extent their problems fall outside the scope of this work. Most disguised unemployment, it would appear, occurs in farm families other than those at the very bottom of the income scale, and among those families there has up to the present time been a considerable exit toward more remunerative nonfarm employment. Thus, while between 1948 and 1954 the number of farm families with incomes under $1,000 remained about the same, the number of farm families in the $1,000 to $2,000 range declined from 1.6 million to 1.3 million.[21] This constitutes the continuation of a long-run trend which has been particularly marked in the South. Between 1930 and 1950 the southern agrarian labor force (in the 13 states extending from the Potomac to the Rio Grande) declined by about 2.25 million or almost 40 percent, with at the end of the period some 3.2 million workers or 22 percent of the employed labor force remaining primarily engaged in agriculture, as compared to 43 percent at the outset of the period.[22] Nonfarm employment being scarce during the depressed thirties, most of this decline took place during the 1940-50 decade. During the period 1950-56 the rate

20. *Ibid.*, p. 30.
21. *Ibid.*, pp. 7, 8.
22. B. U. Ratchford, "Patterns of Economic Development," *Southern Economic Journal,* XX (January, 1954), 220. See also Lorin A. Thompson, "Urbanization, Occupational Shift and Economic Progress," *The Urban South,* ed. Rupert B. Vance and Nicholas J. Demarath (Chapel Hill: The University of North Carolina Press, 1954), pp. 40-42.

of transfer of southern farm people into other occupations was even greater;[23] over the period 1950 to 1957 inclusive the decline of the farm labor force in eight southern states (the Carolinas, Alabama, Georgia, Tennessee, Mississippi, Arkansas, and Louisiana) averaged 4.4 percent per year, as compared with 3 percent in the rest of the nation.[24]

However, this development in the recent past should not make us complacent with respect to the problem of rural underemployment. Neither a careful evaluation of what has happened nor an estimation of what can still be accomplished along the same lines warrants such an attitude. Regarding the second point, a warning note has recently been sounded by Bachmura. Noting that the bulk of nonagricultural job opportunities that have given rise to the movement off southern farms has occurred in urban centers in and outside the South, this author writes: "High birth rates in both farm and nonfarm areas during 1940-50 will shortly bring increasing numbers of entrants into the national labor force. Particularly since the net farm emigration of the last 19 years took place in a situation in which nonfarm entrants of nonfarm birth were relatively scarce, the farm sector was in a more favorable situation for the reduction of its redundant labor supply than it will be in the next 19 years. Because nonfarm entrants are already on the scene when an employment opportunity appears, they are likely to preempt many nonfarm opportunities. . . . It is clear that the competitive importance of nonfarm entrants will become increasingly great with the passage of time. Postponement of the eventual solution will thus make the solution more difficult."[25] In this context Bachmura even mentions in passing the possibility of subsidizing local industry (along with that of subsidizing migration), pointing out the manifest preference throughout the South for local industrialization over migration ("particularly when the latter involved interregional movement by whites").[26] This brings us to our first point, one already touched upon in Chapter I: to the extent that the global statistics quoted above are determined by "forced" migration resulting from lack of employment opportunity in the preferred region, they conceal a dimension of the underemployment problem about which in the declining areas there is much concern. There are no

23. E. L. Baum and Earl O. Heady, "Some Effects of Selected Policy Programs on Agricultural Labor Mobility in the South," *Southern Economic Journal*, XXV (January, 1959), 328.

24. Brewster, *op. cit.*, p. 136.

25. Frank T. Bachmura, "Man-land Equalization through Migration," *American Economic Review*, XLIX (December, 1959), 1013.

26. *Ibid.*, pp. 1013-14.

statistics, nor can there be, to indicate what proportion of the migrants would have preferred to stay in their own districts had there been employment opportunity at a wage level such as would have caused this opportunity to exist for all who wanted it. We do know, however, that in many depressed rural areas "opportunities for off-farm employment are only a small fraction of the number needed to provide full employment for the available able-bodied manpower of working age."[27] The aim should be to accomplish further transfer of workers out of agriculture into the more productive occupations with less interregional migration by bringing industry to the people rather than the people to industry. And if the local people themselves are willing to pay for their legitimate aspiration of bringing employment opportunity to their communities, it is rather presumptuous to tell them that this is in some sense "wrong." It is to refuting this widespread notion that this volume is devoted. With such a purpose it is important to understand the local feeling about migration in the areas sustaining population losses, and therefore at the end of this chapter some more will be said regarding that problem.

It may further be pointed out that migration out of farming in recent years, important as it has been, has not resulted in any increase in real farm incomes. On this subject Brewster presents some interesting data.[28] In 1957, average real income per farm family in the nation as a whole was about the same as in 1951, but between the period 1947-49 and 1957 that part of the incomes of farm families derived from farming itself had steadily declined. Average net real income per farm family from that source in 1957 was approximately equal to what it had been in 1941. Between 1947-49 and 1957 average real income of families living on farms was just about maintained due to the increasing importance of off-farm employment, which in 1956 constituted some 45 percent of their total income as compared to 30 percent in the 1947-49 period. From further information presented by Brewster it may be inferred that in the South during the 1950's the gap between the average income of farm families and nonfarm families has increased. Quoting McElveen,[29] he observes that only during World War II and the immediate postwar years did the economy generate enough demand for farm products and open up enough opportunity

27. Joint Committee on the Economic Report, *Characteristics of the Low-Income Population and Related Federal Programs*, p. 10.

28. Brewster, *op. cit.*, pp. 138-40.

29. J. V. McElveen, "Changes in the Structure of Farming in the South," a paper presented at the annual meeting of the Association of Southern Agricultural Workers, Little Rock, Arkansas, February 3-5, 1958.

for farm people in nonfarm employment to cause any marked increase in the per capita income of farmers relative to the nonfarm average. As to the future, various considerations lead Brewster to conclude: "It is difficult to see how even the farmer's utmost efforts can succeed in preventing a widening of the already conspicuous income gap between himself and nonfarmers."[30] This implies that, especially in the South, the problem of underemployment on the farm is likely to be with us for years to come, a conclusion which warrants further investigation into the possibility of providing a stimulus to the development of rural areas by means of special inducements to industry.

Declining industries, localized unemployment, and subsidies. Moreover, such inducements used at the local level may become powerful weapons in the fight against localized unemployment stemming from the depletion of an area's natural resources, the removal of a town's principal industry, a declining market for the products a community produces, etc. Unemployment has long been substantial in textile regions of New England and in coal-mining areas. In these cases high union wage-scales (and in some instances a record of bad employer-labor relations) have often aggravated the problem. In other cases an area may simply not have sufficient industrial growth to absorb an expanding labor force; this problem is not exclusively one of agrarian regions. But it is of course most likely to exist where the region or community has a high stake in an industry which, for basic underlying factors on the demand and the supply side, does not have a great potential for the employment of additional workers. Of these agriculture (to a very different extent in different branches) is merely a rather extreme and conspicuous example, one of the rare cases in recent years of an important industry in which adjustment has required an absolute decline in the labor force. This has been due to great advances in production technique on the one hand, enabling far fewer people than before to produce an ever increasing quantity of produce, and to the fact that, as real incomes rose, per capita demand for farm products in general has not risen nearly as much as that for the produce of other industries and in some cases (the traditional staples) has considerably decreased. Furthermore, the birth rate on farms has always been higher than in urban areas. Finally, as we have seen, progress in the industry has been quite uneven geographically, causing some areas to be more depressed than others. All this is well-known, but it may bear repetition within the context of our discussion because

30. Brewster, *op. cit.,* p. 140.

it indicates forces at work that may also affect other industries. The textile industry, for instance, is in some respects similarly situated. Already of late the number of workers in the most important branches of this industry has declined, and there is little hope that in the future this trend will be reversed. This industry, which has contributed so much to the industrial development of the South, and which now to a very large extent is located there, shows signs of becoming a more or less perpetually depressed industry. Moreover, as in the past it has migrated from New England to the regions where it is now located, so in the future it may move on to greener pastures in the deep South and Puerto Rico, in search of lower wage scales. In that event the present textile regions will be faced with problems akin to those facing New England now.[31] It is here contended that local subsidies to industry may be used to advantage in such a contingency, smoothing an area's adjustment to structural changes that otherwise are likely to cause persistent unemployment.[32]

Should the South attract "high wage" industries? If there is to be question of deliberate efforts to induce enterprises to choose a southern location, the problem arises as to what kind of industry should be particularly encouraged. The answer to this question is implied in the discussion of later chapters, but here I wish to comment specifically on the argument that the South ought to be particularly keen on securing a larger share of the nation's "high wage" industries. In this connection it is usually pointed out that a considerable part of the North-South wage differential can be explained in terms of the preponderance in the South of industries that pay relatively low wages regardless of

31. There already is a good deal of concern in the South about extreme dependence upon the textile industry. Thus local development groups in Alabama, when asked what type of industry they were trying to attract, mostly answered "any type," but some indicated that they should like the town to diversify from textiles. See *Alabama Goes Industry Hunting*, a study prepared by the Alabama Business Research Council and the School of Commerce and Business Administration, University of Alabama (University, Alabama, 1957), p. 30. Another example of this concern is Gastonia, N.C., which has an industrial diversification commission specifically charged with bringing in industry to complement the existing textile industry (*Subsidized Industrial Migration; the Luring of Plants to New Locations*, Recommendations for legislative action by the Subcommittee on Migration and Subsidization of Industry, National Legislative Committee, American Federation of Labor [Washington: American Federation of Labor, 1955], p. 25).

32. It might be countered that the widespread use of subsidies would itself become (and to some extent already is) a factor causing dislocation, which would then have to be remedied by further subsidies. This issue will be discussed in Chapters VI and VIII, where I shall demonstrate that this kind of competition is in principle beneficial.

their location, as opposed to intra-industry wage differentials between regions.[33]

In Chapter I it has been argued that an industry paying wages well above local standards may lessen the attraction of a locality to other industries seeking relatively low labor cost.[34] But, so we may ask, if attracting high wage industries is our aim in the first place, does this matter? And also, in the context of our argument in favor of subsidies, would not a given amount of subsidy contribute more, dollar for dollar, to the income of a community when it is used to attract an industry that pays high rather than low wages? These questions cannot be ignored, for essentially, when we say that subsidies are useful to effect a transfer of labor from occupations such as agriculture (and at a later stage perhaps textiles, etc.) where labor productivity is low to others where it is higher, we are saying that subsidies derive their justification from furthering a transfer of labor from "low wage" to "high wage" industries. Yet there is a catch in the argument and it is the following.

If the market were to work in accordance with the competitive model, there would be no "high" and "low" wage industries as such regardless of the geographical location of the firms in it. Wages would vary with job content and the scarcity of the skills required relative to the demand for these skills in each area, but in any given locality the unimpeded transfer of workers capable of fulfilling tasks in one industry as well as in another would equalize differentials in net-

33. For instance, in 1947 some 39 percent of the differential in average earnings per worker in manufacturing between Virginia and the nation was attributed to Virginia having a heavier weight of industries that pay low wages wherever located (Virginia Department of Conservation and Development, Advisory Council on the Virginia Economy, *Labor Resources and Labor Income in Virginia,* Vol. II: *Labor Income and Per Capita Income* [Richmond, July, 1953], p. 5). This has led to statements such as: "To achieve the best kind of economic growth, of course, Virginians should increase their efforts to attract the high-wage industries" (Fiscal Study Committee, Advisory Council on the Virginia Economy, *A Report on Virginia's Economy* [Richmond, November, 1957], p. 12). This opinion, which is widespread among planners at the state level throughout the South, is usually simply defended on the ground that high wages contribute more to income than do low wages. Hoover and Ratchford (*op. cit.,* pp. 366-67) also argue that what the South needs is high-wage industries, "the only industries that can raise per capita incomes in the amount required." This, they maintain, is not contrary to the principle of comparative advantage (which on its face might lead one to believe that low-wage industries might on the whole be more suitable to the southern environment) because southern industry may be able to exploit "quasi-monopoly power." But this power does not exist and even if it did its exploitation would be contrary to the national interest and to that of the southern workers who would remain underemployed.

34. *Supra,* pp. 16-17.

advantage of jobs between industries. Thus, for similar or equivalent work equal wages would be paid by different industries in any one place, and wages at any skill level would vary between regions rather than between industries. In that case the South would, to an even larger extent than is now the case (for interregional wage differentials do of course exist in reality and are quite important in most industries), attract industries in which labor cost weighs heavily, i.e. industries with a relatively low capital investment per worker. As will be shown later in this work, under a system of widespread local subsidization of industry, a competitive labor market tends to be simulated.[35] In this it will be assumed that at any time the local community acts in its best self-interest as an independent entity, and it will be demonstrated that the overall effect would be beneficial to the South and to the nation as a whole. But even if we abstract from the changes which would be brought about in the event that the extension of inducements to industry should be widely adopted with an intensity sufficient to solve the underemployment problem of the South, we ought to recognize that, with the presently existing labor cost differentials between the South and the rest of the nation, the South by and large holds a comparative advantage to industries in which labor cost looms large. And this of course explains the present industry-mix of the South with its preponderance of labor-intensive industries.[36]

And it now so happens that these industries are also, under the present circumstances, mostly low wage industries. In fact, the relation between heavy capital investment per worker and high wages seems to be so firmly established in an empirical sense as to be almost axiomatic, which serves to illustrate to what extent our labor market deviates from the competitive ideal.[37] In considerable part, no doubt, this is caused by the fact that the bargaining strength of unionized

35. Particularly in that entrepreneurial labor cost would tend to be the same as in a competitive labor market. If at the present stage this assertion raises various questions, the reader may be assured that they will be answered in due time.

36. Compare J. M. Buchanan, "Note on the Differential Controversy," *Southern Economic Journal*, XVII (July, 1950), 59-60. In this note Buchanan attacks the apparently widely prevailing notion that regional industrial structures develop largely as a result of non-economic forces.

37. Often simply indicating that capital investment per worker in an industry is high (or low) is deemed a sufficient explanation of wages in that industry being high (or low), no further elaboration of that point being required. Backman, for instance, writes: "Wages are generally lower in retailing than in manufacturing [because] . . . there is smaller capital investment in retailing ($5,000) than in manufacturing ($12,000)" (Jules Backman, "Why Wages Are Lower in Retailing," *Southern Economic Journal*, XXII [January, 1957], 304).

workers is greater when labor cost in an industry is relatively small.[38] Perhaps also, "heavy" industry requires in general higher skill levels. At any rate, for a considerable time to come the southern environment may well continue to be attractive primarily to low-wage industries, in which nevertheless wages are very high relative to labor productivity in such occupations as agriculture. It is therefore likely that in many instances local development groups will find that a relatively modest amount of subsidy may suffice to attract a low wage industry, while inducing a high wage industry to establish itself in the community would require a great deal more outlay. In other words, returns in the form of increased community income per dollar invested in subsidies is likely to be greatest, in general, when the outlay is used to attract a so-called "low wage" industry, and "low wage" industries (such as shoes, textiles, and clothing) have in fact been among the most frequent recipients of subsidies. Although most authors on the subject write as if this spells something ominous, it merely indicates the sound business sense of the subsidizing agents. But of course the South is not a homogeneous region; natural conditions in some areas may be advantageous to a type of industry which is in the habit of paying high wages while still requiring some special inducement if it is to be attracted. A sensible subsidization policy should be subject to the requirement laid down by Buchanan for public policy in general: "to exploit rather than to overlook the inherent economic advantages which the region possesses [including an abundant labor supply willing to work at a relatively low wage rate], while at the same time providing as many sound inducements to the establishment of heavy industry as possible."[39] And in this, it must adapt itself to changing circumstances. Thus while today attracting a textile industry may bring the greatest income gain to a community desirous to eliminate disguised unemployment in agriculture, at some time in the future means may have to be found to alleviate unemployment caused by a decline of employment in existing textile mills or to further the transition of workers out of textiles into some other industry where labor productivity is greater. The usefulness of the subsidization approach is not now limited to the contribution it may make in solving

38. To a smaller extent than is actually true, relatively high wages might be paid in capital-intensive industries even in the absence of unions by deliberate choice of the employers. This could be explained on the basis of the relation between wages and labor productivity, stressed in Chapter I. Such an explanation, however, would lead us too far afield here.

39. Buchanan, *op. cit.*, p. 60.

the farm problem, nor will it end if and when this problem will be substantially eliminated.

Un- and underemployment in specific regions within the South. Since this study is concerned with local solutions to local problems that result from certain defects in the working of our economic system, it may be useful to present some more detailed information regarding the impact of these defects in certain typical areas where un- or underemployment is endemic. This provides us with a more vivid picture than global statistics can give of the conditions that have brought forth action of community groups attempting to bring in new industry, of the considerations by which these groups are led, and of the pressing humanitarian problems they seek to solve.

The following is pertinent as regards the causes and effects of unemployment in a coal mining region—Virginia's southwest triangle comprising the counties of Buchanan, Dickenson, Lee, Russell, Scott, Tazewell, and Wise. In 1950 per capita income in this six county area was 57 percent of the state average and in 1953 it was less than half. Yet coal mining is a high wage industry: annual earnings per employed Virginia coal miner in 1950 were 10 percent higher than average manufacturing earnings in the state and in 1953 the differential had increased to 18 percent. In agriculture however, the second most important occupation in the area, earnings per farmer were roughly half the state average for all employment. The principal cause of the low per capita income was the small proportion of the population that was employed. Especially for women, there was insufficient employment opportunity in the area's leading industries: coal mining, agriculture, and lumbering. As a result, of the females 14 years and over only 11 percent were in the labor force as compared to 28 percent for the state and 45 percent in Danville, where textile jobs were available. A number of manufacturing plants, producing electrical equipment and clothing and employing mostly women, had moved in in recent years, but manufacturing was only one-fifth as important as in the state as a whole. It was felt of vital importance to attract more industry employing women if income levels in the area were to be raised.[40]

In view of widespread and increasing unemployment in the mines, in this area as well as in the neighboring states of Kentucky and West Virginia, the need to attract manufacturing industry employing men

40. Virginia Department of Conservation and Development, Division of Planning and Economic Development, *Virginia's Southwest Triangle, Past and Present* (Richmond, May, 1956), pp. 13-15.

would appear equally urgent. When a mine closes down in areas such as these, destitution becomes acute. A recent example of this occurred in the little town of Derby, Wise County, Virginia. After the Stonegal Coal and Coke Co. mine shutdown, most families had no income except the $20 to $30 in emergency funds allotted to members of the United Mine Workers Union by the Derby local, and emergency feeding stations were set up for children. A group of miners met and overwhelmingly approved the idea of proposing to the company to return to their jobs at a lower pay scale. The company answered that such a proposal had to come from the U.M.W. national headquarters, and nothing came from it. Sometimes, however, the union will permit members to form a company for the purpose of digging coal in the mines, which is then sold to the mining enterprise. Earnings of miners working on this basis are typically less than half the official union rates, but payments into the union welfare fund are nevertheless required.

It is frequently argued that this type of region, because of geographical characteristics, low educational level of the population, and general backwardness, is so unattractive to industry that the development of manufacturing can simply not be expected. However, this has also been said about other areas in the South and proved mistaken. Disadvantages of location can be offset by special inducements, and an area, no matter how poor, can afford to offer these inducements if in terms of alternatives open to it much is to be gained by attracting new industry. It appears that in the depressed mining regions in the mountains the people are exceptionally attached to their surroundings. If that is so they certainly can afford to "buy payroll," for this may be the only alternative to near-starvation. It is hard to see why a program freed from restraints that stem from prejudice against this method of improving local prosperity could not succeed if it starts with the idea that suitable prospects will be given what is necessary to get them. Suppose for instance that completely equipped factories would naturally grow in such an area. Would it not, in spite of everything else, be considered well-endowed with natural resources? Yet the cost of *building* such factories is small relative to the payrolls they would bring. And after all, with the feeble inducements now in vogue or even without them some manufacturing plants *have* settled in these regions. There is therefore no reason to believe that in terms of preferred alternatives the cost of inducing others to do likewise would be prohibitive.

Returning to our survey of specific areas we note that an abundance of labor *in practically all sections of the state* is reported in South Carolina[41] and in North Carolina. In the latter state the so-called recruitable labor force, i.e. people immediately available for manufacturing or other jobs paying a similar wage, in 1957 was estimated to comprise 200,000 people residing in the state and an additional 50,000 who had migrated but were desirous to come back to their home town if they could get an industrial job there. Twenty percent of the 200,000 were unemployed and the remaining 80 percent consisted of people in low-productivity occupations.[42] Similarly, "there are many and widespread areas in West Virginia where low-income open country rural families are underemployed."[43] A report from Mississippi indicates conditions that are characteristic of many other sections in the deep South as well: "All areas of Mississippi have low-income (underemployed) families in the open country. This is mainly due to high ratios of population to the land supply. In most areas of the state there are very low alternative employment opportunities, so that most families are not able to leave the open country for industry or nonfarm work."[44] As to Virginia, its position is similar to that of its neighbors, although underemployment is perhaps no longer so great a problem as in some other southern states:

Virginia could expand its labor supply from its own sources by approximately 300,000. This potential expansion is a result of . . . new entrants in excess of those being separated from the labor force, the availability of women in rural areas who now lack job opportunities, and a continuation of the movement of farmers into non-agricultural employment. Will employment opportunities in Virginia expand at a rate sufficient to absorb these people, or will they migrate to the labor-hungry metropolitan areas of the nation or remain underemployed?[45]

Community development groups throughout the South stress the availability of labor.[46]

41. South Carolina State Development Board, *Industrial Data on South Carolina* (Columbia, S.C., 1959), p. 11.

42. Julian Scheer, "Labor: Ready, Willing, and Able," *New York Times,* November 17, 1957, section 10, p. 9.

43. Joint Committee on the Economic Report, *Underemployment of Rural Families,* p. 25.

44. *Ibid.*

45. Virginia, Subcommittee on Finances, Industrial Development Study Commission, *Should a State-wide Industrial Development Credit Corporation Be Organized in Virginia* (Richmond, May, 1957), p. 4.

46. As a typical example, the town of Ripley, Tenn., advertises "LABOR in Abundance, Of High Quality, With Loyal, Steady Response For Which There Is NO Compe-

Testifying before the Senate subcommittee on S. 722 (which proposed a program of low-interest loans and grants to depressed areas) on behalf of the Tennessee Municipal League and the American Municipal Association, Messrs. H. J. Bingham, T.M.L. executive secretary, Hugh Heatherly, City Recorder of La Follette, and Dwain Peterman, Mayor of Livingston, indicated the present (early 1959) extent of the un- and underemployment problem in Tennessee.[47] Mr. Bingham stated that much of Tennessee is economically depressed, with *chronic* unemployment in three of the largest cities and in at least six smaller industrial centers, and underemployment in some 54 out of 95 counties, including the municipalities in them. Mr. Heatherly stated in part:

Campbell County has been losing population steadily, at an alarming rate. The reason, of course, is that there has been no economic opportunity in Campbell and adjacent counties to hold our productive, ambitious younger people. Our county's population in 1950 was 34,400. By 1956, it was down to 33,200—a decline of 1,200. However, we had an excess of births over deaths totaling 3,700. So our net loss through outmigration from Campbell County was 4,900 or 14.2 per cent of our entire population. This is indeed a disturbing figure and a symptom of something seriously wrong.

In spite of this outmigration, per capita income in Campbell County was only slightly more than half the Tennessee average and about two-fifths of the average for the nation. Moreover: "In the La Follette-Jellico-Tazewell area, comprising Campbell and Claiborne Counties, there was a civilian labor force of 16,350 as of last October. We had some 14 percent unemployed or 2,250 persons known to be looking for work and unable to find it. This figure, of course, does not represent all of our unemployment."

In the state of Tennessee as a whole, the number of employees in manufacturing industry increased from 222,300 in 1947 to 261,200 in 1954 or by 17 percent as compared to a 16 percent increase in the thirteen southeastern states (where the increase in manufacturing employment ranged from 5 and 6 percent in Alabama and West Virginia respectively at the bottom to 56 and 21 percent in Florida and Georgia

tition," while on the same page Dyersburg also advertises "Abundant labor" (*Tennessee Town and City*, VIII [July, 1957], 16). In Alabama, every one of 31 brochures studied by the Alabama Business Research Council emphasizes that a sizeable labor pool of redundant farm labor exists, and that these people need cash and want jobs in industry (*Alabama Goes Industry Hunting*, p. 37).

47. "Federal Aid for Depressed Areas," *Tennessee Town and City*, X (April, 1959), 6-7, 21.

at the top).[48]   The rate of industrial expansion in Tennessee is therefore fairly typical for the Southeast as a whole.   The average increase
in Tennessee for the nine-year period 1947-56 was 5,100 industrial
workers per year, but the 1954-56 yearly average was 11,900 or more
than double that of the average over the longer period.   However,
even while employment opportunity was created at this top rate, 55,000
people left the state in the year 1956.   Between 1950 and 1957 Tennessee's net outmigration rate was double that of the 1940-50 decade
and exceeded that of any decade since 1870.   Without these migration
losses the state's population gain would have been about 12.3 percent
in this period, but the actual increase was only 4.3 percent.   This gain
was piled up solely in the four large cities and northeastern Tennessee,
the great majority of the 95 counties suffering sharp losses.[49]   Not
only farming areas but also mining regions in the Cumberland plateau,
where in the past decade employment in coal mining was reduced by
50 percent, were affected by this movement.[50]

Concern about population losses.   In the declining areas there is
great concern about population losses, which do not only adversely
affect remaining business enterprise (e.g. retailing) that is dependent
upon local demand, but tend to impoverish and undermine the social
and cultural life of the community.   "The realities of economic life in
many parts of this country are harsh indeed.   Too many of our smaller
cities [and rural communities] offer little opportunity for the young-
sters they have educated.   Growing up for many generations has
meant leaving home and 'seeking one's fortune' elsewhere."[51]   Personal investigation by means of interviews and correspondence[52] has
confirmed for me that this statement accurately reflects the feeling
about outmigration in communities offering insufficient employment

48. G. I. Whitlatch, "Qualified Towns Planned for Progress and New Industry,"
Tennessee Town and City, VIII (July, 1957), 27.
    49. "A Look Ahead," *Tennessee Town and City,* X (January, 1959), 5.
    50. Robert S. Hutchinson, *Migration and Industrial Development in Tennessee,*
Report to the Industrial Development and Migration Subcommittee of the Tennessee
Legislative Council, October, 1958, p. 5 (mimeographed).   This report contains a
detailed account of migration patterns in Tennessee.
    51. William D. Carlebach, "State and Local Governmental Responsibility for
Economic Development," *Tax Policy,* XXIV (January, 1957), 16.
    52. Thus I have a letter which reads in part: "Georgia, in common with a number
of other states, faces this problem: As a result of mechanization on the farms and
other revolutionary developments which have decreased employment in agriculture,
many persons are leaving the farms for the urban centers.   This has caused a number
of counties to lose population, and it is vitally necessary to these counties that they
secure industrial plants to provide additional employment.   Georgia therefore is
conducting a steady drive for new industry. . . ."

opportunity, and that the growing efforts of local development organizations are in large part a reflection of this feeling. "For generations lack of opportunity was accepted, like drought or a warm summer. . . . Occasionally and fortuitously, like the rain that breaks the drought, a plant would come to town and grow and suddenly there was opportunity at hand. The realization that plant location decisions of great and remote corporations were decisions that could be influenced by community activity did not become widespread until very recently."[53] Or, less poetically, with respect to rural towns and counties: "With the farmers strongly sold [to industrial payrolls as a means of keeping their children at home], with them seeing industry as a means for restoring rural community life, propping up the rural church, etc., effective financial and moral support can be obtained from county government."[54] And again: "A frequently stated purpose of local agencies is, 'We want to keep our young people at home and help the town to grow.' Lawyers need clients, retailers need customers, banks need depositors, and doctors need patients."[55]

Nor do the people who are forced to migrate generally seem to like the change afterwards. With regard to them we read: "From what could be gained from conversations with oldsters in a number of towns, these people would positively come back and be glad to work for as little as half what they are making 'up North.' . . . the impression you get from those who have gone to greener climes is that they are anything but happy, no matter what their salaries."[56] This is consistent with the fact that many migrants actually do return to work in their home town when there is an opportunity.[57] There may be a certain exaggeration in the above statement in that undoubtedly there are also those who are satisfied in their new surroundings, but it is certain that migration induced by lack of local employment opportunity is a problem that demands a solution as much as that of un- and underemployment (of which it actually is a manifestation).

This is not meant in the sense that all net migration from one area to another is necessarily unhealthy. Even when, as a result of reasonable local effort, full employment would come to prevail throughout the economy, income differentials between localities (determined in part by the burden of this effort, which would vary from

53. Carlebach, *op. cit.*, p. 16.
54. *Tennessee Town and City*, VIII (July, 1957), 12.
55. *Alabama Goes Industry Hunting*, p. 46.
56. "Migration at All Time High, Three State Comparison," *Tennessee Town and City*, VIII (July, 1957), 21.
57. *Supra*, p. 15, footnote 21.

place to place, and also by wage differentials) would continue to induce workers to seek their fortune elsewhere. Perhaps in some communities this would always remain more important in alleviating population pressure than local development. Under such circumstances a program of rendering financial aid to people desirous to migrate but unable to bear the initial expense of the transfer, as proposed by various authors, may have merit in principle. Yet certain practical aspects of the matter should be considered. It is, for instance, hard to see why an able-bodied man capable of joining the labor force elsewhere would not also be capable of somehow moving on his own, sending for his family, if he has one, later. The roads of America are full of men in search of work driving or hitchhiking to their destination, and even a trip by bus is not a very great expense. People who do not have the initiative and wordly knowledge to do this probably are very poor risks as regards adaptation in a new environment and may be better off where they are. When subsidized to move, these people may be embarrassed to return. It would therefore seem somewhat irresponsible for an organization or public authority to be instrumental in such a matter. The migration of those fit to migrate does not require subsidization. On the other hand, the dissemination of more adequate information about employment opportunity in all parts of the country is highly desirable.

In conclusion, industrialization need not mean and, given the mainfest preference pattern of those directly concerned, should not mean depopulation of the countryside and an ever-increasing concentration of people in metropolitan centers. To a far greater extent than has been the case, industry can and should be induced to come where the people are and *want to be*. One can philosophize about the relative merits of city and country life and the implications of one kind of development as compared to another for the future stability of our society, but in last analysis this is irrelevant for policy in an individualistic society. Only when there is a great and clear-cut national interest at stake is it fully consistent with the principles of liberal democracy for a nation to decide collectively that a development in important respects contrary to the preference pattern of individuals as such will be imposed. Regarding the question of industrial location in view of the nuclear threat, decentralization should indeed be considered a matter narrowly connected with our prospect of national survival. That on this ground alone decentralization has not been given more attention and that in fact nothing has been done to bring about a more decentralized location pattern of private industry is truly amazing. It so happens, however, that no conflict exists with respect to this question between the peaceful interest of individuals and the interest of national survival in case of war. For this reason there exists what in essence amounts to a market solution, even though this will require the creation of a framework within which the market can operate to the greatest benefit of the people. At present the market is characterized by imperfections the nature of which has been reviewed in Chapter I, while the present chapter has been devoted to a survey of the effects of these imperfections. These effects add up to a very serious distortion in resource allocation, causing much frustration in our society. It has been implied that the organized effort of local communities can play an important role in rectifying this situation by throwing the weight of the preferences of its members in the balance of market forces. In the next chapters an attempt will be made to give the reader an impression of the extent of current and past efforts in that direction.

CHAPTER III

Approaches toward Subsidization: Case Studies of Local and Regional Efforts to Attract Industry

Local action to attract industry by means of inducements other than the services traditionally rendered by municipalities or counties has been undertaken by local governments as well as private groups. When I first started with the research for this work, not having a large staff at my disposition for extensive data gathering community by community, it appeared impossible to gain more than a very sketchy impression of the extent and quantitative importance of this type of activity throughout the nation. Quite recently, however, our knowledge of this aspect of the matter, although yet far from complete, has been much enriched by the appearance of two studies containing a wealth of material based on extensive surveys of nationwide scope.[1] On these studies I have gratefully drawn to round off the picture which I had already obtained on the basis of widely scattered and incomplete information contained in previously existing published material, through correspondence, and by means of a limited amount of personal field investigation. Mostly, however, I wish to refer the reader to the two publications in question, which form a perfect complement to my own study. For the present study is primarily concerned with analysis and evaluation, even in its more descriptive parts,

1. U.S. Congress, Senate Committee on Banking and Currency, *Development Corporations and Authorities,* 86th Cong., 1st Sess. (Washington: Government Printing Office, 1959); Donald R. Gilmore, *Developing the "Little" Economies* (Committee for Economic Development: Supplementary Paper No. 10, April, 1960). The Committee on Banking and Currency publication is a compilation of reports (some of which are analytical and regional in scope but including also a report by Victor Roterus based on a nationwide survey by the U.S. Department of Commerce of community-sponsored private development corporations), statutes, and other materials on state and local development corporations and authorities, while the C.E.D. study is the first comprehensive survey ever undertaken of the wide variety of area development programs both public and private operating in the United States.

and often uses the "what is" as a starting point to make comments regarding "what could be" as well as to exchange opinions with other commentators.[2]

Because in local efforts to attract industry action of private groups has often been narrowly intertwined with that of local governments, the latter operating within limitations imposed by state governments, a separation of material according to the private or public character of the endeavor is not expedient for the purposes of this treatise. Nevertheless, the problems that arise in connection with the allocation of public funds for what amounts to the subsidization of private industry deserve special attention. These problems are discussed in Chapter IV, while the present chapter is largely devoted to what might be termed case studies, which, it is hoped, will give the reader an appreciation of the nature of the local efforts made viewed in the light of the considerations set forth in the preceding chapters. In this I was fortunate to find available a number of intensive studies dealing with particular areas, localities, or industrial development organizations. Chapter V, the last of the empirical chapters, is more extensive in character and surveys past and current attempts of local communities as well as state-wide organizations to attract industry by means of special inducements. Also included in that chapter is a brief survey of federal programs designed to help solve the problems of surplus labor areas.

A few introductory remarks may precede our case studies. While private initiative motivated by profit making in the ordinary sense may make important contributions to local industrialization, for instance in the form of planned real estate development, we are here solely concerned with the activity of groups that are motivated by the expectation of *indirect* benefits to the community at large and themselves in particular which new industry brings in the form of payrolls, increased retail sales, increased demand for services rendered locally in general, higher real estate values, and the like. In other words, we shall look into activities which spring from a realization that industry means employment opportunity, better business, and strengthening of community life.[3] Moreover, from our point of view all activities aim-

2. By contrast, the C.E.D. study states in the introduction: "The reader is left to conclude from this survey all that the data and his reason will allow. . . . It concentrates on the facts and tries to tell a straight story. If it reads something like a telephone book it is just that the figures must tell their own story. An attempt has been made to eliminate all economic, political, and social philosophy; the report was designed only to report the facts."

3. This includes the activities of the great majority of community development corporations organized as regular business corporations. Whether these organizations

ing at industrial development and community promotion are not equally interesting. Little will be said about such promotional efforts as advertising, establishing contact with prospects and trying to interest them in a locality, giving information about local conditions and help in finding the proper site for an establishment, etc. All this is, of course, very useful in principle in that it makes available knowledge which aids entrepreneurs in making rational location decisions.[4] But this work deals specifically with the financial inducements that private groups and governmental units are willing to extend to new or expanding enterprises in order to secure location in their area.[5] These have included outright subsidies in the form of gifts of money or sites and sometimes industrial buildings and equipment, as well as implied subsidies in the form of low interest loans or loans unobtainable through the conventional channels, easy terms on the lease of industrial buildings, the sale of sites and buildings below market value or construction cost, tax exemptions, the provision of utilities below cost, etc.

However, although often present, protestations to the contrary notwithstanding,[6] subsidization is not in all cases a necessary element

are established as charitable trusts (as a few are), non-profit corporations, or business corporations, the primary objective usually is to stimulate local economic growth.

4. Discussions of the full range of activities of local development corporations, local governments, and other agencies as well as of the form of organization of these agencies can be found in the works cited in footnote 1, p. 47 and, as regards the community development corporation, also in Gordon F. Davis, *The Community Development Corporation in Kansas* (sponsored by Kansas Industrial Development Commission), Bureau of Business Research, School of Business, University of Kansas (Lawrence, Kansas, 1954).

5. Development corporations frequently act as intermediaries between entrepreneur and local government to negotiate tax exemptions and other concessions that are within the power of governmental units to make. They may also try to secure for their prospects capital funds from local sources on a businesslike basis.

6. These protestations are indicative of the inhibitions prevailing in the matter of industrial subsidization. The following examples may illustrate this point. Robert E. Black in "Localities Organize for Industry" writes about the financing of industrial enterprise by development corporations in Virginia: "The financing, while sound, is more liberal than what would be possible under strict commercial practice. The community's chief interest is the new payroll, which is new blood in the local economic lifestream." And a few paragraphs later: "The Virginia development corporations cited here do *not* offer any industry as[sic] subsidy, openly or in any disguise. Thinking on this matter follows this line: businesses that ask for concessions in order to come to a particular town are likely to be weak companies and a potential or real liability. . . ." (Italics in the original.) See Commonwealth of Virginia, *Report of the Commission to Study Industrial Development in Virginia to the Governor and the General Assembly of Virginia,* Senate Document No. 10 (Richmond: Division of Purchase and Printing, 1957), pp. 103, 105. Similarly, a letter in my possession says: "Georgia does not put emphasis on gifts and subsidies. The industrial opportunities and advantages are so clear-cut in Georgia that we have not found it necessary to emphasize give-away plans. However, it is possible and even probable

of success, nor can it always be indicated where communities interested in securing an industry have participated in the financing of an industrial establishment. In the first place, an industrial development corporation, while primarily concerned with the indirect benefits of acquiring industry for the community, may take useful initiative along the lines of site improvement, etc., similar to that of interests solely concerned with the profits derived immediately from such activities, and in the process create conditions so attractive to industry that subsidization is rendered unnecessary. Secondly, municipalities often can raise money in the bond market more cheaply than industrial concerns because municipal bonds are exempt from federal taxes. It may therefore be advantageous to an enterprise to obtain municipal financing of its capital requirements on conditions that will enable the municipality to amortize bonds issued for this purpose and meet the interest charges in full. For this reason, such arrangements are frequently made, and this does not constitute subsidization of the enterprise by the municipality. But of course the federal tax exemption does constitute subsidization by the tax payer at large. This issue will be further discussed in Chapter IV.

On the other hand, it should be admitted that when an entrepreneur is given a loan which he cannot obtain through the ordinary channels for lack of equity or whatever other reason, he is being subsidized. Much has been written to the effect that legitimate capital needs of small enterprises (especially for equity capital) are not adequately met. In many of these writings it is pointed out that an increasing proportion of personal savings is nowadays channelled through financial institutions which are unable or unwilling to make funds available for equity financing of small business. Hence the expansion of small enterprises has come to depend more and more upon internal financing, but this is greatly impeded under the present tax structure which bears heavily upon the profits necessary to accomplish this process. One may agree that this is a highly undesirable and socially dangerous situation, but it does not follow, as some authors seem to imply, that providing small enterprises with funds they cannot obtain in the market from financial institutions or individuals guided by the profit motive is free from an element of subsidization. There is absolutely no evidence that these institutions discriminate against small enterprise—if it were profitable for them to allocate more funds to

that nearly every community industrial development corporation in the state of Georgia has made or would be willing to make some reasonable concessions to bring in a good and substantial industry."

small business they would do so. It may be argued that the *system* discriminates against small business, but not the market, which, for better or worse, always operates within the framework of restraints and under conditions of supply and demand determined by the overall system. Again, therefore, it may be argued that in the above lies perhaps a justification (quite apart from the main justification of industrial subsidies with which this work is concerned) for making capital available to small business through special agencies, but it cannot be maintained that this is not subsidization. This is practically a matter of definition or proper usage of a word. Since it is a word that more often than not evokes emotional rather than rational reactions, it is particularly important to insist that it be used properly. Instead of denying that a practice, when rational, constitutes subsidization, we should insist that subsidization may be rational. As the first of our case studies, we shall now discuss a development corporation that has specalized in making loans to small businesses that did not meet the standards of ordinary financial institutions.

The Louisville Industrial Foundation.[7] This institution is one of the oldest and best-known development corporations in the country. It was founded in 1916 at a time that business in Louisville was depressed and workers were leaving the city to find work elsewhere. Other cities at the time responded to a similar challenge by raising community funds to advertise community advantages, subsidize industry, and to combat unionism, but Louisville business leaders decided to follow a different approach. They organized a drive for a "Million-Dollar Factory Fund" for making loans to enterprises "on a business-like basis," including current interest charges. In this way the money could be used over and over again to help establish other enterprises and finance expansions. However, the idea was to accommodate solely manufacturing enterprises unable to obtain "the equivalent amount of capital on comparable terms from other sources in the same area."[8]

By means of newspaper publicity, speeches, and enthusiastically worded pamphlets, an appeal was made to both enlightened self-interest and civic patriotism. The funds were raised by the sale of common stock in $100 denominations. Largest contributors were the Louisville Gas and Electricity Company and the Louisville Railway

7. The information on this foundation presented here is derived from Ernest J. Hopkins, *The Louisville Industrial Foundation, A study in community capitalization of local industries* (Atlanta: Research Department, Federal Reserve Bank of Atlanta, 1945).
8. *Ibid.,* p. 4.

Company, followed by department stores, banks, and other large enterprises, professional men, retailers, etc. A large number of other individuals also subscribed, but it soon became apparent that many of those had done so under pressure brought upon them by their employers or under the mistaken impression that dividends could be anticipated. (In fact no dividends were ever paid, the interest being used for reinvestment in new loans and to meet expenses.) "In the heat of the campaign, some unwise promises were undoubtedly made and some extreme things done."[9] Later it was recognized that it would have been better to restrict the solicitation of funds to individuals and business concerns that were clearly in line to benefit from an increased industrial payroll in the community.

By 1945, the Foundation had extended loans to 44 manufacturing enterprises not eligible at the time for ordinary types of financial accommodation, using its capital as a revolving fund. Thus it has been performing "a strategic role in rounding out and supplementing Louisville's structure of organized finance."[10] With only four exceptions the borrowers ultimately repaid their loans, from which Hopkins infers that "the actual risk presented by the off-standard business situation may be, at times, less than theoretical credit standards might imply."[11] Yet on its face the evidence—too limited in any case to warrant such a generalization—does not seem to bear out this conclusion, for, in addition to the failures (10 percent of all cases), in numerous instances payments had to be deferred and additional aid rendered in order to enable the enterprises in question to survive. Of more interest, therefore, is Hopkins' observation that even the investments that failed represented gain to Louisville as a community: "The companies that did not survive created employment while they lasted, which was generally several years; also, the factory buildings erected for these enterprises from Foundation funds in all cases proved available for new manufacturing occupants and are used as factories today."[12]

Various other aspects of the Foundation's activity may be mentioned briefly. It collects and distributes data concerning the Louisville area, answers business enquiries, and at times compiles reliable briefs for site-seeking manufacturing concerns. In this way it has been able to secure many enterprises for Louisville without contributing to the financing of these firms. As a logical complement to its investment policy—financing "marginal" needs of mostly locally-owned small

9. *Ibid.*, p. 18.
10. *Ibid.*, p. 4.
11. *Ibid.*, p. 57.
12. *Ibid.*, p. 23.

enterprises—it has where necessary taken a continued interest in its clients, guiding them with advice, establishing valuable business contacts, and sometimes putting in additional funds in order to help them along in difficult periods so as to secure the ultimate repayment of loans originally granted. In this as in its lenient attitude toward firms encountering difficulties in meeting their obligations, the Foundation has gone much farther than most other development corporations.

While this approach seems to have been successful in Louisville, it may be questioned whether such a policy is practicable for similar institutions in the smaller cities and rural communities where nowadays the great majority are located. It may be advisable, in the general case, to submit an industrial prospect to a careful investigation as to the probability of its meeting the conditions upon which financial assistance will be rendered rather than to get involved with marginal enterprises. The idea here is that an enterprise may be perfectly sound and not stand in need of any special financial concession for its expansion but may nevertheless require concessions if it is to locate in a particular community desirous to secure a payroll. However, this is not a subject to be treated in a dogmatic fashion. When the talent and the civic spirit are there to make a success out of enterprises considered overly risky by ordinary financial institutions, or when difficulties unexpectedly arise, it may be in the interest of a community to foster the development of such firms and to safeguard investments once made by the extension of guidance and further aid. Moreover, since the erection and subsequent leasing of factory buildings is the most frequent type of financial assistance rendered, development corporations usually are in a position to attract another industry without making further investments should the building become vacant through default of the lessee. A 1954 study of a number of development corporations active in Georgia and Tennessee indicated that most leases had been granted to small and lesser-known firms.[13] Once operations become profitable, such enterprises often exercise a purchase option on the leased building. In a sense the risk involved in financing this type of firm should be considered the equivalent of greater outright concessions a community may have to make in order to attract a more established concern, and this risk is mitigated by the possession of (a mortgage on) the factory building. Besides, communities do not always have a wide range of alternatives and may have to make the best of such opportunities as arise. To find a new

13. Harry Brandt, "Another Look at Development Corporations," *Monthly Review,* Federal Reserve Bank of Atlanta (September 30, 1954), pp. 3-5.

occupant of a vacated building a corporation may of course have to accept rental terms less favorable than it originally intended, but since, as I shall show, subsidies are in general not carried to anywhere near their logical limit, there is nothing particularly disturbing about this. To the subject of leasing factory buildings we shall return later.

The revolving fund approach. Revolving funds have the obvious advantage of perpetuating the usefulness of money once raised. In Louisville, for instance, the 1916 campaign was never repeated but the Fund in 1945 was larger than ever, having aided 44 enterprises. By the same token, however, the approach certainly limits the amount of subsidy that can be given at any moment. Since the purpose is to maintain the original capital intact, the capitalized value of the subsidy element cannot on the average exceed that of the interest foregone on loans extended on this principle and may be less—at least to the extent that expectations are realized. A community should of course not give away more than is necessary to obtain the industry it is after, but strict adherence to the revolving fund principle is not suitable for communities where circumstances require a more drastic type of action. The Louisville Foundation itself has been criticized for being too conservative. During the depression of the thirties for instance, at a time that the employment situation would have warranted an increased volume of industrial subsidies (which in some other areas of the country was in fact forthcoming), the Foundation remained relatively inactive. Most applications for loans received in this period were rejected on the basis of the philosophy that, while it was the task of the Foundation to add as much as possible to the employment opportunity in the city, no action should be taken that might put into jeopardy the preservation of its capital.

Among the development corporations in Georgia and Tennessee mentioned above, a rather similar attitude seems in evidence. The survey comprised thirteen corporations, mostly established shortly after World War II. In 1954, six of these were found to have rendered no assistance to business firms, while three out of the seven that did managed to maintain their capital intact and add to it. It is true that open and implied subsidies in a great variety of forms (donation of sites, loans at lower-than-bank rates, free or reduced rentals on facilities, tax concessions, etc.) played a role in the activities of all of the corporations studied that actually rendered assistance to entrepreneurs. However, rentals in the majority of cases were large enough to provide some return on the corporation's investment in addition to repayment of the principal, and the occupant commonly paid property taxes, insurance, utilities, and maintenance charges.[14]   Although these corporations did not adhere to the revolving fund principle as consistently as did the Louisville Industrial Foundation, they appear to have been motivated by a desire to do so, and this goes far as a likely explanation of the rather modest degree of success in some of the seven active cases and the failure to achieve anything at all in six cases out of a total of thirteen.   It is, however, not astonishing that this should be so in view of the fact that development corporations (as well as municipalities) are commonly severely criticized for such modest subsidizing as they do engage in, especially when this leads to a loss of principal.[15] In most of the thinking on this subject there is a curious inconsistency. On the one hand it is recognized that the role of a development corporation is to serve the community by bringing in additional payrolls, with contingent benefits in the form of increased business activity. On the other hand, however, the notion persists that the money invested in this type of activity should at least be kept intact and if possible yield direct returns.   One is kept wondering why the indirect benefits (payrolls, etc.) that form the acknowledged justification of a corporation's activity in the first place may not themselves be considered as the returns on a permanent rather than a revolving investment in a community's prosperity.   And if there is to be subsidization, why should the interest foregone in meeting financial requirements of prospects be the upper limit, as the revolving fund approach implies?

There is not much logic to this, but an explanation can be readily found.   It consists of two parts.   The first and least rational—and probably the most important—aspect of the matter is that as long as the subsidies are in some way hidden, it is easier to rationalize them. When more than commonly risky loans are made or facilities are made available at a price not quite covering interest charges but enabling the subsidizing agent to amortize its investment, calling the transaction "business-like" will serve to placate the undiscriminating observer as well as the man who knows that "subsidies" are wrong but nevertheless intuitively senses the appropriateness[16] of the action in question.

14. *Ibid.*, pp. 4, 5.

15. A typical statement in this respect is the following: "Subsidies have unfortunately played a considerable part in foundation activities.   Furthermore, development corporations have often been unable to keep their capital funds intact.   This situation arises from subsidization rather than granting of money to enterprises which failed" (*Ibid.*, p. 5).

16. The term "appropriate" in this context must be interpreted from the point

This situation would be much less disturbing if the attitude it reflects had not also often interfered with the extension of more "extreme" subsidies in situations where this was indicated. It is for this reason that it is so important not to evade the issue but to call a spade a spade. The subsidization question stands in dire need of being decided in principle. That alone will make it possible to indicate rational limits to the practice.

The second part of the explanation lies in the insistence on the part of the proponents of the revolving fund approach that repeated appeals to the community for funds are not likely to meet with much success. On its face one is inclined to doubt this assertion. Especially in a small community, one would think, people could not fail to observe the benefits accruing to them from an initial successful effort. They would therefore be eager to repeat the experiment if the employment situation still warrants it. However, this must be decided empirically. Evidence that in fact people react this way will be presented in this treatise.

The widely prevailing conservative attitude has had two effects: first and foremost, that much less has been done to alleviate un- and underemployment by means of subsidizing industry than would have been possible, and secondly, that the indirect returns on subsidies that were pushed through have almost invariably been very large indeed.[17] This implies that under the present circumstances any community not completely devoid of natural attractions can both eliminate local unemployment and gain tremendous returns on the funds invested in acquiring payrolls. In due course this assertion will be further explained and substantiated.

of view of an individual community. This and the following two empirical chapters are not much concerned with a justification of local subsidies from the point of view of the economy as a whole. That task is deferred to the last part of this book. Local subsidies must also be defended against attacks that question their merit from the purely local viewpoint.

17. The question of returns to subsidies is discussed systematically in Appendix V. Here one indication of their magnitude must suffice. We have seen (footnote 15, p. 55) that Mr. Brandt, reporting on thirteen development corporations in Georgia and Tennessee, deplored their use of subsidies and particularly the fact that some did not maintain their capital intact. The seven active foundations in this group together secured for their communities a total of 25 companies, employing an estimated 5,500 workers and disbursing an aggregate annual payroll of over 16 million dollars. Moreover, in at least two cases suppliers of raw materials located in these communities as a result of the establishment of industries the development corporations had brought in. With these results may be contrasted the fact that, as Brandt states, "the initial amount of capital raised in each case was small, the average being less than $75,000" (op. cit., p. 3). Deplorable indeed that some fraction of this initial outlay had to be written off against a lasting annual return exceeding 16 million dollars!

Doing what it takes—the experience of Lafayette, Tennessee. This small rural town is an outstanding example of what can be achieved when a community is determined to halt economic deterioration. Its experience, which will be briefly outlined below,[18] admirably illustrates the point that when the beneficial effects of the establishment of new plants are there for everyone to see, appeals to the community for further contributions so as to bring in more industry are likely to be met with enthusiastic response.

The program to promote industry in Macon County (where Lafayette is located) was started when the Tri-County Electric Membership Corporation, a cooperative organized locally when the utility company serving the area refused to provide open-country farms with electricity, found that it had lost 3,500 customers through out-migration after borrowing to build service for them. A sum of $42,500 was donated by the town and its businessmen to a garment manufacturer from Chattanooga who had indicated that he was willing to consider Lafayette as the location for a new branch plant if the inducements were right. The money was used by the manufacturer as part payment for a plant many times the size the local money would have bought. As William Parker, the local banker who took a major part in this and subsequent promotions, writes: "This brought new industrial load to the electric power lines, and also it brought new business to the bank."[19] The factory now employs about 350 people, with an annual payroll of about $700,000.

Encouraged by this initial success and apparently proceeding without the prejudice against outright subsidization so common in other communities, the bank and the electric cooperative built up community support to secure a dairy products processor. It was felt that the benefits of such a plant would contribute income to any farmer "who had enough energy to milk a few cows." In this case 25 people put up $1,000 each to erect a cheese factory, which was leased to a nationally known food manufacturer.[20] This created payrolls and, more important, led to a steady increase in milk sales in the district, from 1.5 million pounds annually in 1946 when the factory was established

18. For more detailed accounts see: William Parker, "Operation Bootstrap," *Burroughs Clearing House,* XLI (June, 1957), 37-39, 92-96, and " 'Buy Industry' or 'You May Not Get It,' says Lafayette Mayor Who Learned the Hard Way," *Tennessee Town and City,* VIII (July, 1957), 6, 46. Some additional information presented here was supplied by William Parker.

19. Parker, *op. cit.,* p. 38.

20. This fact is underlined because it is often alleged that only disreputable "fly-by-night" enterprises are interested in financial inducements. This assertion lacks any foundation in reality as many other examples to be presented in this work will illustrate.

to 36 million pounds by 1957. As early as the third year of operation the factory paid more than $1 million for the milk it processed, and farm employment tending dairy cattle rose from 150 to 600. In 1957 the cheese factory, together with a strawberry processing plant attracted in 1954, provided a market in farm products of $5.1 million in addition to from 15 to 300 factory jobs, depending on the season. It will have to be admitted that in comparison to these results the initial investments were negligible.[21]

Next, a hardwood flooring manufacturing company, representing local initiative, was helped with loans and aid in securing additional capital financing. Today it has a payroll of about $240,000 annually, buys rough lumber from local sawmills and sawlogs from woodlot owners, and is bringing a sizeable increase to the income of the area. It is now leased to a Chicago company, which plans a two- or threefold expansion.

At this juncture the Macon Industrial Corporation was formed to continue industrial promotion. It has repeatedly solicited voluntary contributions for the purpose of bringing in additional plants and other community improvement projects. The strawberry processing plant mentioned above was located by it and also, in close cooperation with the bank, a shirt factory which employs about 600 to 700 people with a payroll of nearly $1 million per year. The corporation erected the building at a cost of some $400,000 and leased it to the operators against a stipulated rental over a thirty-year period, at the expiration of which ownership will pass to the company. The rental does not quite cover amortization plus interest, but apparently the differential is not great. The financing of this project required some complicated manipulations, including private donations, gifts and loans from city and county, bank credit on behalf of the corporation secured by endorsements of a group of substantial citizens, and a loan from the federal government's Small Business Administration.

As a result of these promotions industrial employment in Macon County rose from 20 plus a few sawmill workers to more than 1,200 in 1957.[22] Of these some 650 were women, and it was felt that more employment opportunity for men was needed "to hold the local boys who now have to go elsewhere for employment, and also to take care of the decrease in farm employment which anyone viewing the situa-

21. Perhaps at this stage a question of causation has arisen in the mind of the reader. This question will be fully discussed during a later phase of our argument.

22. The population of Macon County in 1955 was 12,620 and that of Lafayette approximately 2,500.

tion realistically is bound to expect for at least a few years more." For this purpose a trades training program in woodworking at Macon High School was planned as well as the financing of additional industry employing men by means of special bond issues of a half million dollars by the county and the city each.

The community leaders in Lafayette are justifiably proud of their achievements and have some realistic advice for other small towns. Mayor Tooley, addressing the small cities and towns panel at the 1957 Tennessee Municipal League convention, put it as follows: "The little town that wants industry to stop the flow of young people away from its surrounding rural area does what is called 'buying industry' or it does not get any." The "high sounding talk" about not offering inducements is the worst advice that can be offered a small town, he added, and: "I am awfully tired of hearing the fine theorists of industrial development say to the little town desperate for a payroll: 'only a sick industry wants a subsidy.'" Similarly, Macon County Agricultural Agent Luck, also on the panel, said: "You listen to the experts tell you 'No!' Then if you are wise you do whatever it takes to get the plant, and I mean just that, 'whatever it takes.'" This was also the keynote of Banker Parker's address, in which he informed the audience that doing "whatever it took" produced in ten years an estimated $1,775,000 in annual industrial and food processing payrolls for a town of 2,500.[23] These leaders are convinced that what Lafayette did other towns can do too.

A study of 41 Tennessee communities. In 1937 Robert E. Lowry undertook a survey of the subsidization practice in 41 Tennessee communities scattered throughout the state and ranging in population (basis: 1930 census) from 800 to 25,000 with a median of 3,700. Comprised in the sample were four cities with a population of more than 10,000. The study in which the results are laid down[24] deals primarily with the situation prevailing at the time of the investigation, but also includes information on the development of the subsidization approach since the 1920's. The impression one gains is that, especially in the thirties, subsidizing industry in small communities was a widely prevalent practice in this area.

Lowry points out that in the 1920's the attraction of large urban centers offering industrial employment, combined with a decline in rural buying power and a growing tendency of people to drive to the

23. " 'Buy Industry'. . . ," *Tennessee Town and City,* VIII (July, 1957), 6.
24. Robert E. Lowry, "Municipal Subsidies to Industries in Tennessee," *Southern Economic Journal,* VII (January, 1941), 317-29.

larger centers for their shopping, began to undermine the economic basis of small-sized rural market towns—creating a situation quite similar to that still existing today. It was then that "factory employment and pay rolls began to appeal with a new intensity as the most direct way out of business stagnation. Industrial promotion became the small town shibboleth; thousands of dollars were raised by private subscription and poured into development companies which built factory buildings for the casual occupancy of any operator that could be induced to come in."[25]

The somewhat critical tone of this passage apparently originates in Lowry's finding that during the subsequent depression most of the original occupants vacated the buildings constructed for them, so that other occupants had to be found. It seems, however, that most communities were successful in this, for Lowry mentions that of the 13 factories contained in the sample that were built before the depression only two were vacant at the time of the survey (while two others were still occupied by the original tenants). This turnover is not so unnatural in view of the depressed business conditions of the early 1930's, but what Lowry particularly takes exception to is the fact that in the general case continued subsidization proved to be necessary in order to secure occupancy (all but two occupants still receiving substantial subsidies in 1937). This theme, that subsidization limited to a given initial period may not suffice to hold an industry, frequently recurs in the literature as a warning against the practice.[26] It is therefore necessary to digress in order to discuss this question.

Continued subsidization is in principle justified. The economic justification of subsidization based upon a discrepancy between the

25. *Ibid.,* p. 317.

26. For instance: "If the community is so lacking in attractions that it must violate sound principles of taxation, or its own tax laws, in order to attract new industries, it will be better advised to maintain undisturbed its existing status, for it cannot hope permanently to keep up the competitive pace with other communities possessing these attractions" (Kenneth J. McCarren, "Luring Industry through Tax Exemption," *Tax Exemptions,* Symposium conducted by the Tax Policy League, December 28-30, 1938 [New York: Tax Policy League, 1939]). Compare also the following dialogue: *Mr. Suffrin.* "There is always the danger that if you set up some very special type of agency, it will get all the lemons. People who aren't good enough risks to get capital through the normal facilities, will get capital through some extraordinary way; then they become a tremendous burden on the community. All the capital is not lost, but they become a burden on the community. They build up some employment and the operation goes kaput. This is why one must be terribly careful." *Mr. Batt.* "It is a risk worth taking if they employ a couple of hundred people for several years" (U.S. Congress, Subcommittee on Low-Income Families, Joint Committee on the Economic Report, *Hearings, Low-Income Families,* 84th Cong., 1st Sess. [Washington: U.S. Government Printing Office, 1955], p. 561).

marginal productivity of labor and the wages paid in industry is *not* limited to those cases in which the beneficiary can be expected to become self-sufficient after certain initial difficulties have been overcome or, once established in response to special inducements, can be expected to prefer that location over all others when the inducements cease to exist. In practice this may often be the case during times of normal business conditions for several reasons indicated below, but that does not subtract from the principle.

In the first place, there may in fact be initial difficulties, such as a scarcity of trained labor and many others, that tend to keep industry away from a certain location unless special inducements are offered to compensate the enterprise for temporarily higher costs. In the course of time these disadvantages may be removed and the enterprise finds that operating cost in the location of its choice compares favorably with that in other places.

Secondly, moving is expensive, even for so-called "foot-loose" industries which are labor—rather than market—or raw material oriented. To such enterprises investment in capital equipment may represent only a relatively small proportion of production cost, but there are also intangibles, such as workers having been trained to the special requirements of the enterprise, local connections that represent a business value, etc. Therefore, everything else equal, the location in which an enterprise is established has a special advantage to it over all other locations that may be quite important. In other words, it takes more to induce a firm to come (even when the establishment represents an expansion rather than a relocation because at that time no location has the special advantage of being the location where the plant is established) than to prevent it from leaving. For this reason too, then, an initial subsidy may secure the permanent establishment of an industry.

And third, when the initial inducement consists of the gift of a building or a long lease at below-cost rental, it is really a permanent inducement or at least one that maintains its force as long as the building has not become obsolete. Even when written off in the books, a factory building still represents an economic value to the extent that its free occupancy enables an enterprise to carry on production in the place where it is located at lower cost than elsewhere. The original (subsidized) occupant, when he has obtained ownership, may of course decide to sell the building to another entrepreneur who places a higher value on it, but the community should be indifferent to this if the payroll disbursed by the new owner is comparable to that of the former occupant, as in the general case it probably would be. Thus the original subsidy may be transferred to a new operator in the form of the sale of a factory building at a market value below replacement cost. Similarly, in the event that the community itself has retained ownership and the original occupant decides to discontinue its operations, the community is in a position to subsidize another enterprise without incurring additional outlay simply by making the building available to the highest bidder[27] at a price below replacement cost.

Subsidies, however, may be given in forms other than providing a building below cost, or, to retain an industry, more than that may be required. Therefore it may be stressed once more that our argument does not rest upon any presumption that a temporary subsidy or once-and-for-all donation will be sufficient to hold an industry indefinitely. A town that wants to keep the payrolls initially attracted by means of a special inducement should face the fact that it may have to pay indefinitely the difference between the industry's long run production cost without subsidy in that town and the industry's production cost in the best alternative location. And it should realize that as long as other industries cannot be secured on more favorable terms while departure of existing firms would cause unemployment (other than of a strictly temporary nature), *it remains in its interest to accept this burden*. This applies with more than ordinary force in a depression, which is a period during which the difference between actual wage rates and the rates that would cause full employment is generally great.[28] In such a period the causes of un- and underemployment that operate in declining rural areas are compounded, and more than ordinarily heavy subsidies are in order. This would include the continued subsidization of enterprises which, having received a gift at the time of their initial establishment, might have remained without further special inducements had not the general business climate changed for the worse.

I venture to speculate that an insufficient realization of the above may be partly the cause of such changes in occupancy of community-

27. Should there be a predictable difference in payroll between interested parties this should of course be taken into account.

28. The reader will recall that it was pointed out in Chapter I that the ideal payroll subsidy would cover this discrepancy, which of course changes continuously through time. To what extent the various forms of subsidization actually used approach this ideal in their effects (in kind if not in magnitude) and what practical reasons may exist to prefer the existing methods over the fluctuating payroll subsidy are subjects discussed in Chaper VIII.

built factories and, worse, of such prolonged vacancies as have occurred. This would also apply to communities that have exhibited a practical sense in their readiness to meet the subsidization requirements of new industry. Deceived by a conception that the subsidy would have to be a one-time affair only and disappointed in a prospect which, having received a donation, proves to be impermanent unless more is forthcoming, the community may refuse to have further dealings with that firm, while still willing to repeat its largesse in the case of newcomers.[29] If, in addition, other communities are not disinclined to give a firm desirous to relocate the red-carpet treatment reserved for newcomers, a condition exists conducive to a certain amount of displacement that is socially wasteful. However, the meaning of this statement should be clearly understood. The condition is wasteful as compared to one in which there is no discrimination in principle on the part of the subsidizing agent between new and established enterprises, *not as compared to a situation in which subsidies would be entirely absent.* And again, this latter statement may require further clarification. Discrimination in the sense the word is used here is objectionable in that it is irrational from the point of view of the subsidizing community and because it causes unwarranted dislocation. But the community *should* discriminate between enterprises that require subsidization or else will disappear and those that will stay without, and in each individual instance it should endeavour not to give more than is required for its purpose. I am not arguing, as some have done, that it is unfair to refuse to established firms what is given to new ones and that therefore subsidies, if given at all, should be given to other enterprises in the community as well.[30] This notion is wrong, because the subsidies are not given to enrich entrepreneurs but for the benefit of the community itself and should therefore be given only if they have that effect. Another question is that the community, when operating through its government, might consider compensating individuals that otherwise would be made worse off as a result of the subsidy. These issues will be discussed more fully in the next chapter, which deals with public policy questions related to subsidization.

Thus we conceive of a situation in which some enterprises find such advantageous location conditions in a community that they will come

29. Of course, a certain amount of turnover is rational. A badly managed firm for instance, or one whose location in the community was a mistake in the first place, should not be subsidized indefinitely. In such cases a community is in a position to obtain an equivalent payroll at less expense by attracting a different firm.

30. More specifically, this has been argued with respect to subsidies, concessions, etc., involving public money or the public revenue.

and remain without special inducements,[31] while others can be attracted and retained only by means of such inducements. Without a
marked deterioration in the position of an industry or in the state of
business in general, enterprises that came without subsidy can on the
whole be retained without subsidy, and if so of course should not be
given any. A general depression, however, can change this picture
temporarily. On the other hand, a rise in the marginal productivity
of labor in an area or locality to the prevailing wage level as a result
of economic development would make it in the interest of a community to discontinue the practice of subsidization. This is true even
if this should lead to the loss of certain individual plants, for the stipulated condition implies that then new plants would come in without
subsidy, absorbing the unemployed.

*Lowry's study of 41 Tennessee communities continued—participa-
tion of municipalities during the depression.* It should therefore not
surprise us that during the depression there was a more than ordinary
amount of subsidization activity going on throughout the nation. The
inducements offered also seem to have been greater than before or
afterwards (as is for instance clearly brought out in a Wisconsin study
discussed below), and there was more active participation of local
governments. In such communities as studied by Lowry, where
frequently public officials were also local businessmen, the provision
of factory buildings by municipalities free of charge or at a very
nominal rental was a natural outgrowth of the earlier private activities
of development corporations. Cities and counties had already co-
operated with these corporations to the extent of waiving taxes against
corporation-owned industrial property. In the depression, tax concessions and the provision of utilities to industry free or at reduced
rates practically became a matter of course.[32] These tax concessions
were given in the form of low assessment, nonassessment, or formal
exemption of industrial property, the latter usually for a specified
period of time. In one case in eastern Tennessee the exemption of
two plants, located in the same county, represented a sum of $70,000
during the year 1935 alone. Among 27 of the 41 communities studied
formal exemption of industry was practiced, and most of the others
had granted exemptions in the past or were willing to do so in the
future if the opportunity to secure a new industry by this means should
arise.

31. If this were not so there would, in the absence of subsidization, be no community.
32. See also Robert E. Lowry, "City Subsidies to Industry Wane," *National
Municipal Review*, XXXIV (March, 1945), 112-15.

To maintain their legal status as "municipal buildings" the structures provided by local governments sometimes housed the city fire department and other public offices, but the main part of the building was leased to private operators. On the whole the arrangements with the occupants were largely the same as those made by the development corporations in this period: the typical contract called for use of the property by the entrepreneur free of rent for a period of 10 to 25 years, usually with renewal option, the occupant being obligated to provide a given payroll or volume of employment. However, in contrast with the remarkable turnover in the occupancy of buildings constructed by private corporations, all of the 20 municipal buildings existing in 1937 in the sample communities were at that time still occupied by the original tenants. This may undoubtedly be explained by the fact that the municipal plants had all been established since the early thirties, i.e. during the depression, so that the occupants were not subsequently faced with a deterioration in the business climate that endangered their existence. The initial concessions were adequate for the circumstances under which they had to operate. Also, the time passed since these buildings were first leased had only been a few years on the average.

For nine of the 20 municipal buildings the funds had been raised by the sale of general obligation bonds, secured by the taxation power of the town. In order to assure the town's liability, approval of the issue had to be obtained from the state legislature. After that, the question was put before the local voters, Tennessee law requiring a three-fourths majority. Up to the present day a proposal to finance an industrial building by means of a municipal bond issue has been defeated only once in Tennessee history. In Lowry's sample approval was unfailing: in 12 communities where elections were held the average ratio was 27 to 1 in favor of the issues. Such majorities, which have been equalled and surpassed elsewhere, not only show that public opinion in communities suffering from insufficient employment opportunity is squarely behind the efforts of their governments to bring in industry, they show that those upon whom the burden of taxation falls are willing to pay the cost. And this should not surprise us. In the nine towns among the 41 investigated which in 1937 had factory buildings financed by the sale of municipal bonds (mostly to local investors), the amount raised in this manner varied from $20,000 to $110,000 and the resulting increase in per capita debt ranged from $6 to $40. Thus the annual cost per inhabitant, represented by the interest on this debt, is to be counted in pennies rather than dollars, amounting to a few dollars per family in the most extreme case. Unfortunately, in this case data from which the increase in per capita income could be calculated are lacking, but that it would be many times the cost of the subsidies should be obvious.

In 11 communities with municipal factory buildings the funds were acquired without bond issues by a variety of means including the sale of municipal property, the use of surplus funds, the sale of notes and of mortgages on the factory to finance part of the original outlay, and in some towns these municipal funds were supplemented by private contributions.

The property tax levies to meet the factory building obligations ranged from 20 cents to 50 cents per $100 of assessed value; only in a few instances was the debt being partly liquidated through rental payments by factory occupants. However, eight buildings were being paid for in part at least by levies on the wages of employees. Applicants for work in these factories had to agree to pay a specified portion of their wages into a building fund; failure to do so would bring dismissal. In the various towns included in the sample where this method of financing the building was practiced, the assignments ranged from 3 to 6 percent of the employee's earnings.[33] The practice was specifically permitted under several of the private acts passed by the Tennessee legislature to approve municipal bond issues.

This latter manner of financing the subsidy is extremely interesting in several respects. In the first place, the fact that say 6 percent of the payroll of people previously un- or underemployed constitutes at least a significant part of what it takes to finance that payroll itself (as well as the indirect benefits that accrue to the business community) again indicates the great gains that industrial subsidies can bring to a community. Secondly, the practice serves to illustrate a point made in Chapter I, namely that the people who are subsidized may themselves contribute toward the cost of the subsidy. (It will still be demonstrated that the subsidization actually practiced is in its effect similar to a payroll subsidy.) And third, this kind of arrangement makes possible a wider application of the subsidization approach as a solution to the unemployment problem than would otherwise be the case. After all, it is no more than equitable that the workers, to whom the greatest and most certain benefits of the subsidy accrue, should take a share of its cost for their account. Although property owners and the business community have generally shown an appreciation of the

33. In a study not restricted to these 41 communities Lowry says that employees might be required to assign from 3 to 10 percent of their earnings for this purpose (*ibid.*, p. 113).

advantages they also may derive from the coming of industry, their inclination to participate in a subsidization program will undoubtedly be greater if the newly employed can be made to shoulder part of the burden. The more this burden is distributed in proportion to the income gains made, the smaller is the probability that the use of municipal tax power will cause some people to lose while others benefit greatly. A program that reduces this possibility to a minimum is likely to command the greatest possible support in the community.

In conclusion, a few statistics may be cited that clearly indicate the difference in economic destiny between communities willing to use special inducements to attract industry when depressed business conditions warrant this approach and those that are not. In the 41 communities under consideration at least 50 of 86 plants[34] active or under construction in May 1937 had received concessions, but of these only two were located in the four cities of over 10,000 population (although these cities contained 20 of the 86 factories). Thus subsidization was essentially a small town phenomenon, and among the small towns in the sample the practice had become virtually universal since 1930. Among the 66 manufacturing enterprises located in the towns with less than 10,000 inhabitants, 35 occupied buildings constructed or vacated since January 1930; all but one of the former and all but three of the latter had been subsidized. Of the 31 factories in the smaller towns that had been under the same operators and in the same building since before 1930, 17 were known to have been subsidized—still a majority.[35] Significantly, none of the factories built since 1930 was in the cities of over 10,000 population, and in these larger cities there were only four new occupants of vacated buildings. (Besides, these buildings most likely were acquired below replacement cost, which, as has been argued above, is the equivalent of a subsidy.) Whether it was more difficult to organize action or whether their governments were impeded by a higher sense of "responsibility," it is clear that these cities lost out against the smaller towns because they did not offer special inducements to industry. By perfect contrast,

34. These included all or nearly all establishments other than those serving purely local needs or employing less than 50 persons.

35. However, it is important to note that a substantial proportion of established enterprises could be retained without subsidy at a time that it was virtually impossible to attract new enterprises without substantial inducements—inducements that were undoubtedly available to those who remained where they were should they have decided to relocate. This bears out a point made above that will be of some significance in our future considerations, namely that in the general case it takes far more to attract a new industry than to keep an established one.

more than half of the factories active in 1937 in the small towns had been established since 1930, when the subsidization practice began to gain momentum, and there the pace of industrialization had markedly accelerated, despite the depression. It may still be mentioned that in Lowry's sample as elsewhere shoe and textile (including garment) manufacturers were among the most frequent recipients of subsidies, and that the majority of subsidized plants were of non-local origin, a little more often northern than southern.

A Wisconsin survey. Elsewhere in the country stepped-up subsidization activity was also in evidence during the depression. As one author, writing in the thirties, says: "Under the stress of the depression [the practice of municipal subsidization of private industry] has apparently been pushed at an unprecedented pace throughout the nation—often supported by law, frequently in violation of law."[36] One of the few systematic surveys in this field covers 130 cases of industrial subsidies in 40 Wisconsin communities during the period 1930-1946.[37] This study concludes:

The subsidies typical of the earlier part of the period covered were sizable and costly and consisted in large part of the provision of buildings for low rentals; these subsidies were largely municipally financed in cities which had lost an important part of their previous industrial employment. In more recent years there has been a larger proportion of privately financed and self-liquidating subsidies, particularly in industrially undeveloped cities.[38]

This indicates that what a community can afford and is willing to pay to attract industry does not depend upon its prosperity (it is sometimes argued that depressed areas are too poor to help themselves so that outside aid is needed), but upon the income gains that can be expected to result from the subsidies. Just as capital can be attracted for a prosperous business venture, so it can be attracted by municipalities for profitable investment in the community on a businesslike basis.[39] The burden of subsidization does not have to be borne in a

36. Milton Derber, "Municipal Subsidy of Private Industry," *The Municipality,* XXXII (June, 1937), 125.

37. W. D. Knight, *Subsidization of Industry in Forty Selected Cities in Wisconsin 1930-1946* ("Wisconsin Commerce Studies," Vol. I, No. 2 [Madison: The University of Wisconsin, 1947]).

38. *Ibid.,* p. v.

39. The present discussion does not take into consideration state-imposed legal impediments that may prevent such action by municipalities. To the extent that effective restrictions of that nature exist and are taken as immutable, it might be argued that the states should accept the responsibility for the depressed conditions in their municipalities.

period preceding the reaping of the benefits; the obligations incurred can be financed out of these benefits. Besides, an alternative to borrowing is to subsidize an enterprise on a current basis as in the case of tax concessions, provision of utilities at a reduced rate, etc. And finally, if the prospective gains are great even people in poor communities are willing to make sacrifices in order to secure these gains, making contributions to development corporations, etc. The main point, however, is that not even a temporary reduction in consumption levels is necessary to improve community living standards if this can be done through investment of funds yielding returns higher than the going interest rate. American municipalities are open, not closed economies. This rather simple point seems to be somehow overlooked by those who can think of no other solution to the problems of depressed areas than pouring in federal aid.

The prospective gains from industrial subsidies are naturally greatest when unemployment and underemployment are widespread, and experience indicates that there is a definite relation between the degree to which these conditions exist and the subsidization practice. But the mere prospect of gain does not always seem sufficient to induce a community to effective action. This is most likely to be the case when the economic situation is actually deteriorating, and especially when the impact of the forces causing this deterioration is sudden and catastrophic.[40] Even then, however, in the face of legal and organizational difficulties that must be overcome and in the presence of preconceived notions that condemn all subsidies to private enterprise, the response may not be equal to the emergency. This is not to say that during a severe depression affecting the entire economy subsidization on a scale required to achieve full employment would be feasible. It may, however, be feasible to carry subsidization of industry to the point where it materially contributes to the elimination of localized unemployment and underemployment in an otherwise prosperous economy, as it already has in individual instances. But here we are anticipating the results of further analysis.

The types of subsidy revealed by the Wisconsin study are those already familiar to us. Starting with the most "extreme" and costly types, Knight classifies them as follows: gift of building, low rental, tax concession, cash or equivalent, advance of capital. On the average,

40. Knight found that especially in those cities which had lost large amounts of previous industrial employment there was "tremendous popular pressure" upon municipal officials and civic leaders to take effective action to bring new industry into the community (*ibid.*, p. iii).

cash donations were less than $5,000, but one privately financed dona-
tion amounted to $90,000 and one municipal gift to $19,750. Among
the recipients of subsidies shoe and textile companies loomed large,
but many other kinds of industries were procured in this way as well.
In this connection Knight remarks: "It is often contended that . . . the
firms most readily attracted by subsidy are likely to be small, under-
capitalized and poorly established. There have been some instances
of such firms among the cases studied, but the typical shoe promotion
included in this report has involved the decentralization of a large,
well-established Milwaukee firm, which moved to a relatively unin-
dustrialized town where there was a supply of surplus labor, in search
of lower labor costs."[41] He concludes, moreover: "Covering 130
cases of industrial subsidization in 40 Wisconsin communities during
the period since 1930, this report concludes that, in general, these
promotions seem substantially to have accomplished their purpose in
terms of employment and payroll."[42]

The quantitative results of this important survey are incorporated
in Appendix V, p. 229. It may here be added that in his foreword
Knight indicates that at the beginning of his investigation he shared
the widespread belief in the unsatisfactory and unstable nature of firms
likely to be attracted by subsidization and in the wastefulness of spending money for this purpose. This preconceived thesis, he says, was not
confirmed by the facts. However, opponents of the practice have
continued ever since to make unwarranted assertions with respect to
firms that will locate where subsidies are available, with a great show
of authority but a minimum of evidence.[43] Of course there are, as in

41. *Ibid.*, p. 181.   42. *Ibid.*, p. v.
43. The attitude here is that the matter is self-evident and needs no factual support,
or else that a single instance will suffice to establish the general case. Among in-
numerable examples one that is fairly typical may be cited: "It [i.e., offering special in-
ducements] is *obviously* more apt than not to attract weak industries which pay low
wages and make small profits. The South has specialized in this type of industry long
enough" (Italics mine) (Harriet L. Herring, *Southern Industry and Regional Development* [Chapel Hill: The University of North Carolina Press, 1940], p. 3). In addition
to the charge of instability there is in most cases also involved the notion that an
industry which pays relatively low wages is undesirable for that reason. The reader
will recall our discussion of that question in Chapter II. As Levitan says: "Some students of the problem have suggested that in some of these communities new jobs have
been secured [by development corporations] by downgrading labor and that the new
jobs pay lower wages than prevailed formerly in the community" (Sar A. Levitan,
Federal Assistance to Labor Surplus Areas, a report prepared at the request of the
chairman of the Committee on Banking and Currency, U.S. House of Representatives,
85th Cong., 1st Sess. [Washington: U.S. Government Printing Office, 1957], p. 66).
This rather neatly sums up the attitude of an unfortunately large number of students
of labor problems. Presumably it is downgrading for workers to accept wages at which

Knight's sample, instances of subsidized firms that failed or moved or perhaps were unsatisfactory to a community in other ways, but to my knowledge nobody has shown yet that these cases are more numerous than among other enterprises. As in so many other spheres where prejudice prevails, a pernicious tendency toward unwarranted generalization is in evidence here. When a subsidized firm is unsatisfactory, attention is focussed upon the whole category, but when some other enterprise goes bankrupt people do not say that it was an *unsubsidized* enterprise. They merely say that it was the XYZ company. Using this kind of reasoning one could as easily "prove" that the private enterprise system is no good. And even if it could be shown that subsidized firms have a worse record than others, this would not condemn the practice of subsidization. In the presence of conditions that have induced communities to engage in this practice, deliberately taking a certain risk is completely justified. As we have seen, this may be considered the equivalent of paying larger sums to attract more established firms. Besides, although there may be instances of neglect, it is but a normal precaution for a community to investigate a prospect thoroughly prior to concluding any deal with it. It must be concluded, therefore, that no importance can be attached to this so-called "practical" objection which has been raised against the subsidization practice.

Mississippi's BAWI plan. One of the most publicized organized efforts to attract industry is that of the state of Mississippi, where under the so-called BAWI (Balance Agriculture With Industry) plan political subdivisions (municipalities, counties, etc.) may issue bonds to construct industrial buildings for lease to private firms. Although BAWI is one of the favorite targets of the opponents of industrial subsidization, it is in essence merely enabling legislation which at best permits only a very mild form of subsidization. For while the bonds are of the general obligation type (i.e. secured by the tax power of the municipality), they must be amortized, interest and all, out of the rentals paid by the occupant of the building. When the plan was first launched this was not so, but nowadays nothing like the practices

---

they can be employed, but not to be unemployed and live on the dole at the expense of the rest of the community (which may include a large number of people with incomes far below the wages the unemployed are holding out for, or rather, are forced to hold out for by their bargaining agents or by the government). These writers are prone to denounce "sweatshops" without asking what the alternatives are, or, if challenged on this point, refer to the body of literature obligingly provided by economists which in essence tries to show that there is no relation between employment and real wages.

prevalent in Tennessee at the time of Lowry's study is allowed under BAWI.

It all started in 1936 when Hugh L. White became governor of Mississippi.[44] He wanted to apply the experience of his home town, Columbia, throughout the state. Early in the depression White had been forced to retire from the lumber business as the result of a combination of reduced demand and depletion of the local timber supply. Feeling some responsibility for the resulting distress, he had been instrumental in bringing a garment plant to the town by means of an $80,000 subsidy, raised through a chamber of commerce campaign among local businessmen. The plant soon employed 700 workers from the town (1930 population: 4,833) and surrounding area. The payroll was mostly spent in the town, and business prospered. This was not the first instance of its kind in Mississippi but it was widely publicized, and White found himself invited to tour the state to explain the procedure to chamber of commerce groups. This had the effect that by 1936 "over 20 new industries [had] been established, representing investments of $5,000,000, giving employment to some 5,000 individuals, with an annual payroll exceeding $2,500,000, as the result of the Columbia method."[45] Columbia itself, repeating the original procedure, added a cannery and a plant to process pine stumpage. In 1936 dollar sales in this town were 26 percent above the 1932 level, while in comparable towns that failed to attract industry they had declined by an average of 32 percent.

White's purpose in establishing BAWI was to enable local governments to participate in raising the funds necessary to attract industry. The Mississippi constitution explicity prohibits this practice, and the Supreme Court had enforced this provision on several occasions. However, the 1936 Mississippi Industrial Act establishing BAWI proclaimed that providing industrial employment was a public purpose. The State Industrial Commission, created under the Act, was empowered to issue certificates of "public convenience and necessity" for approved municipal bond issues. These certified issues have been held constitutional by the courts. When BAWI was temporarily terminated in 1940 it was by legislative repeal.

Advantages and disadvantages of municipal participation. One of the reasons why White wanted to open up the opportunity to allocate

44. The information on the first phase of BAWI's operation is derived from Ernest J. Hopkins, *Mississippi's BAWI Plan, an experiment in industrial subsidization* (Atlanta: Research Department, Federal Reserve Bank of Atlanta, 1944).

45. *Ibid.,* p. 13.

public funds for industrial subsidies was the poverty of many communities that needed industry. With the backing of the municipal tax power, credit could be obtained more easily. In Columbia part of the contributions pledged by private individuals had been paid in immediately and for the remainder notes collectible in installments had been made out to the chamber of commerce. These notes were subsequently discounted by a bank in New Orleans, the loan being further secured by a master note bearing the signatures of 40 Columbia businessmen. Other communities had followed a similar procedure, but it had been a real effort for the more active citizens to contribute or pledge the needed subscriptions, and in some instances the banks had not been willing to liquidate the pledge notes.

White also pointed out that when the method of voluntary subscription is used there always is a number of individuals among those standing to benefit from the payrolls who will nevertheless refuse to contribute. This "free ride" argument in favor of compulsion does have validity but should not always be taken as decisive. Factors entering in the scale should be the social merit of the purpose to be accomplished (i.e. the gains—which may be negative—of society as a whole as contrasted to that of the individuals immediately involved) as well as the objections pertaining in each case to compulsion as such. Sometimes these objections are slight. When it is a question of raising funds for a worthwhile purpose, the great majority of people may be perfectly willing to contribute provided they can be assured that others will do likewise, and may therefore wish to rely on taxation. A striking illustration of this attitude, connected with the subsidization of local industry, is afforded by an incident that occurred in New London, Wisconsin, in 1926.[46]   In this city a petition urging the city government to raise $100,000 for the payment of a bonus to a shoe plant was circulated among the owners of taxable property, the money to be recovered by a 2 percent special tax on the assessed value of all property. It was signed by 92 percent of the owners and the city proceeded to levy the tax. In the course of subsequent litigation involving the legality of the assessment, the city attorney maintained that the petition signed by the citizens constituted voluntary subscription. The city had merely acted as a collecting agency, using its tax machinery for the purpose. To conclude, as the attorney did, that therefore in fact no public funds were involved is perhaps pressing the point too far, but the incident certainly indicates that taxation may be the most effective way of marshalling in an equitable manner funds

46. This case is described in Knight, *op. cit.,* p. 22.

which a great majority of those liable to be taxed are willing to contribute. Furthermore, state laws requiring that municipal bond issues be submitted to the electorate for approval tend to protect the public against excessive and inequitable assessment. In Mississippi a majority of the qualified electors must vote on each factory bond issue, and two-thirds of those voting must favor the issue.

Although it may seem far-fetched, it will hardly surprise anyone that opponents of industrial subsidization by municipalities have condemned the practice on the ground that it constitutes "socialism." Thus one of Virginia's leading newspapers, the *Richmond News Leader,* described the Industrial Revenue Bond Act of 1952, introduced unsuccessfully in the Virginia Assembly, as "socialistic," adding somewhat incongruously that "nothing is to be gained on the weak and rotten crutches of state capitalism."[47] Yet all this act would have done is to allow municipalities to issue revenue bonds for the financing of industrial buildings. Similarly, a Mississippi banker said about BAWI: "The thing was outright Socialism and should never have been attempted, much less held constitutional."[48] More reasonable was the attitude expressed by another banker: "I'm so much concerned about real forms of Socialism that I can't worry much about that municipally owned but privately operated factory down the street." As a town mayor put it: "I am chairman of a municipal corporation and if this corporation wants to lease a building to another corporation, I don't see that any high-sounding principle whatever is involved."[49]

While the mayor's statement certainly constitutes a warning against slogan-throwing, undiscriminating dogmatism, there may nevertheless be a question of principle involved: not that of private enterprise versus socialism but that of personal freedom versus the use of coercive political power in a wider sense. An incisive discussion of this question with respect to the scope of local government activity is to be found in Henry Simons' essay "A Political Credo," the introduction to his *Economic Policy for a Free Society.*[50] This author writes:

Individualism and collectivism are usually discussed largely in terms of political (coercive) versus voluntary (free) association and of government-

47. Cited in "Municipal-Industrial Bonds," *Monthly Review,* Federal Reserve Bank of Richmond (September, 1953), p. 6.

48. Hopkins, *Mississippi's BAWI Plan,* p. 61.

49. *Ibid.*

50. Henry C. Simons, *Economic Policy for a Free Society* (Chicago: University of Chicago Press, 1948), pp. 12-14.

monopolistic versus private-competitive organizations. The range of aggregate governmental activities, however, is hardly more important, as a political problem, than their distribution between small and large, local and central, governments. Extensive local socialization need not be incompatible with, or very dangerous to, a free society. Local bodies are themselves largely voluntary associations; people have much freedom to choose and to move among them; they are substantially competitive and, even if permitted to do so, rarely could much restrain trade. The libertarian argument against "too much government," consequently, relates mainly to national governments, not to provincial or local units—and to great powers rather than to small nations.

Simons also discusses the alleged inefficiency and corruption of local government, which may appear greater but is in reality beyond comparison less than that of the federal government. The reasons for this have never been stated better than in the words of Thomas Jefferson: "Our country is too large to have all its affairs directed by a single government. Public servants at such a distance, and from under the eye of their constituents, must, from the circumstances of distance, be unable to administer and overlook all the details necessary for the good government of the citizens, and the same circumstance, by rendering detection impossible to their constituents, will invite the public agents to corruption, plunder and waste."[51] Local governments on the other hand, especially in small communities, are closely scrutinized by their constituents, who can do so with an understanding of the issues involved and of their interest in these issues. Being close to the people, these governments, as Governor White pointed out, may be considered a ready medium for doing what the people want. From all this we may conclude that there can be no reasonable objection in principle against participation of local governments in community action to secure new enterprise when this may make an important difference in the prosperity of the community, and that there should be a minimum of interference with this on the part of the states. As

51. Paul Leicester Ford (ed.), *The Writings of Thomas Jefferson*, (New York: G. P. Putnam's Sons, 1896), VII, 451. The quoted passage is from a letter to Gideon Granger. Jefferson also said: "Were we directed from Washington when to sow, and when to reap, we should soon want bread" (*Ibid.*, I, 113). Opposed to this stands the paternalistic or totalitarian attitude which, today as in Jefferson's time, poses such a constant threat to freedom and prosperity. In the words of a Mr. Suffrin, appearing before the Subcommittee on Low-Income Families of the Joint Committee on the Economic Report: "People in these smaller towns need somebody to hold their hands. They need somebody to tell them to do this, that, or the other thing" (Joint Committee on the Economic Report, *Hearings, Low-Income Families*, p. 548). As we shall see, it is on this principle that BAWI has been run.

will be shown in the next section, the great mistake made under the BAWI plan was not that it gave local government units the opportunity to finance industrial expansion but the stifling control by state authorities to which municipalities desirous to do so were submitted.

Centralized control of local efforts to attract industry under BAWI. The BAWI plan of 1936 did not require that the bonds be amortized out of lease payments by the occupants of municipal buildings as is currently the case, and in most instances of financing under the plan that occurred in the early period only a token rental of $1 or $5 per year was demanded. The occupant had to pay a penalty if at a stipulated date a given minimum payroll or number of employees was not reached, but in practice these minima were attained well ahead of time in virtually all cases. In some cases the contract provided for the building to become the occupant's property free or at a very low price, after a given period of providing employment. In addition, the state of Mississippi extended an already existing practice of granting a five-year tax exemption for all privately owned equipment. Thus the original plan left adequate room for subsidization and might have yielded great results but for the vigorous screening of applicants by the State Industrial Commission.

This Commission, it will be recalled, was founded to circumvent the constitutional prohibition of allocating public funds for the purpose of subsidizing private enterprise. However, it was also intended to "protect" the municipalities from engaging in "unsound" deals. For this feature "the BAWI is generally praised today, even by its former opponents." Still, the following questions have been raised: "Was the winnowing process of the State Industrial Commission too vigorous? Were some good propositions, especially those calling for the formation of home-owned companies to process local agricultural and mineral products, perhaps thrown out along with the propositions of the poorly financed or less reputable applicant concerns? Some Mississippians think that the commission 'leaned over backward to be safe.' "[52]

The facts provide the answer. The Commission bought safety as a traffic policeman might by halting the traffic almost completely. For one thing, it ruled out as a matter of routine the subsidization of all new local enterprise on the ground "that neither the time nor the managerial and labor-skill situation in the state warranted a public subsidization of new hazards."[53] Snowed with propositions (some

52. Hopkins, *Mississippi's BAWI Plan,* p. 10.   53. *Ibid.,* p. 23.

3,800 were received within a very short time, but this was less than expected) and lacking all knowledge of both entrepreneur and the locality where the plant was to be established, it is not surprising that a centralized board should not have time to judge each proposal on its individual merits. But that does not imply that the local people themselves would not have had time to work out their own salvation if given the opportunity. As it was, the Commission operated in typically bureaucratic fashion, drawing fast categorical distinctions and telling the communities what they could and could not do. The result of this smothering overprotectiveness was that all in all only 12 BAWI plants were established between 1936 and 1940. A few favored cities benefited greatly from the enterprises that were attracted (although if left on their own they might have acquired more industry), but the great majority were left to suffer the pangs of depression, barred from helping themselves by the dictatorial power vested in the Committee.

Of course, a useful function may be served by a central agency acting as an intermediary between enterprises seeking a favorable location for a new plant and communities offering inducements. Such agencies, which may also shoulder the task of investigating prospects with a specialized staff maintained for the purpose, need not be run by the state; in fact, private plant locating services have long existed. A state agency would soon be subjected to political pressure, be accused of favoritism, and is likely to arrogate or be given discriminatory power even where this is not originally intended. At any rate, the final decision should be made by people who possess an intimate knowledge of the ever-changing details of the local situation. Without this knowledge, which is simply not accessible to anyone but the people on the spot (who acquire it without effort), it is impossible to make well-informed, rational decisions. Moreover, these decisions should be made by people whose interests are at stake, for they alone can evaluate the alternatives in terms of their preference schemes, and self-interest is still the strongest inducement to be "right." If it be objected that local governments should not be identified with "the people," it may be countered that at least these governments are closer to their constituents, from among whom they are chosen and to whom they are directly responsible, than a state agency. In fact, all the usual arguments in favor of decentralized decision making apply as much to this situation as to the question of who is to make the decisions that in our free enterprise system are made by private entrepreneurs. It is strange that people who would vigorously resist any attempt by the government to interfere with private enterprise should be complacent in the face of interference by state authorities with the economic decisions of its subdivisions, even though legally the states have the right to do so.

If it could be shown that subsidization constitutes a "beggar-my-neighbor" policy, it would still be another matter. Higher authorities should of course not tolerate that municipalities levy tolls on uncrowded rivers, etc. Obviously, interference should then take the form of prohibiting the practice in question. However, it is clear that this consideration has not played a role in the case of BAWI. The Mississippi legislation is neither inspired by this motive nor consistent with it. We are simply faced here with an unwarranted assumption of their own superiority on the part of the state authorities. And this is tolerated because too many people share the mistaken belief that the larger the governmental unit, the more respectable it is and the better it can perform any task.

Further discussion of BAWI. The plants attracted in the 1936-40 period all belonged to highly rated concerns, mostly in the hosiery and garment industry but including a fairly large shipbuilding operation in Pascagoula. The largest bond issue occurred in Natchez, where $300,000 was raised to build a factory for lease at a very small rental to the Armstrong Tire and Rubber Company. The ownership of this company was equally divided between the Armstrong Rubber Company of West Haven (Conn.) and Sears, Roebuck and Company. As Hopkins somewhat reproachfully remarks, yet bringing out the so frequently denied basic logic of industrial subsidization: "The Armstrong Tire and Rubber Company does not appear to have been in need of subsidization from any source, but as to Natchez' need of industrial employment, there could be no question."[54] It is said that the payroll,

---

54. *Ibid.*, p. 46. In the same vein, Hopkins discusses the fact that wages paid in most BAWI plants were low. On this subject he observes: "That the new enterprises in some cases took shrewd advantage of these background circumstances [large labor surplus, absence of any legal or organizational floor under wages, etc.] is regrettable rather than remarkable" (*Ibid.*, p. 30). Suppose, however, that entrepreneurs should take a more lofty position in this matter and operate as charitable institutions, refusing subsidies when they can get them and paying wages in excess of what their pecuniary interest demands they pay. The result would be exactly the same as that of minimum wage laws and union rates: no incentive to come to areas where payrolls are most needed, a distortion of resource allocation, and a decrease in national output. The market would simply not be able to fulfill its function. But if these are the effects of such an "ethical" attitude, would it really be ethical to operate that way, or would it be just sentimentality?

It may be added that there seems to be a dawning realization of the fact that even

which soon far exceeded $1 million per annum, revived the city. In all cases the counties and municipalities were able to meet their BAWI bond obligations. As Hopkins points out, this fact indicates the strengthening of the communities' ability to carry indebtedness, resulting from the income effect of the payrolls. The point deserves emphasis, for it is frequently argued that communities that incur obligations to finance industrial subsidies, grant tax exemptions, etc., are undermining their financial position and will not be able to provide adequate municipal services. This opinion is in large part responsible for restraining legislation in the various states and allegedly even affects the attitude of entrepreneurs toward communities offering municipally financed subsidies. It is therefore important to discuss it fully, and we shall return to it later.

After a four year suspension period, BAWI was revived in 1944 with communities still under the tutelage of what was now called the Mississippi Agricultural and Industrial Board. In this respect, the plan has not materially changed. However, municipalities have been further curbed by the new requirement that industrial bonds must be amortized over a period not to exceed 25 years with lease payments by the occupant covering principal and interest. Land and building may be leased for 99 years with only nominal payments after amortization is completed, the attraction of this arrangement being that the industry saves property tax payments. (Under Mississippi law municipalities and counties are also empowered to give a five year exemption from the local property tax to new industry not availing itself of BAWI financing.) Thus, tax advantages and, in the case of small enterprises, avoiding possible difficulties and relatively high charges in obtaining capital from private sources constitute the main advantages of the program. Returns on municipal bonds being exempted from the federal income tax, municipalities can borrow in the bond market at lower interest rates than otherwise would be the case, and this advantage can be passed on to industrial prospects in the form of relatively low rentals on municipal property.

Taken together, the advantages to industry under the present BAWI arrangement may or may not be sufficient to attract industries

perfectly respectable enterprises are in business for profit and may require some form of concession as a condition for their establishment in a particular community. Thus during a recent meeting of the Industrial Committee of 100 of the Chattanooga Chamber of Commerce which I attended, it was brought out that such a requirement was very common. A mimeographed paper distributed to the participants says in this context: "CAUTION—Do not be misled into believing that "fly by night" industries are the only ones that require financing."

to communities in need of payrolls—no doubt in a great many cases they are insufficient. To that extent the Mississippi legislation, in that it prohibits further concessions municipalities may be willing to make, is repressive of local initiative. On the other hand, the Industrial Board has approved more industrial bond issues than did the State Industrial Commission during the early period. As of December 21, 1959, a total of 225 industrial projects, including 161 new plants and 64 expansions, had been financed (since 1944), and the total value of approved bond issues was $64,303,500.[55] These figures may seem impressive, but on a per capita and annual basis the implied subsidization (considering also the corresponding tax concessions) can hardly be called large. A bolder approach would seem appropriate for a state like Mississippi, which still suffers from widespread underemployment in virtually all rural areas. Moreover, with such feeble inducements as are now permitted, the location of an industry may certainly not in all cases be attributed to the subsidy. In this connection it should be noted that the great majority of plants established in Mississippi during the post-war period have bypassed the inducements offered under BAWI. In the two-year period covered by the 1956-58 Biennial Report of the Agricultural and Industrial Board, for instance, 166 new plant constructions and expansions occurred in Mississippi, of which 31 used BAWI financing.[56] But it is said that BAWI has helped create a favorable, industry-conscious atmosphere in Mississippi, which also attracts many enterprises that undertake their own financing. Popular support of industrial bond issues has certainly been great: in all but two cases the issues were approved by the required two-thirds majority, often with virtual unanimity.[57]

55. Information extended by the Mississippi Agricultural and Industrial Board.

56. State of Mississippi, *Balancing Agriculture With Industry,* Seventh report to the legislature by the Mississippi Agricultural and Industrial Board (Biennium 1956-58), p. 10.

57. Examples of election results in favor of bond issues by Mississippi communities: 690-0, 2408-68, 3843-16, 3044-13. Source: Mississippi Agricultural and Industrial Board, *Mississippi's BAWI Plan* (Pamphlet).

CHAPTER IV

Problems in Using Public Funds for Subsidies to Industry

Municipal concessions and the law. Although municipal subsidization of industry has been widely practiced in several regions prior to any enabling legislation (and, where the latter existed, often also in defiance of the terms of such legislation), the legality of the practice where not specifically sanctioned by the state has always been in question. The constitutional obstacle lies in the general principle that public funds shall not be appropriated other than for a public purpose and in the narrow interpretation of what constitutes a "public purpose." The classic statement of this principle (or rather, its counterpart) is found in the case of *Citizens Savings and Loan Association v. Topeka,* in which the U.S. Supreme Court says in part: "To lay with one hand the power of government on the property of citizens and with the other to bestow it on favored individuals to aid private enterprises and build up private fortunes is nonetheless a robbery because it is done under the form of law and called taxation."[1]

However, when Mississippi's BAWI plan was tested both the U.S. and the State Supreme Court adopted a broader view of public purpose, and the act under which the plan was established was found constitutional. It will be recalled that the act was specifically designed to overcome constitutional obstacles,[2] declaring in its preamble that "the present and prospective health, safety, morals, pursuit of happiness, right to gainful employment and general welfare of its citizens demand, as a public purpose, the development within Mississippi of industrial and manufacturing enterprises."[3] In arriving at its decision,

1. 87 U.S. 655 (1874), cited in W. D. Knight, *Subsidization of Industry in Forty Selected Cities in Wisconsin 1930-1946* ("Wisconsin Commerce Studies," Vol. I, No. 2 [Madison: The University of Wisconsin, 1947]), p. 6.

2. *Supra,* p. 72.

3. Ernest J. Hopkins, *Mississippi's BAWI Plan, an experiment in industrial subsidization* (Atlanta: Research Department, Federal Reserve Bank of Atlanta, 1944), p. 19.

the Mississippi Supreme Court took into consideration the avowed objectives of eliminating unemployment and raising the standard of living, and also that a close check was to be exerted by the state over the selection of industry and the terms of the contract. Many people nevertheless felt—not quite without justification—that this was riding roughshod over the state constitution, which explicitly forbids the appropriation of funds or the extension of credit by the state or municipalities in aid of a private corporation or association.[4] In other states that have enacted enabling legislation municipal factory bond issues have also been upheld by the state courts, and the U.S. Supreme Court in its more recent decisions has made it clear that it refuses to interfere with state determination of "public purpose."

In states lacking such legislation, however, the courts have in several instances withheld their approval of municipal appropriations to private bodies or enterprises for the purpose of furthering industrial development. Thus in 1952 an appropriation by a North Carolina municipality for the local chamber of commerce was held invalid because of lack of public control over the expenditure,[5] and in that state the use of public funds as an inducement to industry as well as the waiving of taxes at both the state and local level are considered illegal. Similarly, in Florida the Supreme Court held in 1952 that the city of North Miami might not finance an industrial plant with revenue bonds. At that occasion the Court declared:

Every new business, manufacturing plant or industrial plant which may be established in a municipality will be of some benefit to the municipality. But these considerations do not make the acquisition of land and the erection of buildings for such purposes a municipal purpose.

The financing of private enterprises by means of public funds is entirely foreign to a proper concept of our constitutional system. Experience has shown that such encroachments will lead inevitably to the ultimate destruction of the private enterprise system.

There is no similarity between this case and those where the legislature authorized a municipality to establish a sewage system, a water system, an electric light plant, or to furnish some other public utility or service essential to the welfare of all the people of a municipality, or for the exercise of the police power for slum clearance.[6]

4. Knight, *op. cit.*, pp. 8, 9; State of New York, *Report of the Joint Legislative Committee on Commerce and Economic Development,* Legislative Document No. 28 (Albany: Williams Press, Inc., 1954), p. 34.

5. New York, *Report . . . on Commerce and Economic Development,* p. 33.

6. *Ibid.,* pp. 33-34.

This statement is worth commenting upon, but rather than digress at this point we should first look into the legislation that controls the subsidization of financing of industry by municipalities in the various states.

Partly for constitutional reasons and also to curb municipal "excesses," several states have followed Mississippi's example of specifically allowing local governmental units to finance the construction of plants for industry. By 1958 general legislation permitting municipal bond issues was in effect in eight states: Alabama, Illinois, Kentucky, Louisiana, Mississippi, New Mexico, Tennessee, and Wisconsin. A Pennsylvania law permitting the establishment of "local authorities" for specific purposes has the same effect, and some other states, including Massachusetts and Maryland, have enacted special laws sanctioning particular municipal issues. In Kansas a law enacted in 1923 permits cities with a population under 40,000 (at the time of enactment 20,000, but in 1939 the present limit was adopted) to create a special tax fund for the purpose of securing new industry. From 1939 to late 1953 the plan was approved in 34 cities, but three had never levied the tax. The total amount collected over this period was $352,360.[7] In some other states, for instance Oklahoma, municipal participation in the financing of industry is condoned in the absence of specific legislation dealing with the practice. Thus Oklahoma municipalities have issued revenue bonds for the construction of municipal buildings which were then leased to industry in part or in their entirety.[8] Other states however, including New York, Virginia, and Florida, expressly prohibit the extension of financial aid in any form by municipalities to industry.

As to the nature of the issues, only in Mississippi, Louisiana, and Tennessee does the law permit the use of general obligation bonds, secured by the tax power of the community. Louisiana and Tennessee further imitate Mississippi's BAWI plan in providing a central authoriy to review the soundness of the proposed undertakings. If these boards approve, the issue is submitted to the voters. In each of these states the law requires that rental payments be sufficient to cover the entire obligation incurred by the municipality, so that the full faith and credit character of the bonds is of importance only as a guarantee to the bond holder in case the lessee fails to meet his contractual obligations toward the municipality. Further restrictions are the Louisiana stipulation that the factory bonds must not exceed 20 percent of the total assessed

7. Mabel Walker, *Business Enterprise and the City* (Princeton, N.J.: Tax Institute Inc., 1957), p. 49.

8. New York, *Report . . . on Commerce and Economic Development*, p. 32.

value of all property within the subdivision and the corresponding Tennessee stipulation which imposes a maximum of 10 percent. The constitutionality of the Tennessee act was not determined until 1957, and by the end of that year only one plant had been financed under this arrangement.[9] At this time 14 Louisiana communities had issued municipal bonds totaling $2,790,000 since the legislation here described had materialized in 1952.[10] In the other states that have general enabling legislation only revenue bonds are allowed.[11] Although issued by municipalities, counties and other political subdivisions, these bonds are *not* secured by the tax power of these units. Thus no public funds are involved and because of the greater risk interest rates usually are higher than on general obligation bonds. In this they resemble more the obligations of private corporations than of municipalities. Their only *raison d'être* is their tax-exempt feature. The issuance of this type of bonds is not subjected to centralized control, but in some states, for instance Alabama, state agencies may give assistance to local development efforts by establishing contacts between communities and industrial prospects, etc.

Regarding the exemption of industry from state and local taxes, "attacks on the basis of due process and equal protection [guaranteed to all citizens under the U.S. constitution] have not been successful due to the failure of the courts to extend them into the field of tax exemption."[12] The practice has also been attacked under a provision in many state constitutions and statutory laws requiring equal and uniform taxation as laid down in general rules. In several states that had this provision, however, municipalities have carried on the practice with impunity, the courts seldom being called upon to render an opinion. Thus in Tennessee the constitution, as interpreted by the Supreme Court of that state, permits no industrial tax favors. Nor did it permit, during the thirties, municipal bond issues for industrial financing. Nevertheless, in the 1935 and 1937 sessions of the legislature

9. Under an earlier law (1951), Tennessee also permits municipalities to issue revenue bonds for the construction of factories.

10. Gilmore, *"Little" Economies*, pp. 57-59.

11. However, in Kentucky, where the law specifically permits only revenue bonds, the Court of Appeals in 1956 ruled that incorporated municipalities have the right to issue general obligation bonds for financing the construction of plants to be leased to industry, *provided there is substantial unemployment in the community*. In principle these bonds must be serviced by rental payments (State of Kentucky, Department of Economic Development, *The Local Industrial Development Corporation* [Frankfort, Ky., 1959?], pp. 20-21).

12. "Municipal Inducements to Private Industry," *Minnesota Law Review*, XL (May, 1956), 691.

23 local acts were passed authorizing municipal bond issues for factory construction, and in other cases the municipalities in question did not even bother to obtain express legislative approval. In granting tax favors, the rule was for municipalities to act as they saw fit. In this they were fairly safe, for the Supreme Court in a 1934 decision, while reaffirming an earlier decision that tax favors were illegal, had clearly implied that it was unwilling to enforce this rule. Similarly in Wisconsin, where as we have seen both municipal financing of industry and tax exemption were widespread, neither practice was allowed under the law.[13]

Preferential tax treatment, for a long time almost part of the normal pattern due to the discretion exercised in the assessment of property values, is still a widely used device to attract industry. Before the war, a large number of states specifically permitted exemption from municipal taxes by local option, usually for five or ten years. In New England and the South this was the prevailing condition. Since then the number of states that have enabling legislation has diminished. Virginia, for instance, recently repealed its exemption statute and today the practice is prohibited. In Georgia a constitutional provision allowing five-year exemption was withdrawn in 1945, but local exemption is still practiced in that state. Where municipalities pursue this policy without approval or in violation of state law, there is little information on the extent of the practice, which then usually takes the form of preferential or token assessment. Nowadays the general provision requiring equal and uniform taxation "is not an effective limitation because many states have abolished the law and the remaining provisions are now very liberally construed."[14] However, preferential tax treatment of industry is specifically prohibited in a number of states, including Colorado, New York, Tennessee, and Virginia. By contrast, several states still have programs offering exemption from state or municipal taxes (the latter by option of the municipality), or both. In 1953 the following states featured some kind of tax concession especially designed to attract *new* industry (i.e., this does not include states that generally treat industrial property favorably): Alabama,

---

13. Knight, *op. cit.*, p. 11. For the city of New London this state of affairs had bad consequences. In 1930 this city sued the Menzies Shoe Co. for failure to perform its obligation of paying the sum of $1 million in wages to local labor over a 10-year period under a contract whereby this firm had received a $100,000 bonus. The Supreme Court disallowed the city's claim to compensation on the ground that the contract was illegal since it involved municipal subsidies and in spite of the fact that the defense of the company was a "dishonest" one (*ibid.*, pp. 22-23).

14. "Municipal Inducements to Private Industry," *Minnesota Law Review*, XL, 691.

Arkansas, Delaware, Kentucky, Louisiana, Mississippi, Rhode Island, South Carolina, and Vermont. Kentucky, for example, allows any city or town to exempt manufacturing establishments from municipal taxation for up to five years. In Alabama, the state as well as the municipalities may exempt new industries from property taxes (other than school district taxes) for ten years. Louisiana offers exemption from all state and local property taxes on buildings and equipment to new and expanding industry for five years, and this exemption may be renewed for another five years. However, "no exemption shall be contracted for any new manufacturing establishment actually engaged in the manufacture of the same or closely competitive articles without the written consent of the owner of such existing manufacturing establishment."[15]

Opposition to municipal concessions based upon considerations of equity and self-interest—compensation. The above stipulation of the Louisiana constitution and the verdict of the Florida Supreme Court cited earlier[16] may serve as starting points for our discussion. It hardly needs saying that such protection of vested interests against competition as Louisiana provides may be contrary to the interests of the community. The criterion for the granting of open or implied subsidies to industry in any form by a municipality should be whether this means affords an opportunity to increase community income (which it does in the presence of un- or under-employment), not its effect on particular individuals.[17] There is hardly any change in the status quo, whether caused by a private party or a governmental unit and no matter how beneficial in the aggregate, that is not detrimental to some. The removal of tariff barriers or the building of a badly needed bridge are cases in point. By the Louisiana criterion or that of the Florida judges, public funds should certainly not be allocated for the bridge, for it would bring competition upon the owners of a ferry service and thus be harmful to some people. The Florida decision, therefore, which lists as examples a number of municipal activities that supposedly benefit *all* the people as contrasted to the erection of a plant to absorb the unemployed, constitutes evasion of an issue. It is obvious that the measures listed are not exceptions to the rule that on the whole desirable and even essential gov-

15. Constitution of Louisiana as amended by Act 401 of 1946, Article X, Section 4, Paragraph X.

16. *Supra,* p. 82.

17. As the reader will realize when he bears with me, this does not imply a Hitlerian "you are nothing, the state [or community] is everything" philosophy. I am not proposing that the rights of individuals be trampled upon.

ernment measures may be harmful to some, if only because people whose welfare is not directly affected may have to contribute to meet the expense of the measure. Obviously too, this is not in itself a reason to condemn these measures, but we should not accept them under the false pretense that they are universally beneficial in an immediate sense: it is important to be right for the right reason. We accept this type of action because it is deemed important to the *community*, not because in each isolated case every individual is benefited. And it is hard to see why measures designed to alleviate unemployment by attracting private industry[18] should not be considered fully as essential to the welfare of a community as for instance the establishment of a sewage system. For the reasons stated, unanimous approval of proposed government action can seldom be expected (unless, perhaps, deliberate attempts at distributing the burden according to the benefit principle are made and compensation of injured parties is undertaken), but so strong has at times been the popular feeling in favor of municipal factory bond issues *that they afford some of the few instances in which unanimity has in fact been attained in the political process.* On the whole the majorities in these referendums have been such as to leave no doubt regarding the desirability of this type of action in the eyes of the people themselves.[19]

Since the way of thinking with respect to subsidies that has found legal recognition in the Louisiana stipulation and the Florida decision is also widely reflected in the literature,[20] the above refutation may be pursued further. By generalizing an argument it often becomes possible to see whether its implications are acceptable and if not, to conclude that it should be qualified or discarded. In this case, the latter conclusion is clearly indicated (which of course does not preclude the possibility that objections raised on other grounds have validity). For if governments should be guided by the type of reasoning in question—as unfortunately they often are, judging by their

18. As to the alleged impending doom of the private enterprise system resulting from municipal participation in industrial financing, it would be interesting to know what experience the judges are referring to. It is to be feared, however, that the passage in question is merely a dogmatic statement about government action in general of the sort we have discussed in the previous chapter.

19. Compare the evidence presented above, pp. 65, 80.

20. A typical statement: "It is obviously not fair to use municipal funds if one group benefits at the expense of the other" (Milton Derber, "Municipal Subsidy of Private Industry," *The Municipality,* XXXII [June, 1937], 126). This sounds fair enough until we realize that it applies to about every possible kind of government expenditure. However, the possibility of compensation should not be lightly dismissed. For a discussion, see the text below.

actions—the logical consequence would be the prohibition of all change. The government should not only abstain from any "positive" action, such as the subsidization of industry, the repeal of tariffs, measures designed to curb monopoly power, or whatever else may lead the economy closer to the social optimum as usually defined, but it should also interfere with private parties introducing innovations of any kind, and this would become its main economic function. Since the government has the power to suppress as well as to act, we should be consistent and not reserve a special set of niceties with respect to the possibility of individuals being adversely affected in the case of positive government action. If we are prepared to rule out the subsidization of an enterprise by a governmental unit on the ground that it may compete with already existing firms, we should also be prepared to rule out the subsidization of such an enterprise by private groups or its spontaneous establishment if that would have the same effect. There is little difference between the government "causing" and "not preventing" changes in income distribution.[21]   Indeed, many societies have come close to consistency on the side of prohibiting all change that might be detrimental to some and have stagnated as a result.

This is not to argue that income distribution effects should not be considered in the good society. However, acknowledging that this matter should be given due attention is something completely different from categorically objecting to government action that may adversely affect some people, or, if the subsidization of industry is somehow specifically singled out to be charged with this criticism, from objecting to this practice on the ground that it may not benefit all the people. There are several compelling reasons why this ought not to be so. For one, the redistribution of income may itself be deemed desirable. Secondly, while not desirable, the losses suffered by some may be relatively minor and fall quite within the nature of the accepted order, as for instance when a municipality uses its taxation power within normal limits to alleviate a serious unemployment problem by attracting industry. The accepted philosophy about government action essential to the welfare of the community is that *in the long run* practically all the people will be very much better off when the required measures are taken all the time, so that everyone is likely to benefit from the aggregate of these measures. In the absence of severe hardship or concentrated impact, therefore, compulsory contributions to the general welfare are an unavoidable and expected thing, and the account is not settled every time a measure is taken but is expected to

21. A qualification will be given below, pp. 89-90.

straighten itself out as time goes by. The alternatives being stagnation or an inextricable tangle of small claims to compensation, this seems to be a workable and reasonable philosophy to which no exception should be allowed in the case of such an overriding public interest as the creation of employment opportunity. And third, if concentrated losses and hardship for some should be the price of gains far exceeding these losses in magnitude, we should not think in terms of foregoing either the gains or the losses, but instead take the possibility of compensation seriously.[22]

Above it has been stated that there is little difference between the government "causing" and "not preventing" changes in income distribution. This statement must now be qualified. It holds in the sense that it is equally unreasonable to condemn categorically change that might harm some when its implementation requires positive government action as when it does not, and the passage in question was an attempt to point this up with respect to the case that it does by extending the argument *ad absurdum*. However, there may be a difference in that the possibility of some types of change could have been reasonably anticipated and therefore have or should have been taken into account among the factors guiding individuals in their past actions, whereas other kinds of change may be the result of a deviation from long-standing practice.[23] It may be felt that, when, so to speak, the rules of the game are changed, the argument in favor of compensation is reinforced. To some extent changes in the rules of the game may themselves be expected, but there is a difference of degree. There is merit in the argument that when a society adopts new rules because it expects to benefit from this, it should accept the responsibility of compensating those who would otherwise be severely harmed by the unpredictable change. This would apply when the change involves positive government action not hitherto practiced, unforeseen repressive action (e.g. abolition of slavery), or even in the event of drastic changes originating outside the government sphere

22. With all due qualifications afforded by modern welfare economics and its critics, I believe that the concept of Pareto optimality still provides a useful starting point for our thinking in evaluating the economic aspects of government action and of the general framework in which governmental and private units operate. Implicitly, if not always explicitly, this is also the prevailing opinion in the profession, as evidenced by continued general reference to the marginal optimality conditions in a normative sense. In this view a measure "essential to the welfare of a community," at least in the economic realm and if not purely distributional in purpose, is by its nature one under which compensation of those who would otherwise sustain material losses is in principle possible.

23. For this point I am indebted to J. M. Buchanan.

(as when the British government determined that canal owners should be compensated when their property became obsolete almost overnight due to the advent of the railroad). In addition to the question of equity, there is a question of expediency involved here: concentrated opposition to a proposed change may be far less when compensation is contemplated, and therefore paying compensation may be necessary if the change is to be introduced at all or is to be introduced without causing undue strife and resentment.

The implications of these considerations to our problem of municipalities extending concessions to industry should be clear. Should great harm be inflicted upon individuals as a result of the action, the community, rather than to abstain from the action, should look into the possibility of compensating the injured parties. Apart from legal impediments, this alternative would seem real at the local level—the cost of carrying it out would certainly not be prohibitive. However, with the possible exception of heavy taxation—about which more will be said below—the issue of people being unduly harmed while others benefit appears largely academic in the case of industrial subsidies.

With respect to competition in the product market between a new subsidized enterprise and a previously existing firm (the case foreseen by the Louisiana law), this would be of importance only if the market is primarily local in scope. If not, the coming of the new enterprise to the community in question would have about the same effect on the already existing firm as if it should be established elsewhere. Since the type of enterprise attracted by subsidies almost invariably produces for "export," this case may be dismissed as trivial. Competition in the market of production factors supplied locally is a different matter; this of course may also affect enterprises not producing a similar product. Evidently, in the general case this is most important in the labor market, and it is from the side of entrepreneurs employing low-cost labor that the greatest resistance against community efforts to attract new industry may be expected. Thus industry may for instance draw laborers away from the cotton fields, causing the plantation owners to suffer an income loss in their capacity as landowners. In general, this would be a factor when in agriculture a system of tenancy or hired labor prevails. If not, farmers derive most of their income from their labor, and what they may lose as landowners (if anything, family labor often being redundant), is more than made good by the creation of factory employment for members of their families. But when large landowners form an important power, resistance that could divide the community may perhaps be expected.

Such resistance could also come from the side of manufacturers, but in the general case this is likely to be less important. For subsidization is advantageous to a community only insofar as new industry can draw upon the un- and underemployed, and hence the coming of a subsidized industry is not likely to lead to a bidding up of factory wages. When the new industry insists on paying higher wages than those prevailing in other industrial enterprises there may be an unfavorable demonstration effect (discussed in Chapter I) and there may be some competition for special skills, but by and large there will be no occasion to compensate already established manufacturers.[24] And as to the large landowners, this may be a case in which it is generally felt (i.e., by most others) that the redistribution of income is a positive good of itself.

We may conclude this section with an account of a very different interpretation of all this given by Hoover and Ratchford. These authors mention that "this practice [the issuance of municipal bonds to subsidize industry] is almost universally condemned by those who have studied the question thoroughly, yet its persistence is evidenced by its continued use even in the face of constitutional prohibitions." Being unable to see any good in the practice themselves, they offer the following explanation: "Perhaps one explanation is that the leaders of a community, frequently businessmen and landowners, see a chance to make a profit while the cost is being paid by the taxpayers as a whole, many of whom derive no benefit from the transaction. The rank and file of the taxpayers may have no leadership, or they may be ashamed to oppose the measure since it is presented as a 'progressive' move."[25]

It is true that the practice is generally condemned, and yet the

24. By the same token, one would not expect manufacturers to be vigorously opposed to community efforts to attract new industry by means of special inducements. In some cases a realization of the community's need for additional payrolls may even induce their support, in others relatively slight economic drawbacks may tip the scale in the direction of a somewhat unfavorable attitude. This seems to be borne out by the facts, as the following citation indicates: "The active support of community programs for economic development is usually found among wholesalers and retailers, banks, newspapers [important for the formation of public opinion!], public utilities, and transportation agencies with more or less lukewarm cooperation from established manufacturers. The last group sometimes fears that new industries will unfavorably alter the status quo and bring greater competition for sites, materials, services, and labor supply. In fact, it is not unknown for chambers of commerce, when dominated by large manufacturers, to withhold official support or to extend it only indirectly" (C. S. Logsdon, "Some Comments upon the Effectiveness of State and Local Area Development Programs," *Southern Economic Journal*, XV [January, 1949], 308).

25. Calvin B. Hoover and B. U. Ratchford, *Economic Resources and Policies of the South* (New York: The Macmillan Company, 1951), p. 317.

writings of those who have studied the question thoroughly do not support the thesis here developed. The most thorough studies in this field are those discussed in the previous chapter. While Knight, Lowry, and Hopkins have their misgivings as to the desirability of the subsidization practice from the viewpoint of the economy as a whole, they do not argue that it constitutes exploitation of the majority by an organized minority, and at least two of them (Knight and Hopkins) feel that in general the subsidies did benefit the communities that used them. The Hoover and Ratchford thesis would be more plausible if the bulk of the taxpayers had no effective suffrage, but this is not so. As mentioned above, a qualified majority is usually required for the passage of an industrial bond issue, and the majorities actually obtained have generally far surpassed those required. Hoover and Ratchford also overlook that similar activity is carried on by private groups which always comprise a cross-section of the leadership in their community. The fact that in that case the endeavour is financed by *voluntary* contributions of interested parties shows that the explanation need not be sought in terms of the leadership group compelling the others to contribute to a cause they have nothing to gain from.

In reality, conditions are the exact opposite of what Hoover and Ratchford suppose. With the prevailing real estate tax, which to an important extent is paid by those who also represent the community leadership, the people who benefit most directly and in largest measure from the subsidies (the workers hired by the industries that are brought in) are likely to contribute far less than their proportionate share in the gains. Therefore, insofar as self-interest is the motive of the leaders, we may expect that only the much smaller indirect benefits that accrue to them (compare Chapter VIII) are weighted against the greater part of the subsidy which they pay, and hence that subsidization is not nearly carried to the point where the marginal returns to the community as a whole are equal to the costs.[26] Moreover, as I have indicated, of all groups large landowners are the most likely to be adversely affected when industry is brought into a rural community, and if they are influential they may be able to prevent the coming of industry that would greatly benefit the community as a whole.

Opposition to municipal concessions on the ground of financial considerations. After what has been said in Chapter III about decentralized decision making in connection with the financing of industry by municipalities, it should be self-evident that the same holds

26. However, in Chapter VIII it is also shown that it may not be necessary to do this in order to maximize community income and eliminate un- and underemployment.

with respect to exemptions from municipal taxation. This is a method of subsidization that has the advantage of causing few difficulties in its financial aspects, for there is no problem of raising funds. As Walker points out: "The tax-exemption subsidy is largely paid in the future rather than in the present. It is mainly exemption of a tax upon new buildings and upon enhanced value of land. To the extent these increments of value may have taken place as a result of the tax-exemption feature, the community has lost only the tax upon the value of the property before the development took place. Moreover, even this may be many times offset by the resulting increases in the value of unsubsidized property."[27] It is therefore important that local governments should not be unduly impeded by state laws in the use of this device, along with others, for of itself exemption from local taxes is not likely to be a sufficiently potent factor in most cases.

As we have seen, the subsidization of industry is fraught with legal difficulties as soon as local governments get involved. In this the privately financed development corporation has a great advantage. Municipalities and counties derive such autonomy as they have from the states, and with respect to this matter of subsidization the states have chosen to raise obstacles that in the general case prevent the exercise of true autonomy. No doubt this reflects the contempt in which offering "artificial" inducements to industry is generally held, fear of financial irresponsibility at the local level, and, above all, fear of "unbridled" competition for industry by local communities. All this, I feel, is based upon a thorough misunderstanding of our private enterprise economy. On the one hand this economy is implicitly endowed with the quality of allocating resources in an optimal fashion as if it were perfectly competitive, in spite of its manifest failure to prevent localized and sometimes general un- and underemployment. (Otherwise it could not be taken as self-evident that every local effort to influence industrial location decisions lures industry away from where it ought to be.) But on the other, that which makes a private enterprise economy tick, competition, is regarded a great danger as soon as it is extended outside the private sphere, without a moment's pause to reflect that perhaps such competition might be complementary to that between enterprises. It is hoped that this analysis may contribute to the creation of a legal framework that will give local governments greater freedom to fight unemployment within their own sphere.

However, municipal attempts to alleviate unemployment and raise

27. Walker, *op. cit.*, p. 47.

living standards by bringing in industry have not only been impeded
by the law but have also met with organized resistance by private
groups. In December 1951 the Investment Bankers Association
adopted a resolution condemning municipal industrial bonds as a
menace to public credit, our free economy, and state sovereignty, and
this resolution has been reaffirmed at several occasions, the last time
in May 1959. A similar resolution was adopted by the American Bar
Association in September 1952. The effect has been a boycott of
further issues by members of the Investment Bankers Association,
leading to the cancellation of large projected issues (e.g. those of
Meridian, Miss., and Elizabethton, Tenn.) and the restriction of later
sales to match the absorption capacity of smaller, regionally oriented
security houses and local investors.

Among the arguments brought to bear on the question in this context some are related to the statutory exemption of municipal bonds
under the federal government's Internal Revenue Code. As I have
indicated, under the present restrictions the attraction of industrial
issues by municipalities derives mainly from this exemption.[28] It is
argued that the exemption was not intended for the benefit of private
industry, and that continued use of municipal issues for this purpose
may endanger the immunity of all municipal bonds. It is further
pointed out in this connection that the courts have held that when a
state or local government itself engages in commercial activities (such
as state liquor and mineral water businesses), the usual federal taxes
apply.[29] The point of this reasoning appears to be that the participation of government units in business for purely fiscal reasons is
undesirable.

With this I fully agree, but I feel that the criticism is directed to
the wrong party. No matter how objectionable the law may be that
makes it attractive for municipalities to finance industries that otherwise would do this themselves, these municipalities are not at
fault any more than is an individual who avails himself of tax favors
legally granted that we may object to on general grounds. However,
the present state of affairs may certainly lead to undesirable results,
for under the existing exemption municipalities can subsidize industry
indirectly *at the expense of the general public.* Thus the inducement
to do so is not restricted to cases that will lead to the establishment of
enterprises in localities suffering from underemployment, as is practically assured when municipalities by autonomous decision impose the

28. *Supra,* pp. 79, 83-84.
29. New York, *Report . . . on Commerce and Economic Development,* pp. 34-35.

burden of the subsidy upon themselves.[30]   It is clear that under the present rule the municipal financing of industrial capital requirements is given a systematic advantage over the financing by industry itself (which of course may be offset by other factors, such as greater credit-worthiness of an enterprise itself than of the municipality in which it locates).   While so far this advantage does not appear to have been important enough for the practice to be widely adopted by municipalities that have full employment, this may change in the future; the fact that the inducement exists is in principle wrong.   Municipal governments should not be called upon to extend such facilities to industry when no overall social advantage can be gained by their doing so.   Thus the exemption should either be repealed or be limited to cases in which the employment situation warrants industrial subsidization.   The latter alternative raises the whole question of federal subsidies to areas suffering from lack of employment opportunity, which will be briefly discussed later.   I also believe that the removal of this blemish, with which the financing of industries by municipalities is now often identified, might help to put the whole practice in a more favorable light.   Naturally the state-imposed restrictions that require the bonds to be self-liquidating should then also be removed.

The Investment Bankers Association also argues that "piling up debt to aid private industry in addition to legitimate expenditures can only hurt municipal credit in the long run."[31]   Insofar as in most states the law permits only the sale of revenue bonds that do not involve the general credit of the municipality, this argument seems far-fetched.   Where, as in Mississippi, Louisiana, and Tennessee, general obligation bonds are issued for this purpose, such an effect might conceivably occur in the event of widespread mismanagement, but of this there has not been the slightest indication.   However, if because of the federal tax exemption feature in the long run the financing of industrial expansion by means of general obligation bonds should become the rule, the municipal tax power might no longer be sufficient to give municipal bonds the status they now enjoy.   But the arguments of the financial experts are not all along these lines.   Some of their most violent criticism definitely applies to municipal factory bond issues *per se*, and it is these issues they want to suppress, not merely their exemption from the federal income tax.   Here they frequently draw upon historical evidence, as in the 1951 resolution of the Invest-

30. This is explained in Chapter VI, pp. 150-52.

31. Lester Tanzer, "Dixie Dilemma; Bond Buyers Frown on Public Money Lure for Southern Plants," *Barron's,* XXXII (August 18, 1952), 15.

8## 96 LOCAL SUBSIDIES FOR INDUSTRY

ment Bankers Association itself which states that "similar practices in the past have had injurious effects upon public credit."

The historical argument has been developed by David Wood of New York, a leading municipal bond attorney, who compares industrial municipal bonds to other instances of public subsidizing of private enterprise in the nation's history. Tanzer presents his views as follows:

During 1825-37, many states built or helped build canals and roads or furnished credit for private banks; after the Civil War, municipalities bonded themselves beyond reason to subsidize railroad expansion; and in the 'twenties, municipalities aided the real estate boom by building utilities for privately owned developments. Each of these periods was followed by widespread municipal defaults. When local governments refrained from subsidizing private enterprise, however, Wood notes, the financial condition of states and municipalities was excellent, with rare exceptions, and state and municipal credit was high.[32]

Such an unqualified interpretation of history is impermissible. Mr. Wood might as well have cited the South Sea Bubble to argue against the limited liability of stockholders in corporations (as in fact many influential financiers in the eighteenth and nineteenth century did, with as a result the long postponement of this very useful form of enterprise). All depends upon the circumstances under which the subsidies are given and the returns in the form of community income that can be expected. Much of the sentiment against the subsidization of industry derives from a rather simplistic type of reasoning to the effect that tax exemption and the use of public funds for this purpose will necessitate increased tax rates, is likely to impair municipal services, and may so upset municipal finances as to cause bankruptcy.[33] This overlooks that due to the payrolls which the subsidies may secure and which will lead to increased real estate values, greater sales volume, etc., the tax basis of the community is widened. Depending

32. *Ibid.*

33. To illustrate: "The exemption of particular properties or classes of properties from taxation restricts the tax base and consequently increases the tax burden borne by other property owners or by payers of taxes other than the property tax" (Seward B. Snell, "Tax Exemptions to Encourage Industry," *Taxes,* XXIX [May, 1951], 383-84). It is added that "such business is naturally undesirable." Also: "Concessions given one company may bring in others on a similar basis. Each one would add to the burden of all citizens, industries, and businesses that are paying the tax bills to maintain a good community" (Commonwealth of Virginia, *Report of the Commission to Study Industrial Development in Virginia to the Governor and the General Assembly of Virginia,* Senate Document No. 10 [Richmond: Division of Purchase and Printing, 1957], p. 105).

on the tax structure of the community and the effect of the coming of industry on taxable values, decreased tax rates if we assume equal services are by far the most likely effect of subsidies applied under the appropriate conditions; and even if municipal rates should have to be increased, *the tax would be paid out of a larger aggregate income.* As long as the rates of return on subsidies in terms of community income remain anywhere near as high as hitherto they generally seem to have been, it is hard to imagine that financial difficulties should arise, even with the most restrictive local tax structure. However, it may be desirable to distribute the burden of taxation as much as possible in proportion to the income gains of those who benefit from the subsidy, while one way of practicing the principle of compensation might be to reduce the tax burden on those (groups) who otherwise would become worse off.[34] This would require that towns be given sufficient leeway to devise their own taxes, but in this matter there still is much to be wished for in many states. While reliance upon the property tax remains the rule, a report made by the Municipal Finance Officers Association in 1956 observes that "the most phenomenal development in local finances since World War II has been the increased use of non-property taxes by local units, especially in the urban areas."[35] Other local taxes now in vogue include the sales tax—levied by some 1,500 municipalities in ten states—gross receipt taxes on businesses and occupations (including payroll taxes), and selective excise taxes. In Kentucky and Alabama, liberal municipal tax systems that "authorize the citizens and officials of municipalities to exercise a wide choice in levying broad-based, equitable taxes to finance governmental programs desired by the public, and at the same time avoid excessive levies upon property or excessive demands upon the state for financial aid" have been in effect for more than a generation.[36]

A tax proposal. How, if the necessary freedom should be granted, might small municipalities use it to distribute the burden of subsidiza-

34. Another way of accomplishing this purpose that has much to be said in its favor would be to allow vote trading, as under Greek democracy. It is clear that by this method the market could be inserted into the political process so as to allow full compensation for losses, provided this process requires near-unanimity for approval of measures. This is not contrary to the notion of political equality, for everyone is given a vote free at the outset. However, since this idea is rather foreign to America and probably evokes a host of emotional reactions, it will not be further pursued here. It is discussed in a forthcoming more theoretical work by J. M. Buchanan and Gordon Tullock.

35. "Needed: New Municipal Revenues," *Tennessee Town and City,* X (January, 1959), 25.

36. *Ibid.*

tion equitably? Insofar as the beneficiaries (i.e. not the industry, but those in the community who ultimately stand to gain) are residents of the local units that pay the subsidy, a special income *gains* tax might be levied to service industrial bonds to the extent that amortization and interest are not covered by rental payments. This might be complemented by other taxes, such as a payroll tax on beneficiaries residing outside the county or municipality. (With the prevailing property tax the problem of the political unit that undertakes the financing of the project having no jurisdiction over many beneficiaries may also loom large.) For the purpose of the income gains tax, capital gains would be considered income gains, but income gains derived from sources that could not very well have been affected, directly or indirectly, by the new payrolls brought into the community should be excluded. The latter category would comprise all incomes and capital gains originating outside, and also incomes from inside activities not likely to be favorably affected, e.g. manufacturing for "export," etc. The rate at which income gains would be taxed could be tentatively set on the basis of anticipated returns on the subsidy which the income gains from included sources are taken to represent and would later be adjusted when closer estimates become possible on the basis of results actually obtained. To be covered against failure the bonds would be of the general obligation type, covered by the general tax power of the community. The introduction of a certain progression in the rates at which income *gains* are to be taxed might be considered, for it seems reasonable to assume that large gains within the included categories bear a close and direct relationship to the coming of the subsidized industry, whereas causality may be more doubtful when the gains are small. If so desired, people in the lowest *income brackets* could be excluded from the tax, which might also exempt people with relatively small *gains*.

With returns such as have generally obtained in the past,[37] this system may seem unnecessarily elaborate. However, in order to prevent the collection of trivial sums, the community might set some reasonable rate and proceed to amortize the bonds in a very short period, say a year. Alternatively, it may decide to build a fund for further *tax-free* subsidies of new industry. Indeed, one of the great advantages of the proposed tax is that it would bring home forcefully and unmistakably the high returns on industrial subsidies. If this should lead to emulation and hence to increased competition, tax rates would tend to move upward later, but as I shall demonstrate,

37. Compare Appendix V.

unemployment is likely to be eliminated before they become very high.[38] In any case, communities can engage in this type of activity as long as it is deemed rewarding and feasible to do so.

This tax scheme involves a minimum of compulsion. Ideally it would work almost as if everyone had perfect foresight and contributed in proportion to his expected gain without attempting to get a free ride. If it be objected that in reality it could not quite work this way, it may be submitted that in small communities a good approximation could be obtained, and that any combination of existing taxes would be far more crude. The tax may therefore be well worth the cost of administration, especially since many people (writers and legislators at least) develop very tender sensitivities when it comes to allocating public funds for the purpose of bringing in industry. The only "inequity" that might remain under the proposed scheme would consist of the taxation of people making income gains unrelated to the coming of new industry, and this possibility would be reduced to a minimum. Looking ahead, the income gain approach would mean that nobody can get worse off than he is for the adoption of a subsidization plan except in the event of total failure, which is a remote chance when reasonable care is taken in the selection of a prospect. This should assure great majorities at the polls.

The effectiveness of municipal subsidies in attracting industry as compared to community improvement. Related to the objections on the ground that it will lead to financial difficulties is the notion that spending tax money for subsidies tends to jeopardize the discharge of other municipal functions. Lowry has stated the problem as follows: "The alternatives which face local government wanting to invest public funds in the community's economic future are . . . rather clearly defined. One approach is to extend financial inducements directly to industry, in effect to build the new factory and let the new school building wait. The other approach is to help create a community more attractive to people who staff the industry."[39] The champion of the latter view is apparently the Tennessee State Planning Commission, which has repeatedly spoken out against the subsidization practice. "This Division, as a matter of official policy, always has looked with disfavor upon the subsidization of new industry by community groups, and especially when tax exemption and other forms of public

38. See Chapter VIII, pp. 183-86.
39. Robert E. Lowry, "City Subsidies to Industry Wane," *National Municipal Review*, XXXIV (March, 1945), 112.

subsidization are involved."[40]   It believes that *"a community must first be attractive as a place to live if industry's attention is to be invited."*[41] Thus it emphasizes adequate municipal services of the usual kind, good recreational, cultural, and educational facilities, sound finances, an attractive physical environment, zoning, etc. These amenities are to be obtained by self-improvement programs and community planning. Communities that offer direct inducements to industry but lack the civic necessities and conveniences that progressive management considers in making a location are tackling the industrial development problem in reverse. In Virginia, where this theory is also adhered to at the state planning level, it has been observed that "a responsible industry would rather move to a community that is sound financially, honest governmentally, and attractive physically and culturally, than to have subsidies and tax concessions. It will feel a definite obligation to the community and will want to assume its share of the cost of public services."[42]   According to Lowry, "a new school building, a well equipped playground or a new fire station is displacing the municipal factory building as the most effective means of making the community attractive to desirable industries."[43] Only Seymour Harris, from his New England vantage point, sounds a discordant note, implying that an underdeveloped public sector is a positive advantage in luring industries away from there: "In fact, the competition among states for low taxes and inadequate services as a means of attracting industries has contributed greatly to the loss of industry in vital spots in the Northeast."[44]

As our discussion of the effect of subsidies on tax rates[45] implies, if industries can be secured by means of subsidies, the community will be in a better, not a worse position to provide civic amenities. Further, as the material presented in Chapter III amply demonstrates, industries *can* be secured by means of subsidies. Thus, if industrial subsidies via

40. *Tennessee Industrial Planning Newsletter,* March 1, 1952, p. 2, quoted in Walker, *op. cit.,* p. 51.

41. Tennessee State Planning Commission, *Partners, Industry and the Tennessee Community, a Guide to Community Industrial Development* (Nashville, October, 1947), p. 1, cited in Albert Lepawsky, *State Planning and Economic Development in the South,* N.P.A. Committee of the South, Report No. 4 (Washington: National Planning Association, 1949), p. 82.

42. "What Does Industry Expect in a Community," *Virginia Economic Review,* IV (April, 1951), 3.

43. Lowry, "City Subsidies to Industry Wane," p. 129.

44. U.S. Congress, Subcommittee on Low-Income Families, Joint Committee on the Economic Report, *Hearings, Low-Income Families,* 84th Cong., 1st Sess. (Washington: U.S. Government Printing Office, 1955), p. 655.

45. *Supra,* pp. 96-97.

higher incomes lead to an increased demand for public services *for their own sake,* as undoubtedly they do, and if these public services are themselves such a potent factor in attracting industry as the Tennessee planners and others allege, then we can only conclude that the subsidies will have a cumulative effect and are even more important than they seem on their face. Of course the next defense would be to maintain that industries which subsidies can attract are undesirable and what not, but we have seen on what insufficient grounds this assertion is made, so that this need not detain us here.

Naturally this is not to deny that a beautifully run and equipped community that does not offer subsidies may hold greater attractions to industry than one that is corrupt and where services are poor, but which holds out special financial inducements. The question is: starting with the status quo, which is more effective in attracting industry *per dollar spent,* donations to industry or the building of a playground (this to represent civic amenities in general). The pat prescription of the economist of course is that, given the total volume of expenditure, each type should be carried to the point where the marginal returns in terms of added payrolls are equal.[46] While this is the only true generalization that can be made—and one that is very useful with respect to the current discussion which is of the all-or-nothing type outdated by the marginal revolution—some reflections that perhaps have a little more concrete content may follow.

If we may assume that in general entrepreneurs behave rationally,[47] it is self-evident that with respect to securing any particular prospect a subsidization policy is the most effective. For the enterprise always has the option to use the money (or, if the subsidy is not received in cash, the cash value of the concession) for some civic purpose or service that the municipality might otherwise have provided or to return the gift to the community with or without the stipulation that it be used for a particular purpose. There are instances of this on record[48]—presumably the enterprises that made this gesture felt that

46. Since playgrounds are also valued for their own sake, rational decision-making actually implies that this type of expenditure should earn a lower return in terms of added payrolls alone.

47. For the argument that follows in the text we need not make the more restrictive assumption that the entrepreneur maximizes profits. It is sufficient to postulate that he has some purpose, any whatever, or a combination of purposes that can be attained with money. The only rational exception would be an overriding objection to accepting subsidies, even though these subsidies could be returned to the donor.

48. For instance, I have a letter from a Georgia Department of Commerce official that mentions two substantial donations to industries which returned the gifts to the respective communities where they established themselves. These firms were interested

its goodwill value was more important to further their purposes than anything else the money could buy. That is still not the same as if the community had never offered the subsidy; however, it is conceivable that an enterprise, without regard to the psychological effect of its action, would spend the money in exactly the same way as the community would have should its policy have been to woo industry by means of civic improvement (as the Tennessee State Planning Commission recommends). In that case both policies—that of subsidization and that of civic improvement—would be equally effective. But this is an extreme case and, as Marshall has said in a different context, while conceivable, it is absolutely impossible. In all other cases, where the enterprise would spend the money in a different way, a given sum spent on subsidization is bound to be more effective than if that same sum were spent on civic improvement.

Now it is of course possible that certain types of services that are directly related to the cost of industrial production but that can best be provided on a community-wide scale are very deficient in a particular community, so that a given amount of expenditure in that direction would be more effective in bringing in industry in general than the equivalent sum spent on subsidies to particular prospects. This is true because money spent in that way would not only benefit any particular prospect but other industries as well, while the benefit might not be important enough to any particular recipient of a subsidy to induce him to make these expenditures himself or to require the city to make them in lieu of the subsidy. My main dissatisfaction with the civic improvement approach is not with the possible alternative it points out but the hostility toward subsidization upon which it thrives, a hostility which implies that the situation described above invariably exists. A certain amount of fire protection, law enforcement, etc., *is* of course essential to attract industry, but the American community that is really grossly deficient in these basic services is rare. Beyond that, the relation between municipal outlays for the general public and production cost in industrial enterprise becomes remote and intangible, and is at best very speculative.[49] Making a community more attractive, physically and culturally, to those who staff the industry is a worthwhile endeavour, but whether doing this is an effective way

in an indication of active cooperation on the part of the townspeople, and the gifts indicated that.

49. It will be shown below that most entrepreneurs, while perhaps not going quite as far as Harris implies, feel the same way. Since the problem is how entrepreneurs can best be induced to choose a community for plant location, we may as well face this—to some apparently unpleasant—aspect of reality.

of bringing in the industry in the first place may be questioned. For after all, the great bulk of workers is usually hired locally, and the very presence of these workers on the spot implies that to them the town in question already is the most attractive place to live, although perhaps for reasons other than those visualized by the proponents of the civic amenities approach. Of course, executives and some workers may have to be brought in from the outside, but it seems improbable that an impoverished town can do much within feasible limits to make itself more attractive in the eyes of those outsiders prior to a general rise in prosperity. It is much more likely that a good salary, which a firm could afford to pay when it is subsidized, would overcome any reluctance these imported workers might have.

Occasional utterances of businessmen seem to belie this reasoning. Thus in the course of perhaps the most extensive investigation on this subject, the following reaction was registered: "The offer of a low tax assessment discredited the whole of this city to the manufacturer. ... The company officials indicated that they expected to carry a fair tax load, otherwise 'they did not see how the community could furnish proper schools, recreation, sewers, and city services for their employees.' "[50] Statements like this are frequently quoted to show how shortsighted a subsidization policy is,[51] but they do not represent

50. *Local Government Services and Industrial Development in the Southeast,* a Joint Statement by: University of Alabama, Bureau of Public Administration; University of Florida, Public Administration Clearing Service; University of Georgia, Bureau of Public Administration; University of Kentucky, Bureau of Government Research; University of Mississippi, Bureau of Public Administration; University of North Carolina, Institute for Research in Social Science; University of Tennessee, Bureau of Public Administration in cooperation with the Tennessee State Planning Commission; Tennessee Valley Authority, Division of Regional Studies (University, Alabama: Bureau of Public Administration, University of Alabama, 1952), p. 22.

51. McLaughlin and Robock state that corporate executives are generally convinced that it would be poor business on their part to accept any special concession from a local community (Glenn E. McLaughlin and Stefan Robock, *Why Industry Moves South,* Report No. 3, National Planning Association [Washington: Committee on the South, N.P.A., 1949], pp. 112-13). However, they then indicate that one reason why many manufacturers in their sample were not impressed by local concessions was that the offered grants consisted mainly of free sites or payments on buildings, which accounted for only a small proportion of total plant cost. Here it is important to remember that the bulk of their sample consisted of relatively large plants, fully nine-tenths of which represented investments of $100,000 or over (at prices prevailing just after World War II). Under these circumstances the manufacturers found that the concessions offered were trivial, and that it would be taking undue advantage of the local community to accept gifts that could not markedly influence their location decision. It is clear then that the conclusion of these authors does not necessarily apply to smaller plant establishments or to cases where more significant concessions are offered: when it costs you very little it is easy to be magnanimous. As against this, L. Clinton Hoch of Fantus Factory Locating Service in an address ("The Location

the views of the typical entrepreneur. The typical attitude of the
industrialists included in the survey from which the above citation
was taken toward local taxes was that they are "an expense to be
avoided insofar as possible."[52] As to how industrialists evaluate community services, the following finding emerged upon the basis of
questions addressed to officials of more than 100 plants that had located
in the Southeast since 1945:

They produced conclusions about community services which ranged from
'almost no importance to industry when it chooses a plant site' to the
finding that 'instances where industries have selected communities without
considering the quality of local government are rare.'[53] Judging from
these state surveys, a relation between general community services and
industrial location might seem to be regarded by most of the industrialists
interviewed in the Southeast as either nonexistent or at best intangible
and elusive.[54]

Similar results have been found in other recent studies.[55] Apparently, according to the statements made by adherents of the civic
improvement approach, we should conclude from this that the majority
of industry is "undesirable," "irresponsible," and "unprogressive." This
also seems to be the opinion of the writers of the "Joint Statement"
cited in the text above, for in spite of their finding they conclude that
better community services "are perhaps the only lasting inducement
which local government has it in its power to extend to industry."[56]

Decision," a paper presented before the Semi-Annual Conference, Production Executives Division, The National Association of Shirt, Pajama and Sportswear Manufacturers, New York, June 20, 1957, p. 20 [mimeographed]) said that the ideal
location for a sport shirt plant would be a small community in the mid-South, where
the following conditions prevail: excess female labor happy to work at rates near
the legal minimum, freedom from union interference, willingness to provide capital
for the erection of a building according to the manufacturer's specifications for long-term
lease to the firm, an "equitable" state and local tax picture, willingness to make
local concessions including tax exemption for 5 years, a free site, and the provision
of facilities for the training of applicants.

52. *Local Government Services and Industrial Development in the Southeast*, p. 22.
53. This of course does not necessarily refer to the quality (and quantity) of
"amenities" provided by the municipality. The remainder of the citation seems to
indicate that the concern expressed here is more with honesty, cooperativeness toward
business, etc.
54. *Ibid.*, pp. 7, 8.
55. Thus Charles Quittmeyer, reporting on the Southern Appalachian region, sum-
marily concludes that community accommodations got a blank among factors determining plant location. The results of his intensive investigations have been
provisionally laid down in C. L. Quittmeyer, *Summary Report on Appalachian
Questionnaire*, Charlottesville, Virginia, October, 1959 (Berea, Ky.: Berea College,
1959).
56. *Local Government Services and Industrial Development in the Southeast*, p. 26.

Other policies, such as providing special services to industry at general expense and relying upon new industry to provide itself those services to its plant and employees that the industry feels necessary or desirable, are listed as shortsighted. "All of these alternatives assume that the welfare of the industry can be held apart and separate from the welfare of the community at large,"[57] the latter presumably to be identified with the services provided by the government.

To sum up: It is theoretically possible but in practice most unlikely that, starting from the given condition, a given amount of community expenditure on general improvement would be more effective in bringing in new industry than special inducements offered to prospects. In the general case, this is certainly not so, for those community services directly related to the cost of industrial production are already being provided in the great majority of American communities, and, as extensive investigations indicate, the typical entrepreneur, for better or worse, is little concerned with the more intangible factor of civic amenities. Moreover, even if in the long run the provision of more civic amenities should be the most important factor in attracting industry (which I, for one, do not believe), this approach would still be highly speculative and beyond the financial power of impoverished communities to execute. If in reality the great majority of entrepreneurs were to act as the "Tennessee School of Planning" alleges they do, the situation of such communities would be hopeless indeed. They would be bogged down in a vicious circle of poverty from which perhaps only municipally-*operated* industry could extricate them—or they would have to resign themselves to their fate. It is outright foolish to advise a poverty-stricken community to invest money in playgrounds and the like to the detriment of more important expenditures in the private sphere (for we are here discussing outlays on civic improvement which, although of some value to the community, would not be undertaken solely for their own sake but mainly to serve as bait for industry) on the off chance that this would strike the fancy of some visiting executive's wife and bring in industry. As to entrepreneurs not interested in subsidies, they will presumably come to a community without them or stay away. It is even possible, although of course not proven, that in some cases the fact that a community held out an offer of special concessions was sufficient to discredit it in the eyes of an entrepreneur who would otherwise have settled there. But in my opinion communities that have been bypassed by industry and that suffer from lack of employment opportuni-

57. *Ibid.*

ty are ill-advised if for such a reason they should hold back and wait some more. As I have shown above,[58] the surest way to get the industrialization process started if money is to be spent for this purpose is to offer this money *to a particular prospect,* this being more appealing *to this prospect* than any other way of disbursing the equivalent sum. Perhaps this would then have the cumulative effect described in the second paragraph of this section. Of course this presupposes rational behavior on the part of the entrepreneur, but there is every indication that by and large this postulate is met. At any rate, the facts are that those communities which have gone all-out for industry have been able to procure what they were after by means of subsidization and have prospered as a result, while on the other hand several unfortunate instances of communities losing a prospect due to their refusal or inability to make even the slightest concession are also on record.[59]   As regards civic amenities, the best working rule is to provide them only insofar as they are wanted for their own sake, for both analysis and the response of businessmen to questionnaires indicate that as a means to attract industry they are quite ineffective at the existing margin. Communities that use the more effective subsidization approach will end with more amenities, in the public as well as in the private sphere, than those trying to run costly civic improvement programs that they cannot afford and do not want at their given income level at the outset.

The effectiveness of tax concessions—the tax uniformity proposal. In addition to objections against concessions in general on the ground of alleged ineffectiveness in accomplishing the purpose of attracting industry, tax concessions as such have been specifically criticized on this ground. In a book devoted to the question of the influence of tax structures as they vary between states and localities upon industrial

58. *Supra,* pp. 101-2.

59. A few of these are mentioned in *Alabama Goes Industry Hunting,* a study prepared by the Alabama Business Research Council and the School of Commerce and Business Administration, University of Alabama (University, Alabama, 1957), p. 45. Thus: "A gas stove manufacturer went to Mississippi in preference to Alabama because the town considered was unable to finance the project on an acceptable basis." Also: "A company seriously considered locating in an Alabama area where a local building was to be erected with local capital bearing a five percent interest rate. During the period of negotiation, the interest rate was raised to 6 percent. The company located its new plant in another state." More in general, Clinton Hoch's paper (*op. cit.*) indicates that difficulties can be expected by an enterprise seeking community financing of a plant when the investment per worker is well above the average, *even when a rental sufficient to cover amortization plus interest is stipulated.* Such reticence on the part of communities suffering from underemployment is unbelievably shortsighted.

location, Joe Floyd cautions that "the easy assumption that tax conditions significantly influence the choice of sites for manufacturing plants has been challenged by persons who base their objections either upon theoretical reasoning or upon the evidence of inductive studies." Continuing this author says:

Two important theoretical objections have been made. The first is that public revenues derived from industrial taxes may be used to improve public services which in turn may reduce certain types of industrial costs in the community. The second theoretical objection is that tax costs can have little effect upon plant location because they usually constitute a very small part of the total manufacturing expense. It is conceded that plants will locate where the total of all costs is lowest, but the claim is made that tax costs will have negligible influence in comparison with other expenditures which bulk larger in the total.[60]

As to the first objection, the answer is implicit in our discussion of outright subsidies versus the community improvement approach. Regarding the second point, the taxes that industry does not have to pay are similar in effect to an outright donation, and hence must exercise as powerful an influence upon industrial location as a community can hope to exercise *per dollar it is willing to allocate for this purpose.* It is obvious that if the total amount involved is small or negligible the total effect may also be small—this is no more than saying that a small subsidy is less likely to obtain results than a large one. This can hardly be called a theoretical objection to tax concessions; in fact, it is no objection at all. If exemption from local taxes is not sufficient to make a marked difference of itself, tax exemption can still be used together with other incentives to obtain for a community the payrolls it needs. Since on the whole local and state taxes are not very large cost elements, one is not surpised to hear that "manufacturers have rarely located a plant primarily to obtain the [tax] concession"[61] or that a study carried out by the Federal Reserve Bank of Boston "points to the conclusion that taxes are relatively unimportant as locational factors."[62] Neither these findings nor others that point in the opposite direction[63] have much if any

60. Joe S. Floyd, Jr., *Effects of Taxation on Industrial Location* (Chapel Hill: The University of North Carolina Press, 1952), p. 8.

61. McLaughlin and Robock, *op. cit.,* p. 114.

62. Floyd, *op. cit.,* p. 11.

63. To argue the opposite case on *a priori* grounds it has been pointed out that as between localities or states locational factors other than taxes may often be in substantial balance, and that therefore taxation may well be the decisive factor that tips the scale one way or another. See for instance Clarence Heer, "State and Local

bearing upon the question whether a tax exemption policy is to be recommended for communities that wish to attract industry.

Floyd also argues that, since taxes paid by manufacturers typically do not represent the cost of goods and services used in the manufacturing process, tax considerations may be classed as uneconomic elements in location decisions. So far this reasoning is correct. He then goes on to say, however, that "to promote the optimum industrial development of the entire nation, existing interlocal tax differentials should be modified materially or eliminated."[64]

Supposing that Floyd speaks only of taxes bearing directly on industry, this still overlooks the fact that state and local governments do provide industry with services and that neither the production cost of these services nor their quantity and quality are the same everywhere. Elimination of differentials, therefore, would not solve the problem. Ideally from the location point of view, industry should pay not a tax but a retribution, paying just what it costs a community to provide it with police protection, utilities, justice, extension of streets, sewers, etc. In practice this is impossible because of the cost allocation problem. Moreover, it holds only if otherwise the markets for productive services that industry buys are perfect. The pivotal point of this treatise of course is that they are not. This treatise emphasizes that in the presence of un- or underemployment the market price of labor lies above its opportunity cost. Since from the location point of view industry therefore pays "too much" for labor

Finance in the Postwar Plans of the South," *Southern Economic Journal*, XI (January, 1945), 246-54. This author draws from this the correct conclusion that "the imposition of higher than average taxes on business concerns which are relatively mobile and footloose would, therefore, seem to be a risky policy for states which are seeking new industries" (p. 250). Others have pointed out that, while taxes are small relative to total cost, they can still be substantial relative to profits, and that therefore industry is likely to pay a good deal of attention to them when making location decisions. McLaughlin and Robock (*op. cit.*, p. 107) mention that chemical companies and pulp manufacturers emphasized that low property taxes were especially important to them because of high investments per wage earner in plant and equipment and standing timber reserves respectively. These authors further state that in general companies carefully compare the tax burdens in different states (p. 107). For the importance attached by industry to state and local taxes see also Melvin J. Goldberg, "Industry Fights Back on State and Local Taxes," *Dun's Review*, LXXI (April, 1958), 37 ff. Goldberg emphasizes that "the stakes are growing bigger." Wolkstein mentions (Harry W. Wolkstein, "Recent Problems and Developments in Property Tax Exemptions," *Proceedings of the Forty-fourth Annual Conference on Taxation*, Dallas, Texas, November 26-29, 1951 [Sacramento, Calif.: National Tax Association, 1952], p. 185) that five major industries locating a number of branch plants in South Carolina in recent years valued at over $200,000,000 had made exhaustive tax studies in several states.

64. Floyd, *op. cit.*, p. 113.

in localities where these conditions exist, a competitive policy of subsidization that may include tax exemptions tends to further rather than counteract an economic location pattern of industry. Both *a priori* reasoning based upon an assumption of rational behavior by local governments[65] and existing practice lead us to maintain that the inducement to engage in this practice exists only when local employment opportunity is deficient. On this ground alone, therefore, one may take strong exception to Floyd's recommendation of ironing out tax differentials between localities and states as well as to his assertion that "the long-run results of such competition can only be to produce an uneconomic distribution of industry, to subsidize inefficient enterprises at the expense of more efficient ones, and to disturb the equity and productivity of state and local tax systems."[66] Registering a protest is the more important since this uniformity proposal, in one form or another, raises its head throughout the literature. To give one more example, Wolkstein feels that "all of our individual states should set up reciprocal agreements under which they and their county and municipal governments will agree to abide by certain uniform rules and regulations as to subsidies, tax exemptions, and concessions to private industry with a view to working toward uniformity and proper coordination of tax-exemption policies among our state and local governments."[67] Since cartel agreements between a large number of parties are viable only with the backing of higher authority, we need not worry much about this. More serious is the possibility (and partial reality) of states imposing uniformity upon their municipalities.

State tax exemption programs. To carry out a system of industrial subsidization involving state funds according to the principles outlined in this work is much more difficult in practice than it is to do this at the local level. The basic difference is that states are not homogeneous with respect to employment conditions, so that ideally the state government would have to designate labor surplus communities where the tax exemption would exclusively apply. Politically, this is difficult to accomplish, and in fact it has not been attempted. Yet discrimination is required here if waste is to be avoided and if industry is to be directed toward the labor surplus areas. Furthermore, discrimination is also required in the sense that industries should not be subsidized if they would have come to a labor surplus area within the state anyway, while in the case that subsidization is required to accomplish this the industry in question should not be given more than is re-

65. See Chapter VI, pp. 150-52.   66. Floyd, *op. cit.*, p. 113.
67. Wolkstein, *op. cit.*, p. 172.

quired.[68] Thus bargaining with each individual prospect is of the essence, and while this is feasible (and is the standard procedure) when a local community does the subsidizing, it can easily be seen how such a procedure would bog down in bureaucracy if attempted at the state level. Not only would there be administrative difficulties, but the bargaining agent would undoubtedly be subject to pressure from different regional and local groups within the state. Ideally each prospect should go to that local surplus community where it can be induced to come at least cost to the state, but instead of a competitive mechanism directing it there bureaucratic ignorance and political favoritism would be almost certain to prevent this. Nor could the bargaining be delegated to the municipalities themselves; if local communities should be authorized to hand out favors that cost them nothing it is clear that there would be no weighing of total cost against total benefits. In that case the exemption would be given as a matter of course, and this in practice is the method that states with tax exemption programs seem to have followed, even though formally the granting of the exemption is usually by option of a state authority charged with the administration of the program. While the states may be commended for not having tried the impossible, the fact that they cannot properly discriminate[69] in either of the two ways required under a theoretically sound program casts serious doubt upon the desirability of having a state tax exemption program at all.

68. As Heer points out (*op. cit.*, pp. 252-53), "from the standpoint of their potential influence on the economic growth of a state, business taxes are by no means alike." He distinguishes taxes subject to interstate competition (with respect to location) and taxes on concerns comparatively unaffected by such competition.

69. In a study of the tax exemption program in Louisiana (William D. Ross, "Tax Exemption in Louisiana as a Device for Encouraging Industrial Development," *The Southwestern Social Science Quarterly*, XXXIV [June, 1953], 14-22), William D. Ross of Louisiana State University comes to the conclusion that out of total exempted investments of $355,121,753.60, only approximately $25,000,000 worth of investments (or about 7 percent) would have been lost for the state in the absence of the inducement. This result is based upon questionnaires mailed to officials of the 429 firms that had received exemptions between December 1946, when the current program was inaugurated, and June 1950. (For some comments on Professor Ross's study see Appendix II, p. 215.)

In Puerto Rico, which administers a tax exemption program with savings much greater than are possible under state programs on the mainland, the same lack of discrimination is in evidence. In that island it has been considered necessary for competitive reasons to include already existing firms in the exemption when it was granted to newcomers in the same line of production, and there has been little relationship between the contribution of firms to employment and investment on the one hand and the amount of income-tax subsidy received on the other. See Milton C. Taylor, *Industrial Tax-Exemption in Puerto Rico* (Madison: The University of Wisconsin Press, 1957), p. 146.

To the extent that enterprises that otherwise would have settled elsewhere have located in labor surplus areas as a result of state tax exemption, there has of course been gain. Therefore a policy of exemption or other inducements at the state level may, in spite of deficient administration, be better than a policy of no inducements at all, especially when un- and underemployment are widespread throughout the state. However, there is another alternative available that would make subsidization of industry by the state unnecessary, and that is to allow the municipalities unrestricted freedom in making concessions at their own expense or at least more freedom than they now have. Some may argue that an advantage of subsidization by the state over this alternative lies precisely in the fact that under the former procedure the burden does not have to be borne entirely by the low-income municipalities to which the industries should be directed. We have already seen, however, that in political reality a state program may not accomplish this, while such a program is certain to invlove wasteful concessions. If a redistribution of income between rich and poor regions is desired, this can be accomplished by other means.

It might also be contended that I am inconsistent in objecting to the exemption of industry from state taxes in cases in which the industry would have come to the state anyway, while being in favor of competitive subsidization between local communities. Surely competition between communities will lead to the extension of inducements, it will be said, that might have been avoided in the case of a program administered by the state. On an abstract theoretical level there is some truth in this: if we assume that by central manipulation an exemption (or subsidization) program could be administered in the discriminatory fashion outlined above, full employment might be achieved with less total subsidy than in the case of competitive subsidization between municipalities. However, states would still compete with other states, and with respect to most prospects the degree of monopsony power a state could exercise might not be great. At any rate, the possibly somewhat higher total expenditure incurred in the case of competitive subsidization by municipalities would serve the excellent purpose of allocating the industries where they can add the most to community income, whereas in the case of subsidization by the states there is no equivalent mechanism.

Another matter is possible state action in the event that the boycott of municipal industrial bonds by the financial interests should continue.[70]   This boycott has not been and cannot be complete.   Regional financial interests have continued to invest in them and many have also been placed with local private investors.   But to widen the market and break the boycott, at least one state has considered using state funds to secure an outlet for the bonds of municipalities desirous to finance industrial expansion.   State bonds could be marketed for this purpose, and should the boycott be extended to those (which seems unlikely), the states should not hesitate to raise the necessary funds through taxation.   This, I believe, would be better than direct state subsidization by exempting new industry from state taxes.

70. If the federal government should discontinue its tax exemption of these bonds, there would no longer be any justification of the boycott. Until then, the boycott is useful to point up the presently existing anomalous situation.

CHAPTER V

A Global Survey of Efforts to Influence Industrial Location by Means of Special Inducements

Early community efforts. It has been stated that the practice of municipal subsidization of private industry is almost as old as municipal life in the United States.[1] Perhaps it is better to say "America" because special inducements, bounties, and tax concessions were common in the colonial period. From the earliest times of New England settlement, for instance, townships have held out such inducements as a house and free land to attract skilled artisans, immunities from local taxation, and the payment of bonuses to attract desired industries, etc. The analogy with modern times is close, for in the colonial period also custom as well as price and wage regulations tended to impede the working of the market. Since at that time authorities were inclined to set legal wages and prices below the market rate, "scarcities" were artificially created. This was then counteracted by the municipalities, which held out inducements over and above the price producers could obtain for their products and services. Nowadays the problem is that entrepreneurs have to pay too high a price for labor services in localities that desire to attract industry in order to create employment, and hence the community tends to step in to correct this situation by means of subsidization.

Halting industrial decline. In this modern form the problem of local development began to emerge in the latter part of the nineteenth century. Acting through local organizations—boards of trade, chambers of commerce, trade associations—industrial development was promoted by the local business community, not primarily with a view to direct profit but to protect its investments in the area.[2] Early examples

1. Milton Derber, "Municipal Subsidy of Private Industry," *The Municipality*, XXXII (June, 1937), 125.
2. Victor Roterus, "Community Industrial Development—a Nationwide Survey,"

of formally constituted industrial development corporations include
the Industrial Association of La Crosse (Wis.) and the Louisville
Industrial Foundation, founded in 1910 and 1916 respectively. During
the 1920's the growth in the number of foundations was slow; the
depression years of the 1930's saw a more rapid increase. Often such
an organization represented a community's response to a critical situation that suddenly arose when a city was faced with the loss of a
predominant enterprise. A striking example is that of Manchester,
N.H., which was faced with an emergency that threatened to undermine the entire economic foundation of the city when it largest enterprise, the Amoskeag Manufacturing Company, was forced to liquidate.
In July 1936 local businessmen within a week raised 10 percent of the
$5 million required to buy the assets of what had been the largest
textile plant in the world, formed Amoskeag Industries Incorporated,
and agreed to buy the entire property. Further funds were acquired
by the sale of water rights and dams to the Public Service Company of
New Hampshire and by borrowing from local banks against a mortgage on the property. The balance was provided by a local businessman and former mayor of the city and by the city itself. In its concern to secure occupancy of the buildings, four textile mills were set
up by the corporation itself in 1939, of which three succeeded and
were sold. By the close of World War II all of the remaining space
had been sold, chiefly to textile and shoe manufacturers, and in 1948
the corporation constructed the first of a series of new buildings.[3] In
a similar fashion economic deterioration has been halted in Scranton,
Pa., located in an area where the decline of anthracite mining has
caused widespread unemployment. In this city local effort to bring
in new industry has been organized since 1914, but the achievements
that have made Scranton renowned throughout the country date from
the post-World War II period. By means of public subscriptions, the
sale of bonds, and mortgage borrowing from banks, a large number
of industrial buildings has been constructed by various development
corporations operating in the area[4] and sold or leased to private oc-

in U.S. Congress, Senate Committee on Banking and Currency, *Development Corporations and Authorities*, 86th Cong., 1st Sess. (Washington: U.S. Government Printing
Office, 1959), p. 123.

3. State of New York, *Report of the Joint Legislative Committee on Commerce and
Economic Development*, Legislative Document No. 28 (Albany: Williams Press, Inc.,
1954), pp. 41-42.

4. The reason for the existence of more than one development corporation in a
single area (as in the case of Scranton, where there are four) lies in the statutory
limitations under which banks are not allowed to loan more than a certain percentage
of their funds to any one creditor. When a development corporation has exhausted

cupants. Other instances of successful activity are those of Laconia, N.H.; Franklin, N.H.; Pawtucket, R.I.; Altoona, Pa.; Nashua, N.H.; Portland, Me.; Grand Rapids, Mich.; Greater Muskegon, Mich.; Hopkinsville, Ky.; and in the state of New York, among others, Binghamton, Auburn, Whitehall, Hornell, and Johnstown.[5]   The extension of aid to industrial enterprises by development corporations has not been limited to new firms but has also included assistance to existing enterprises that had trouble or were about to move to another location.

Growing community sponsored development activity after World War II.   As we have seen in the two preceding chapters, the subsidization of industry by local communities was widespread in several areas of the nation during the depression, but no comprehensive nationwide survey of this type of activity seems to be in existence for that period. After the war the need for creating jobs in communities whose economies had largely been geared to defense production and where buildings vacated by war industries were standing idle, the desire to provide local employment for returning veterans, and beyond this the more long-term factor of proceeding mechanization in farming and mining provided a new stimulus for community-sponsored development activity. This has been reflected in a rapid increase in the number of local development corporations. Thus in Texas only 18 community development corporations are known to have existed before 1953, but at least 27 more were established between the end of 1952 and 1955. Similarly in New England at least 75 corporations were formed between 1912 and 1956, of which 34 were established between 1952 and 1956.[6]   For the nation as a whole the Department of Commerce found that of some 1,800 local development corporations active in 1958 the majority had been formed during the preceding five years, predominantly in nonindustrialized areas or in industrialized areas with persistent unemployment. The great majority were located in very small communities, as for instance in Minnesota, where about

---

its borrowing limit with the local banks, an additional corporation may be founded to circumvent this difficulty. Except for their legal separation, these corporations are operated as a single unit. See Roterus, *op. cit.,* p. 126.

5. New York, *Report . . . on Commerce and Economic Development,* pp. 41-44, 55-62; Gordon F. Davis, *The Community Development Corporation in Kansas* (sponsored by the Kansas Industrial Development Commission), Bureau of Business Research, School of Business, University of Kansas (Lawrence, Kansas, 1954), pp. 17-20.

6. Donald R. Gilmore, *Developing the "Little" Economies* (Committee for Economic Development, supplementary paper no. 10), p. 130.

half of these organizations were established in towns with populations of 2,000 and under and 70 percent in towns of 5,000 and under.[7]

Several studies afford some glimpses of these postwar development efforts. Thus a 1946 report of the Federal Reserve Bank of Atlanta[8] states that the establishment of industrial development corporations was gaining popularity among the towns and small cities of the South and indicates that at least 24 communities within the Sixth Federal Reserve District had founded such corporations or were planning to do so. A survey was made of thirteen of these corporations located in Georgia and Tennessee. The usual practice (or intention) was to acquire a site and to construct or remodel a building according to the requirements of an accepted industry to which the property was then leased, a common arrangement being lease at a monthly rental equal to 1 percent of the cost for ten years. At the end of that period the enterprise would have acquired the title to the building. In one case, however, the industry's rental payments were to be scaled down as its employment would rise and only a nominal sum was required at

7. Roterus, *op. cit.*, p. 124. It may be mentioned here that for the state of Minnesota a serious discrepancy has been indicated between the number of corporations in existence at the time of the survey conducted by the Office of Area Development of the U.S. Department of Commerce and the number included in this survey. The latter figure, put globally at 130 by Roterus, is apparently based upon information provided by the Minnesota Department of Business Development, which in its January 1958 newsletter states that Minnesota started 1957 with 125 community industrial development corporations and ended that year with 143. In reality, according to Fjelstad, only about 70 corporations actually existed, the department having added communities that were hoping to have such corporations to those that had already organized them to get the figures presented (Ralph S. Fjelstad, "Local Development Corporations in Minnesota," *Development Corporations and Authorities*, pp. 39-40). A discrepancy of this magnitude for one state of course also casts serious doubt upon the accuracy of the overall estimate for the nation given in the Office of Area Development study. At any rate, it should be realized that the situation is changing rapidly all the time. As Gilmore indicates: "The increased interest now being placed upon economic growth at the subnational level has brought with it the formation of a large number of new organizations almost weekly as well as changes in organizational structures and activities, thus limiting the accuracy of this report to the time when the survey was made" (Gilmore, *op. cit.*, p. 9). This chapter merely presents such figures as are available that may, together with the qualitative information contained in it and the two preceding chapters, give a global impression of the spread and nature of local, regional, and federal development activity designed to influence the location of industry in labor surplus communities by means of financial inducements—a picture of perhaps questionable accuracy, at least in its quantitative aspects but necessary and, I believe, sufficient as a background for our theoretical and practical considerations. From this point of view the knowledge that in recent years many hundreds of local development corporations have been in existence and that their number is rapidly growing is of greater interest than the exact number at any particular time.

8. C. H. Donovan, "The Spread of Development Corporations," *Monthly Review*, Federal Reserve Bank of Atlanta, XXXI (October 31, 1946), 105-09.

the anticipated employment level. The shareholders of the corporation were to be reimbursed out of property taxes levied through the county, and title to the building would remain vested in the county and city jointly. The results of another investigation of the same corporations eight years later, in 1954, have already been related in Chapter III.[9] It may be recalled that by that time only seven of the 13 had actually participated in industrial financing and that of these seven but three had managed to do so while maintaining their initial capital intact. Besides, the municipalities also extended favors in a number of cases.

In 1947 at least two dozen industrial development corporations were reported active in Missouri. Their formation was promoted by the State Department of Business Administration. Funds were obtained by private subscription for the purpose of constructing factory buildings that were leased or sold to industry, rentals usually permitting a 3 percent return on the corporation's investment. Tennessee counted some 22 such corporations of which half a dozen had proved successful, and elsewhere in the South their existence was reported in Arkansas and South Carolina.[10]

A nationwide survey of development corporations was conducted in 1948 by the Tulsa Chamber of Commerce. Of the 228 cities answering the questionnaire 72 had active local development corporations, 9 had had such an organization at some time in the past, and 17 cities were contemplating the formation of an industrial foundation. Among those in existence over 40 percent offered subsidies in one or more of the following forms: free sites (33 percent), tax exemption (20 percent), free use of buildings (12 percent), some form of free utility (9 percent).[11] Of the responding corporations less than five years old 84 percent had located one new plant or more, 42 corporations having had a hand in the establishment of 148 new firms. In addition, 12 corporations over five years old had brought in 67 plants.[12] In contemplating these results it should of course be realized that communities with successful corporations probably responded much more frequently than those whose development efforts had failed as a result of not holding out sufficient inducements. The survey also indicated that not only small concerns but also large and nationally known business institutions had received aid.

There are some indications that in the years just following the war

9. *Supra,* pp. 54-55.

10. Albert Lepawsky, *State Planning and Economic Development in the South,* N.P.A. Committee of the South, Report No. 14 (Washington: National Planning Association, 1949), p. 70.

11. Davis, *op. cit.,* p. 16.   12. *Ibid.,* p. 18.

and perhaps also later offers of substantial subsidies to industrial prospects by community groups may have been more common than the published activity of development corporations would suggest. These groups of interested businessmen do not always operate through development corporations but may act in a more informal manner. The conditions under which plants are attracted are then often treated as business secrets, and even when municipal concessions are involved the results may not be publicized. One must therefore rely upon indirect evidence. Thus in 1946 the Louisiana Department of Commerce and Industry made it known that a well-rated Louisiana manufacturer of men's clothing wanted to establish a branch plant, possibly within five hours from New Orleans. The firm required that the community put up a building for its use on a ten-year lease against an annual rental amounting to 4 percent of the construction cost minus a sum equal to one percent of its annual payroll. Thus a $100,000 building would rent for $4,000 per year against which, assuming a $250,000 annual payroll, would apply a credit of $2,500. In that case the net rental would be $1,500. It was stressed that the firm had already received such offers from two communities in Arkansas, two in Mississippi, one in Alabama, and one in Louisiana.[13] Similarly, McLaughlin and Robock state (1949) that shoe and apparel companies in the South usually only consider communities willing to offer substantial inducements in the form of cash or contributions toward the construction of a factory. The industry then agrees to operate the plant for a certain minimum period, usually ten years, and over this period guarantees a certain minimum payroll. The community retains title to the building until the company has fulfilled its obligations. These authors mention that whereas before the war the community usually paid the total construction cost, contributions since the war had as a rule been restricted to about $100,000. The two large shoe companies, International Shoe and the Brown Shoe Company, both emphasized that in almost all cases their payrolls had far exceeded the guarantee, and they justified the subsidy by pointing to the indirect benefits to the commercial and professional people of the community.[14]

A report by Robert A. Andrews,[15] based on questionnaires and

13. Lepawsky, *op. cit.*, pp. 122-23.

14. Glenn E. McLaughlin and Stefan Robock, *Why Industry Moves South*, Report No. 3, National Planning Association (Washington: Committee on the South, N.P.A., 1949), pp. 113-14, 142.

15. Robert A. Andrews, *Community Industrial Financing Plans in Operation* (Stanford, November, 1950) (mimeographed).

correspondence during the period April-July 1950, lists a total of 291 privately financed community development plans in 40 states, of which 40 had been discontinued or were inactive. Of the 247 active plans, 180 supplied industry with funds in the form of financing industrial buildings or sites, while 38 others were classified as direct-financing plans (i.e. plans with a policy including the extension of direct loans to industry or the purchase of stock in industrial corporations). In addition, one plan operated by guaranteeing loans made to business concerns by outside financial institutions, one by supplying management assistance to client firms and arranging financing from outside sources, and 27 others in ways unknown. Reports from 28 plans with total means of $3,289,000 indicated the sources of equity capital: 24.2 percent had been obtained from individual citizens, 56.9 percent from business firms, 9.3 percent from banks, 6.9 percent from public utilities, and 2.7 percent from other sources. Among the information supplied regarding the results of these plans may be mentioned that 614 firms had been aided under 45 plans reporting on this question (average number of years plans had existed: 10 years). Data on capital losses suffered were made available for five plans only, whose combined results were as follows:

Total aid extended	$3,955,853
Total capital losses	$ 259,321
Ratio of losses to total aid	6.5%
Average number of years in operation	20

One year later, in 1951, the results of a state by state survey of communal inducement practices, based upon questionnaires circularized by Harry W. Wolkstein, were presented at the annual conference of the National Tax Association.[16] Apart from listing official tax exemptions and municipal industrial bond issues in states permitting this practice under enabling legislation,[17] the survey indicates that it was possible to obtain special rental terms and interest-free loans as well as favorable tax assessment of industrial property at the local level in Georgia. In that state development corporations existed in many communities, and some were prepared to offer free sites and buildings. In Kentucky, private development corporations would often arrange for free rents, water, and power, interest-free

16. Harry W. Wolkstein, "Recent Problems and Developments in Property Tax Exemptions," *Proceedings of the Forthy-fourth Annual Conference on Taxation,* Dallas, Texas, November 26-29, 1951 (Sacramento, Calif.: National Tax Association, 1952).

17. This legislation was reviewed in Chapter IV.

loans, favorable rents, and, in some cases, free sites.[18] For Virginia
the report indicates the occasional occurrence of the subsidization of
new industry by local governments (gifts of land, interest-free loans,
low rents) and mentions the industrial foundations established in the
Hampton Roads area, which are ready to aid in the financing of new
industrial plants in that region. In West Virginia, according to this
report, development corporations were mostly active on the level of
publicity, providing information to prospects, etc. In Florida some
communities might—illegally—offer free sites or free water and occasionally also exemption from local taxes; in Missouri and Kansas
the financing of new industry by local development corporations was
widely practiced, and low initial assessment of industry was generally
provided by local communities in the former state. In Pennsylvania
many communities had development corporations to help finance
new industry and local tax incentives were sometimes offered
in spite of legal prohibition. Similarly, in Michigan tax exemption
might be arranged locally. The report also mentions activity of industrial development corporations in Maine and special inducements
of various kinds in several other states, most of which are very minor
and need not concern us here. It is clear, however, that the picture
presented by Wolkstein is far from complete. For the state of Tennessee, for instance, the state enactments covering tax exemptions and
municipal factory bond issues are mentioned, but nothing is said about
the activities of private groups or about extra-legal inducements offered by counties and municipalities. As indicated above, information
regarding these activities is not readily imparted.

A study by Albert E. Redman of the Ohio Chamber of Commerce, dating from early 1952,[19] also mainly contains information
pertaining to state legislation and throws little light on private community development activity and illegal or extra-legal municipal
action in this field. In addition to data also presented in Wolkstein's
report, it indicates the occurrence of industrial subsidization at the local
level (in the form of gifts of land or buildings, special rental terms,

18. However, this allegedly widespread willingness of Kentucky development corporations to subsidize industry does not seem fully consistent with the more detailed
information on the practices of these corporations provided by the Kentucky Department
of Economic Development. Compare *infra*, p. 128.

19. Albert E. Redman, *Study on Special Inducements to Influence Plant Location*
(Ohio Chamber of Commerce—American Industrial Development Council, Washington,
April 1, 1952) (mimeographed). This study is based on information obtained
from state planning and development agency officials and also incorporates material
released in reports of the Association of State Planning and Development Agencies
(A.S.P.D.A.).

or interest-free loans) in Colorado, Michigan, Minnesota, Mississippi, South Carolina, South Dakota, Tennessee, and Vermont.

In the most recent nationwide surveys, the presence of local development groups is reported in practically all labor surplus areas. Levitan's 1957 report to the U.S. House of Representatives' Committee on Banking and Currency states that some 1,200 corporations—less than 40 percent of the total number—had built at least one plant for industrial prospects, while about 80 percent had indicated their willingness to do so.[20] On its face, the number of corporations implied in these figures is not in accordance with the 1958 Department of Commerce figure of about 1,800 active corporations throughout the nation.[21] A breakdown by states and regions based on the latter survey indicates the presence of industrial development corporations in some 760 communities in the Midwest; 468 in the Southeast with Georgia and Tennessee over 90 each, North Carolina 86, and Mississippi the smallest number, 4; 223 in the West South Central States with the largest number in Arkansas, 90, Texas 74, Oklahoma 34, Louisiana 23;[22] 142 in New England; and 184 in the Middle Atlantic States, of which 112 in Pennsylvania.[23] In addition Roterus states: "We have reports from many sections of the country indicating that local chambers [of commerce] are doing much the same type of job as the formally constituted industrial development corporations—offering plants and sites, loans, and other assistance (not excluding subsidies). In Texas alone there are reportedly 85 chambers of commerce that own industrial sites and buildings and have funds available for industrial development."[24] On the other hand, most development corporations that are separate legal entities are operated by local chambers of commerce. "In effect they serve as the industrial development arm of

20. Sar A. Levitan, *Federal Assistance to Labor Surplus Areas,* a report prepared at the request of the chairman of the Committee on Banking and Currency, U.S. House of Representatives, 85th Cong., 1st Sess. (Washington: U.S. Government Printing Office, 1957), p. 62.

21. The much larger number indicated by Levitan may be the result of his inclusion of corporations not considered "active" by the Department of Commerce and of groups not formally constituted as development corporations. However, elsewhere in the report Levitan says: "Supplementing the work of the official city bodies are about 2,000 privately sponsored community industrial development corporations or foundations . . ." (*ibid.,* p. 61).

22. The Louisiana figure does not include 38 parish planning and development organizations.

23. Roterus, *op. cit.,* p. 124. These are preliminary figures, cited here for their global effect. They deviate slightly from the final list published later in 1958 (compare *infra,* p. 122).

24. *Ibid.,* p. 129. See also Gilmore, *op. cit.,* pp. 114-21.

local chambers. They are usually housed in chamber headquarters and their programs are managed by the chambers' paid staffs or voluntary workers."[25] It may finally be added that Gilmore indicates that in 1958 at least 1,952 communities in the United States had development corporations. This figure was obtained by adding to the 1,801 communities with formally constituted development corporations listed by the Department of Commerce as of June 1958,[26] 151 others not appearing on this list the names of which were received by the C.E.D. in the course of its survey of development activities during 1958 and which were judged to be bona fide development corporations. The C.E.D. estimates that together these organizations spent some $19 million for development purposes in 1957 and that by early 1958 the then existing corporations had raised at least $125 million.[27] In addition there were some 867 local development groups of various descriptions designed to stimulate the economic growth of their communities and generally engaging in activities similar to those of the formally constituted corporations.[28] To estimate the number of development corporations and less formal groups that had been formed through time was impossible "because records have not been kept on many which were established for a single purpose and liquidated after this purpose was accomplished, or which never raised sufficient funds, or for some reason never carried out a transaction and quietly disbanded."[29]

Character and activity of local development corporations.[30] An extensive description need not be given here for we have already discussed many aspects of these organizations and are in general familiar with their mode of operation; some information about them seen en

25. Roterus, *op. cit.,* p. 127.

26. This list includes at least one community in every state except Delaware, New Jersey, and South Carolina. However, development activity by chambers of commerce, committees, and county development boards (South Carolina) was reported in these states. See U.S. Department of Commerce, Office of Area Development, *Communities with Locally Financed Industrial Development Organizations* (Washington: U.S. Government Printing Office, 1958).

27. The latter sum does not include amounts borrowed from conventional institutions and other sources, of which no global estimate is available. However, an impression of the relative magnitudes is conveyed by a Pennsylvania Department of Commerce estimate indicating that between 1945 and 1956 some 52 development corporations in that state raised $19,044,000 of their own funds by sale of stock and bonds, borrowed $23,277,000 from banks on first mortgages, and constructed 104 plants costing $42,321,000 (Gilmore, *op. cit.,* p. 131).

28. *Ibid.,* p. 122.

29. *Ibid.,* p. 131.

30. Mostly derived from Roterus, *op. cit.,* pp. 123-29 and Gilmore, *op. cit.,* pp. 126-33.

masse may complete the picture. The large majority of presently active development organizations have been established as nonprofit organizations; regardless of their form of organization, their major purpose is not to make profits on real estate transactions or lending activities but to stimulate local economic growth. When profits are made they are generally retained for further operations. The most that persons who supply capital to these organizations may sometimes expect is their money back with possibly a small amount of interest. Some are set up on a permanent basis, while many others are one-shot operations that are dissolved when the project is completed or failure to carry out their purpose has become evident. Funds are raised through the sale of stock or bonds in the corporation (mostly the former) and/or the solicitation of outright contributions from the public at large or from a more restricted group of local businessmen. Community development corporations frequently supplement their own funds by means of borrowing from existing financial institutions on a mortgage basis to finance the construction or remodeling of factory buildings.

To attract payrolls various means are used, but the primary activity of most development corporations is to provide factory space for prospects. In the great majority of cases construction or remodeling is done according to the specifications of a particular firm after an agreement has been reached, provided that the building remains suitable for possible later occupants. Lately, however, a number of communities have constructed speculative buildings without any particular prospect in sight, usually unfinished and of a general purpose variety so as to be both readily available and adaptable to a specific occupant's need. These communities feel that equipped in this manner they may have a better chance to locate an industry than if the whole building would first have to be constructed, the time element often being an important factor once a firm has decided to move or establish a branch plant. In 1956 such buildings were held by 62 corporations in 32 states.[31] The facilities are generally leased to the occupant, frequently with a purchase option; rentals have as a rule been set at levels that would enable the development corporation to get all its money back plus interest at a moderate rate over periods ranging from 10 to 25 years.[32]

31. Levitan, *op. cit.*, pp. 62-65. For a discussion of community experience with speculative buildings in New England see "Speculative Industrial Building," *New England Business Review* (November, 1959), pp. 1-4.

32. Compare also Davis, *op. cit.*, p. 20: "Community development corporations, in addition to the part they played in securing new industries and retaining established

Financial assistance has also been rendered in various other forms, including the purchase of company stock by the development corporation in a few cases as well as outright cash grants. According to Roterus the practice of offering cash grants, while still in use, is no longer as common as it once was. Development corporations frequently make nonbankable loans to manufacturers, usually with interest rates similar to those charged by conventional financial institutions but with lower grade collateral than would be acceptable to banks or none at all. These loans may also be extended for longer periods than bank loans and fewer restrictions are imposed upon their use. Some corporations supply second mortgage funds to enterprises that themselves build a plant. Corporation loans have also been used to purchase machinery, cover moving expenses, finance plant expansion, purchase sites, and as working capital. *Frequently a minimum annual payroll or employment volume is specified as a condition of the loan agreement.* Development corporations may act as intermediaries between banks and firms locating in their community and in some instances have undertaken to guarantee bank loans to manufacturers. They may also aid a business concern to sell its stock locally.

Development corporations frequently purchase or take options on land deemed suitable for industry to prevent its use for other purposes or to assemble contiguous small parcels under single ownership. Sites are generally sold at or close to cost, but there are instances of donations. Some development corporations have laid out industrial parks. Other activities include supplying prospects with local information, advertising, and rendering aid to prospects in obtaining favorable municipal decisions with regard to such matters as zoning, providing municipal services, taxation, subsidies, etc. In some cases development corporations furnish managerial and engineering advice to small firms and a few have undertaken comprehensive development programs. In addition to aiding outside firms, development corporations have given assistance to manufacturers already established in their community to enable them to expand or stay in business at that location.

Other development activity at the local level as indicated by the C.E.D. survey. Under the C.E.D. investigation local development groups and chambers of commerce were asked whether their local

concerns, have, in general, conducted their operations with financial profit. This holds true for nonprofit as well as profit corporations. Though these agencies have all been set up with the profit motive relegated to the background, almost without exception they have preserved their capital intact, and not a few have shown a profit."

governments had taken any action specifically directed toward promoting the industrial development of their areas. About half of 141 development groups answering the question reported that this was the case. Types of action mentioned were: construction of roads, sewers, and other municipal facilities for new industrial plants; re-zoning of land for industrial purposes; appropriating funds for a development organization; special tax treatment for a new industry; gifts of land or buildings; and issuance of bonds for the construction of new plants.[33] Similarly, nearly two-thirds of 610 chambers of commerce that replied to the question gave an affirmative answer, listing specific activities as follows:[34]

Activities	Number of times mentioned by 384 chambers
Rezoned land for industrial use	245
Built roads, sewers, etc., for a new plant	204
Appropriated funds for a development organization	65
Offered tax exemptions	46
Made gifts of land or buildings	40
Offered special assessments or tax abatements	37
Appropriated funds for industrial job-training program	33
Issued bonds for construction of factories	17

Other activities written in:

Appropriated funds to provide utilities free or at cost	25
Appointed committees for study and recommendations	16
Paid for promotional material and advertising	9
Financed studies	8
Appointed development commission	7

Among activities of local government units in the development field that are of interest to us for the purpose of this treatise and which have not been covered in the preceding chapters may still be mentioned the existence of municipal or county development agencies in 23 states. Among 249 such agencies polled under the C.E.D. inquiry, 34 supplied usable information; of these only three had been formed before 1950. On the whole their budgets and powers are very limited; the combined 1957 budget of 27 agencies reporting expenditures was $340,000.[35]

33. Gilmore, *op. cit.*, p. 125.   34. *Ibid.*, pp. 117-18.
35. For a more detailed discussion see *ibid.*, pp. 63-69.

By contrast, a prominent part in local and regional development activity has been played by railroads, which in 1957 spent an estimated $65 million for this purpose. Of this sum some 56 percent was allocated to real estate acquisition and property improvement and 19 percent to promotion. "Direct action by railroads in this field reflected the difficulties they had experienced in having suitable land set aside for industrial use, in getting land rezoned for industrial use, and in assembling suitable sites. Many railroads appeared to have concluded that the only way of assuring suitable sites for industry was to provide these sites themselves."[36] Railroads being primarily interested in freight, i.e. in indirect returns to this type of real estate activity, implied subsidization of manufacturing enterprises may have occurred in disposing of their property for industrial use, but I have no specific information on this. That railroads do sometimes subsidize industry is vaguely suggested by Gilmore: "Planned industrial parks formed not primarily to provide real estate profits but to help accomplish the major objective of the sponsor, such as those formed by railroads interested in getting freight traffic . . . can and do offer special inducements to tenants. These inducements may take such forms as sale of improved sites at cost, tax deferments, and free utility installations. These parks are sometimes referred to as 'subsidized parks.' "[37] The central factor here of course is that railroads are a classical example of a decreasing cost industry and therefore vitally interested in the general economic development of their areas. For similar reasons, electric and gas companies also spend relatively large sums on local and area development programs.[38] In spite of this, however, their efforts are mentioned here only in passing because of lack of readily available detailed information on the subsidization aspect of their development activity and because this work is primarily concerned with the subsidization activities engaged in by public and private agencies which by their very nature reflect the fact that attracting industry by means of special inducements may serve the public interest.

Recent community development activity in some southern states.

36. *Ibid.,* p. 94.

37. *Ibid.,* p. 136. Railroads have been responsible for the development of a large number of industrial parks, especially the early ones. Of approximately 300 parks in existence in 1957 only 33 were developed prior to 1940 and 183 since the beginning of 1950. By 1957, railroads owned about 30 percent of the existing parks and private industrial developers 40 percent. The remaining 30 percent had been formed by development corporations, chambers of commerce, governmental agencies, etc. (*ibid.,* pp. 134-35).

38. *Ibid.,* pp. 99-106.

This section contains some piecemeal information on the southern region that may shed additional light on the subsidization practice in particular states and areas.   In part it is based on admittedly limited personal inquiries that have consisted of interviews with people active in local development groups as well as correspondence with state and local development agencies.

For the state of Kentucky, where on the whole the attitude at the state level toward the subsidization of industry is among the most liberal and where even outright donations have found merit in the eyes of the authorities, a fairly comprehensive although condensed survey of current practice has recently been compiled by the Kentucky Department of Economic Development in cooperation with the Kentucky Chamber of Commerce, a number of utility companies and railroads, and the Kentucky Motor Transport Association.[39]   The purpose of the booklet is to provide local business and civic leaders with practical information to assist them in promoting the industrial growth of their communities, and this it does in a manner that deserves to be imitated elsewhere.   It indicates that in 1958 about 35 local industrial development corporations were in operation in the state outside that of Louisville, and that most of these had been organized since 1950 in small communities located in underindustrialized areas or in industrial areas with serious unemployment.   Together these corporations had built some 30 manufacturing plants and had developed and sold numerous plant sites.   More than 9,000 well paying jobs had resulted from these activities.   In at least one case an "enlightened donation" had secured a plant now employing more than 1,400 women.   This occurred in Campbellsville, "where improvement-minded citizens shelled out $105,000 as a donation to an industry.   It was a clincher.   The industry moved in."[40]   This was accomplished under the auspices of the Taylor County Area Development Association, founded in 1948.   The company built a $1 million factory, and "wages paid at the plant, coupled with resultant stimulation of business in the community, has made the $105,000 seem but a drop in the bucket."[41]   The donation was secured by an equity the Association held in the property until $3,500,000 had been paid out in wages, a figure that was reached within a few years.   Summing up the booklet states: "Experts in the field of industrial promotion generally frown on 'give-aways' to attract industry.   In the Campbellsville

39. State of Kentucky, Department of Economic Development, *The Local Industrial Development Corporation* (Frankfort, Ky., 1959?).
40. *Ibid.*, p. 13.   41. *Ibid.*

case, however, the donation was protected by the equity in the plant and the excellent reputation and financial standing of the company. The firm, formerly the Taylor Manufacturing Company, is now the Union Underwear Company."[42] By contrast, "poor results in some instances [of Kentucky development corporations that failed to accomplish anything] can be laid to failure to nail down a good industrial site at an attractive price or to be ready to finance the construction or purchase of a plant."[43] As has been repeatedly emphasized in this work, however, a little more than the mere financing of industry may be required—as in Campbellsville. As the booklet stresses, this case is unique in recent Kentucky experience. In the other cases it describes in some detail there is hardly a trace of implied subsidization in the rental conditions, and while the readiness of the communities in question to put up the money probably was the decisive factor in securing the industry, other communities have failed to attract industry on that basis.

Much the same may be said about the financing of industry by means of revenue bond issues. Through the years 1950-58 fourteen Kentucky cities used this method, which was less than expected. This has been attributed to unfamiliarity of local officials with the law—to my mind a most implausible explanation. Perhaps local officials are not always aware of the law permitting municipalities to issue this type of bond, but if it offered real possibilities to do something substantial in the way of securing industry, the news would have spread like a bush fire. The impression then remains that, while Kentucky communities have achieved important successes by means of financial inducements to industry that have included very little subsidization, on the whole the approach has been timid and consequently a great deal more could have been done to improve the employment situation with relatively small outlays.

One also gathers the impression that this applies to the South in general. Although one Alabama source states that "offers of an attractive industrial site on a railroad, a new factory building and liberal financial inducements . . . have become part of the normal pattern," it appears that in most cases these offers are not made free of charge and that the inducements are frequently limited to temporary exemption from local taxes and the financing of a building on a near-businesslike basis. Thus for Alabama itself we are told that "virtually every community in the state has become an aggressive bidder for the location of new manufacturing enterprise," but about half the spokes-

42. *Ibid.*   43. *Ibid.*, p. 6.

men for the numerous development organizations existing in that state have admitted that their efforts have not been successful.[44] Such an admission, of course, is not readily made, and we may therefore not infer from this that the others have been successful. An official of the Alabama State Planning and Industrial Development Board indicates (in a letter to the author) that some communities have given subsidies to industry other than those authorized for municipalities by law (financing of buildings with revenue bonds and tax exemption), such as free sites and the subscription of stock in the industry by development organizations and interested citizens. However, he emphasizes that "this is not the rule, but is done by a number of municipalities in the state" and adds: "It is often proven that such efforts turn out to be less than competitive with proposals made by cities in other states." This information nevertheless suggests that in an unobtrusive fashion more is going on than is commonly perceived or has found its way into the published results of global surveys.

That community efforts to attract industry are widespread in the labor surplus areas (but often lacking in sufficient intensity to guarantee success) is further confirmed by a recent Chattanooga Chamber of Commerce estimate that 75 percent of all new industrial establishments require some form of local financing. Our source[45] does not indicate precisely what region the estimate refers to, but we may assume that it applies to Tennessee and surrounding areas. Within the state of Tennessee, of 168 new industries locating in 115 cities under 10,000 population during the nine-year period 1945 through 1953, the buildings were financed as follows: 41 by city or county bond issues; 50 by local development organizations; 77 by the industry itself.[46] The relatively large number of municipal bond issues in this state (as compared, for instance, with Kentucky) may perhaps in part be explained by the fact that Tennessee municipalities often used the general obligation bond rather than the higher interest-bearing revenue bond, although legislation permitting this did not exist during the

44. *Alabama Goes Industry Hunting,* a study prepared by the Alabama Business Research Council and the School of Commerce and Business Administration, University of Alabama (University, Alabama, 1957), p. 34. Apparently most of these organizations are not formally constituted development corporations, for only three such institutions appear on the 1958 U.S. Department of Commerce list referred to above.

45. *Industrial Committee of 100 of the Chamber of Commerce,* Chattanooga, July, 1959, p. 2 (mimeographed).

46. This was indicated by a 1954 survey by the Bureau of Public Administration, University of Tennessee. See "Needed: Investment Capital," *Tennessee Town and City,* VIII (December, 1957), 12.

period in question.[47]   However, none of this implies that "the
record of local action in financing local industrial progress is
one of all-out effort by local communities and their governments."[48]
There is nothing to indicate that the number of communities
which have done "all it takes" to attract industry on a sufficient
scale to create employment opportunity for all qualified residents
who desire it has been large.   The Chattanooga Chamber of Commerce also observes that "long-term financing for the site and
building at a reasonable rate of interest will meet ninety (90%) per
cent of the requirements of those industries that require some form
of financing."[49]   What this actually means is that in approximately
that many cases industry *has* located on those terms because more
attractive conditions were not obtainable (and since it was known
that they were not available other than in exceptional cases entrepreneurs may have saved themselves the trouble to look for them).
Naturally the terms that are negotiated depend upon the kind of concessions local communities are willing to make, but more enterprises
would be established in the labor surplus areas and more local initiative and capital formation would be encouraged there if communities
—in their own interest—were really to become aggressive bidders for
industry.

I have not been able to locate a survey of local development
activity in Georgia, but more than 100 development corporations exist
in that state, which reportedly are in general willing to extend "some
reasonable concessions."[50]   This was confirmed during a number of
interviews conducted there by the writer, but no details were revealed.
In North Carolina incomplete figures gathered by the state's Department of Conservation and Development show that some fifty local
development corporations, using entirely private funds, have erected
buildings for lease to industry.   Information on the rental terms was
furnished to the department on a confidential basis.   I was informed,
however, that at rare intervals communities have donated sites but
that special concessions are seldom used "since the people of North
Carolina prefer to promote industry on a business-like basis."[51]   Both
in Georgia and North Carolina the idea of subsidization seems to be
anathema at the state level.   This may perhaps in part account for the
reluctance of local groups to disclose the terms of their agreements

47. *Ibid.*, p. 13.   48. *Ibid.*, p. 12.
49. *Industrial Committee of 100 of the Chamber of Commerce*, p. 2.
50. Letter from a Georgia Department of Commerce official.
51. Letter from a North Carolina Department of Conservation and Development
official.

with industry, although from a business viewpoint this is also under-standable. South Carolina reports that little is done by way of sub-sidization at the local level apart from the donation of sites that usually are not very valuable and the extension of temporary tax exemption by local units, which state law permits. In Florida the financing of new industry by local development agencies is also practiced, with site donation and tax reduction indicated in a few instances.[52] Of course, not all of Florida is a labor surplus area; parts of the state are growing very rapidly without any need for special inducements.

A report on Virginia indicates that in this commonwealth in 1957 development corporations or unified groups ready to finance industry were in existence or in the process of being organized in 44 com-munities.[53] All of the organizations were closely allied with the local chamber of commerce. Some had purchased industrial sites on which they planned to construct buildings for suitable industrial occupants or were holding options to such property. The industrial development foundation of Portsmouth, one of the most successful, had built three factories since 1950 and had contracted for a fourth building. Al-though Virginia includes depressed coal mining regions and has considerable labor surpluses in some farming areas, the report is contemptuous of industrial subsidies and claims that none are cur-rently offered, openly or in any disguise, by development groups in the state.[54] It is nevertheless not denied that the financing of industry by development corporations as a rule takes place on terms more liberal than can be obtained from conventional institutions. A recent success-ful example of this type of action and the community spirit that moves it occurred in the small town of Galax, Va., where popular subscrip-tion in the form of note pledges to the Carroll-Grayson Development Corporation to finance the building of a plant for the Hanes Company of Winston-Salem "roared past the million dollar mark" when the

52. Felix Muehlner and James G. Richardson, "Financing New Manufacturing Plants in Florida," *Engineering Progress at the University of Florida*, X, No. 10 (October, 1956).

53. Commonwealth of Virginia, *Report of the Commission to Study Industrial Development in Virginia*, Senate Document No. 10 (Richmond: Division of Purchase and Printing, 1957), p. 103. It may be added that for 1958 the U.S. Department of Commerce recorded 55 Virginia communities with development corporations.

54. In another report that appeared only a few months earlier this is contradicted: "About a dozen of the [Virginia] corporations will donate a site or offer free rent . . . one or two will offer free utilities, pay moving expenses or buy necessary machinery. No doubt some other corporations might do as much if they were pushed" (Common-wealth of Virginia, Subcommittee on Finances, Industrial Development Study Com-mission, *Should a State-wide Industrial Development Credit Corporation Be Organized in Virginia*, [Richmond, May, 1957], pp. 20-21).

September 1 deadline was reached.[55] The local money invested will draw interest at 4.5 percent.

A question and an answer. One of the country's foremost plant locating services indicates that the question most frequently asked by spokesmen of development groups or municipalities interested in attracting industry is this: "To what extent should we provide inducements to industry?"[56] At a highly abstract level the answer to this question is easy, and so it is at the practical level under present circumstances. As to the former, the abstraction that makes the answer easy (but which at the same time is necessary at the outset to arrive at a realistic answer in the end) is that we look upon the community as a corporation interested in maximizing the aggregate income of its residents (its net communal product). How far does such a corporation carry its outlays? To the point where marginal cost equals marginal revenue. Specifically, as long as the returns to subsidization, consisting of net additions to payrolls plus indirect benefits, exceed the subsidy itself, it pays to bring in industry by means of subsidies. As common sense may suggest and as will be demonstrated in the following chapters, this will generally be the case as long as there is un- or underemployment within the community—before the full employment level is reached outlay at the margin may come to exceed revenue but this is unlikely, and beyond that point marginal revenue drops to zero, assuming a given wage level in industry. At any rate, the problem of exact calculation only arises when there is active competition between truly aggressive bidders for industry, operating on the principle outlined. Under current circumstances, as the empirical information presented here clearly shows, this is not the case. Communities, imbued with overly conservative notions and impeded by legal restraints, do not by and large act as maximizers of their collective incomes in the sense of following the marginal principle insofar as practical considerations permit. As a result, returns to successful subsidization efforts have with hardly any exceptions been very high for lack of serious competition. Therefore, the answer to the question under discussion at the practical level is in virtually all cases: the community should carry industrial subsidies to the point where employment is provided for all its able-bodied residents that desire it at going industrial wage levels, thereby of course looking for the most favorable conditions it can get.

Only very few communities seem to be using this approach nowa-

55. *Galax Gazette,* September 3, 1959.
56. Letter from Ronald M. Reifler of Fantus Factory Locating Service.

days. Clinton Hoch states that currently average community investment in industrial structures in the mid-South area is about $600 per
worker, including mortgage loans.[57]   It is clear that a community
making such an investment receives its money back in payrolls disbursed by the plant alone within two or three months once operations
have started, assuming an average monthly wage between $200 and
$300. This still disregards the indirect benefits that accrue to local
businessmen and the circumstance that a sizeable part of the construction cost itself may immediately return to the community in the form
of wages paid to local construction workers.   As a lasting effect the
community then owns an industrial building which is likely to retain
for the community a payroll for many years to come without any
further investments, even if the original occupant should have to be
replaced by another.   In addition the community derives rental payments from the building in by far the most numerous instances.
However, insisting upon rentals covering the total construction cost
plus interest has been the tragic and fatal mistake of a great many
development corporations that as a result have achieved little or nothing—as if under present conditions the benefits coming to a community
suffering from un- or underemployment when it locates a new industry
are not great enough without any rentals whatever!   And as the reader
will recall, the principle that a community's expenses must be fully
recovered through sale or rentals has been embodied in the laws of all
the states that explicitly permit municipalities to issue bonds for the
financing of industrial buildings.   All this derives from the fact that
the economics of unemployment is simply not understood.

   State-wide development credit corporations.   As the name indicates,
these organizations purport to stimulate economic development on a
statewide basis by means of providing loans to enterprises that cannot
be obtained from conventional sources.   In this respect they are similar
to local development corporations, many of which, as we have seen,
often operate in this fashion.   However, to the extent that the necessary
equity capital that this mode of operation requires has to be obtained
from private sources (there also exists a number of state-supported
industrial financial authorities) there would appear to be less com-

57. L. Clinton Hoch, "The Location Decision," a paper presented before the Semi-
Annual Conference, Production Executives Division, The National Association of Shirt,
Pajama and Sportswear Manufacturers, New York, June 20, 1957, p. 13 (mimeographed). This writer also indicates that resistance on the part of community leaders
may be anticipated when in a particular case the average should be higher, even when
the industry is willing to pay a rent covering amortization plus interest on the
investment.

pelling logic to this type of organization than can be attributed to its local counterpart. On the local level the benefits from the corporation's activity that may accrue to certain business interests within the community are clearly apparent and apt to be of vital importance to the business community. Moreover, since the businessmen themselves or people closely related to them whose interests run parallel to their own are in charge of the corporation's activity, there is a certain assurance that the money they contribute will be spent in accordance with their wishes and interests. This naturally facilitates the solicitation of contributions, which is sustained by enlightened self-interest in the expectation of indirect returns. But in the case of corporations operating at the state level contributing enterprises may be fairly certain of indirect returns only if they themselves also operate on a state-wide level. Therefore, since relatively fewer enterprises operate on a state-wide basis, contributions inspired by the expectation of returns in the form of increased business would have to come from fewer sources. These benefits will also be shared by other enterprises established in the community where a manufacturer financed by the development corporation may locate, but these enterprises have no incentive to make any contributions, since the location of the new industry within the state is not known in advance. Thus the close connection between contributions and benefits upon which local development corporations are based does not exist in the case of state-wide corporations dependent on private funds. In this writer's mind they appear to be somewhat artificial contrivances without real possibilities, although, when launched with great enthusiasm, limited support may be obtained from companies desirous to contribute to the public interest and/or to maintain good public relations.[58]

58. If it be argued that the state-wide development credit corporation provides an ingenious manner of marshalling capital that otherwise would not be available for the financing of business expansion (possibly due to legal restrictions imposed upon other financial institutions), then this type of corporation should be able to operate on a profitable basis—paying dividends to its shareholders comparable to those of other business enterprises—and should be set up on that basis. Alfred C. Neal, president of the Committee for Economic Development and a leader in the credit corporation movement, believes that in fact development credit corporations have a promise of paying some dividend and should attempt to do so. This opinion is shared by Sherwin Badger, a vice president of New England Mutual Life Insurance Company and one of the founders of the Massachusetts Credit Development Corporation, who has stated: "The first criterion, at least in my mind, was that the Massachusetts Development Corporation was going to operate on a profit. We have never said we will pay no dividends. I dearly hope we are going to be able to someday, and it may not be too far away." At the same time, however, Badger describes support of corporations as "enlightened self-interest." This implied reservation with respect to the prospect of direct returns is only realistic in view of the earnings record of the New England

The absence of a true community of interests is reflected in the fact that ten statewide corporations, founded between 1953 and 1957, were unable to point to any achievements by the beginning of 1958. Although a number of these were too new to be listed as failures, some of the reasons given for this inactivity are telling: difficulty in selling stock, inability to recruit members in the financial community,[59] inability to do a public relations job and "sell" the community.[60] Most of the seven active corporations existing at that time (in the New England states with the exception of Vermont,[61] New York, and North Carolina) also had experienced great difficulties in selling stock and as a result had been forced to operate at a smaller scale than had been contemplated. In spite of this rather indifferent success, however, the latest information indicates that in several other states legislation authorizing the formation of a development credit corporation has been passed or is pending and that a number of corporations are in the process of organization.[62] The record of the corporations designated as "active" may be briefly outlined below.[63]

Private development credit corporations acquire funds from two sources: the stockholders and the "members." Equity capital is obtained through the sale of stock, which in practice has mostly been purchased by public utilities and to a lesser extent by banks, insurance companies, and the general public. As in the case of local development corporations, this is virtually equivalent to a donation since dividends can hardly be expected; earnings made in the past have been

corporations, which shows only modest net returns that have been used to build up needed reserves against possible losses. Under these circumstances the New England corporations have found it increasingly hard to interest the business community in providing additional equity funds. See "Development Credit Corporations, a Stimulant for Economic Growth," *New England Business Review* (June, 1958), pp. 1-4.

59. The "membership" of financial institutions in development credit corporations will be explained below.

60. Edward B. Shils, "State Development Credit Corporations and Authorities and Problems of Financing Small Business," *Development Corporations and Authorities,* p. 17.

61. While not listed as "active" by either Shils or Gilmore, the Vermont corporation, founded in 1953, did approve its first loan in 1958. This is also true of the Wisconsin corporation, which dates from 1955 (Gilmore, *op. cit.,* p. 142).

62. "Status of State Development Corporations and Authorities," *Development Corporations and Authorities,* pp. 150-61.

63. For a more detailed discussion of state-wide development credit corporations the following works may be consulted: Shils, *op. cit.;* Gilmore, *op. cit.,* pp. 140-51; Robert S. Hutchison, *Migration and Industrial Development in Tennessee,* Report to the Industrial Development and Migration Subcommittee of the Tennessee Legislative Council, October, 1958, pp. 241-47 (mimeographed); Virginia, *Should a State-wide Industrial Development Credit Corporation Be Organized in Virginia,* pp. 9-16; "Development Credit Corporations," *New England Business Review* (June, 1958), pp. 1-4.

devoted to building up reserves and to expanding the corporations' lending activity. State-wide development corporations are chartered by special legislation which makes it possible for state-regulated financial institutions to become members and as such to supply operating funds on a commercial basis in the form of loans to the corporation; the corporation's equity capital serves as a guarantee for loans obtained from members. In some cases the relation between equity capital and borrowed money is stated in the charter, while in other cases it is not. In practice a 1-8 or 1-10 ratio of equity to debt is at any rate maintained. On the condition that sufficient equity funds will be available, the members pledge a line of credit on a call basis. In the past, the bulk of this credit has been pledged by commercial banks. Members rather than stockholders as a rule elect a majority of the directors, which is usually explained on the ground that the members also supply most of the funds. These funds are used to make non-bankable loans to enterprises locating or expanding in the state or to help established firms overcome financial difficulties; interest charges on these loans have generally been somewhat higher than bank rates. In several instances loans have been made in conjunction with local development corporations, and in one case participation of the federal government's Small Business Administration was cited.

By 1958 the seven active corporations, which were founded during the years 1949-55,[64] had sold $2,694,000 worth of stock and had received pledges totalling $33,015,000 from 594 member institutions. However, only about $11,245,000 or about one third of the amount pledged had been called, due to the fact that insufficient stock had been sold to enable the corporations to utilize their full line of credit. The amount of loans disbursed was $20,075,146 (indicating a certain amount of turnover) and that of loans approved $32,513,434. Altogether 292 loans had been made and 407 approved.[65] It is generally agreed that selling stock rather than securing membership funds is the major problem facing the state-wide development credit corporation.[66] As an exception may be mentioned the case of North Carolina, where the $1,000,000 in capital stock sold (the full amount authorized under

64. The oldest state-wide development credit corporation is the Development Credit Corporation of Maine, founded in 1949; the Massachusetts corporation, dating from 1953, is the largest.

65. Gilmore, op. cit., pp. 142-43.

66. Hutchison, op. cit., pp. 244-45; Shils, op. cit., p. 30; Gilmore, op. cit., pp. 143, 148.

the corporation's charter) compared favorably with the pledged loan potential of $4,482,000.[67]

State-supported industrial financing authorities. If efforts to stimulate economic development in labor surplus areas by means of providing funds for industrial expansion that cannot be obtained through the ordinary channels are to be undertaken on a state-wide basis, it makes sense that these efforts should be financed by public appropriations—at least if anything commensurate with the requirements of the situation is to be achieved. As compared to a state tax exemption program this approach has the advantage that discrimination in its application would seem to be assured since actual disbursements out of a given fund allocated for the purpose are involved. However, whether the taxpayer in general should be burdened in a situation where the local communities, should they be freed from state-imposed legal restrictions on the use of public funds and their own conservative notions regarding the subsidization of industry, are in the general case quite capable of helping themselves is still an open question. The prevailing notion of course is that local communities suffering from localized unemployment, being poor for that reason, are not capable of supplying or attracting all of the necessary capital themselves, and starting from this premise, state-supported financial authorities have been conceived to come to the rescue by means of extending financial aid to local development corporations.[68] However, those local corporations (and municipalities) whose success has hitherto been limited or which have accomplished nothing appear to have been impeded more by a lack of prospects under the conditions offered than by a lack of funds. Furthermore, "lack of funds" may in reality be the effect of spreading funds too thinly. In Chapter III we have discussed the unfounded preoccupation with fund maintenance, leading to the revolving fund approach. It is clear that a subsidy representing a given present or cash value (which measures the strength of the inducement) requires a very much greater initial amount of money when the subsidy is extended in the form of a non-bankable loan than when it is given as an outright donation, even when in the

67. Hutchison, *op. cit.*, p. 243.
68. Thus, pointing out that about one-fifth of the people of Pennsylvania in 1956 still lived in chronic labor-surplus areas in spite of the considerable achievements of local development corporations in that state, Gilmore typically remarks: "It was apparent that the total job to be done was beyond the resources of community development corporations alone. Communities looked to the state for help. The state government responded by . . . establishing the Pennsylvania Industrial Development Authority to participate with community development corporations in financing new industrial plants" (Gilmore, *op. cit.*, p. 52).

former case the corporation supplements its equity funds by borrowing from banks or other financial institutions. Thus, many development corporations may never get started at all due to what they claim to be insufficient community response to their fund raising campaign, while actually if the money raised or pledged were to be disbursed in more concentrated form one or more industries could be attracted—after which, as I have argued, *with success demonstrated* repeated appeals are not likely to go unheeded. Moreover, even if the initial amount raised without any particular prospect in sight should be insufficient but a prospect can be interested with a realistic proposal, *with success clearly in sight* further contributions may be solicited more easily. In this light a good portion of the complaints about "lack of funds" should be interpreted.[69] Even so, it should be recognized that at times fund raising may prove difficult, especially in larger communities if it has to be done without municipal support on an entirely private basis. In a small town, where the community is closely knit and the common interest is readily apparent, it should be easier to obtain substantial contributions from local businessmen on a private basis than in a sizeable city.[70] In these cities, therefore, the arguments in favor of municipal participation expounded in Chapter III apply *a fortiori*. Since municipalities are barred from effective participation by state law, it is within the power of state governments to change this condition. This would eliminate any need for allocating state funds to aid local development corporations in their efforts to attract industry by means of special inducements.

As distinguished from misgivings about the allocation of state funds to aid local development corporations, a strong objection may be raised

69. Thus some comments received by Andrews (*op. cit.*, p. 6): "From a city of 12,000 with a fund of $30,000: 'We have started our program too small, without enough financial backing to take care of needs and requests and opportunities that have been available. . . .' "

"From a city of 54,000 with a fund of $55,000: 'Lack of funds is hampering progress.' "

"From a man who has had close contact with several plans: 'The basic amount of money raised should not be less than one million dollars.' "

That especially the latter statement can only be made with the fund maintenance approach in mind (and even then is wildly exaggerated) should be clear from the examples of successful activity described in this treatise. It may be added that Andrews, who quotes these statements in apparent agreement, himself recommends the revolving fund approach (*op. cit.*, p. 12).

70. Thus the Tulsa study indicated little correlation between the capitalization of local development corporations and the populations of the cities where they were located. Frequently, small cities reported large capitalizations, while an occasional large city had a small capitalization (Davis, *op. cit.*, p. 33). Andrews (*op. cit.*, p. 5) writes: "Apparently it is easier to get large per capita contributions in small towns than in large cities."

against the approach used by the state programs currently in effect. This objection runs parallel to that advanced against most local programs themselves: in no case is there any recognition of the need of many surplus labor areas for a more drastic type of subsidy than that offered under the various currently prevailing financing plans offered by local communities. As the outline of the various programs of the state financial authorities given below will indicate, the conditions upon which their aid is extended leave no room for a more intensive form of subsidization than the revolving fund approach permits. This does not imply that there will be no demand for the financial services of the state authorities: in as much as they provide the local corporations with a relatively easy and inexpensive way to obtain funds, the latter will naturally avail themselves of this opportunity in the event that a prospect can be attracted by financial inducements of the prevailing kind. But since the main difficulty is that sufficient industries cannot be attracted on this basis, the current state programs hardly constitute an adequate answer to the problems of the labor surplus areas.

Such programs have been adopted in New Hampshire, Pennsylvania, Maine, Rhode Island, Kentucky, and Arkansas.[71] The oldest is that of New Hampshire, where the New Hampshire Industrial Park Authority was created in 1955. It participates with local development corporations in the establishment of industrial parks upon which buildings for sale to manufacturers may be constructed. When the authority was founded the state provided an appropriation of $675,000. Funds may further be acquired by borrowing from the state treasury and by the sale of notes and bonds in the market; to back the bonds the authority may pledge the credit of the state. By the end of 1957 the New Hampshire Industrial Park Authority had cooperated with two community development corporations in the establishment of industrial parks and the construction of three plants in these parks, and it had constructed a fourth building on a speculative basis with a third community development corporation.

In 1956 the Pennsylvania Industrial Development Authority was established to aid local development corporations in their efforts to fight chronic unemployment. To these organizations it may loan up to 30 percent of the cost of constructing a plant for a committed firm on a second mortgage basis. The local corporation puts up 20 percent and is the owner-builder, and local banks provide the remaining

71. Descriptions can be found in Gilmore, *op. cit.*, pp. 49-56; Hutchison, *op. cit.*, pp. 247-50; Shils, *op. cit.*; "Needed: Investment Capital," *Tennessee Town and City*, VIII (December, 1957), 12-13.

50 percent, secured by a first mortgage. Rentals must be sufficient to cover amortization plus interest of the entire investment, and loans made by the authority to the local corporation must accordingly also be repaid with interest. Interest rates have ranged from 2 to 5 percent. By the end of 1957 the authority had made 44 loan commitments totaling $5,685,812 for the construction of new plants or plant expansions costing $17,120,586. Due to this new plant capacity an estimated 8,500 would be employed. The authority is not allowed to construct industrial plants itself, borrow, pledge the credit of the state, or engage in other types of activity. To finance its lending activity the state appropriated $5 million in 1956 and an additional $3 million in 1957. Closely resembling the Pennsylvania authority is one created by the Kentucky legislature in 1958. However, the assembly that established the authority did not appropriate any funds to it.

A different approach was followed in Maine, where the Maine Industrial Building Authority was founded in the latter part of 1957. It received a $500,000 appropriation from the legislature to serve as a mortgage insurance fund on a revolving basis. Under this plan the credit of the authority may be pledged by the authority to guarantee loans by private lending institutions to local development corporations for the purpose of constructing buildings for approved industries. For this service the authority charges an insurance premium of not less than one half and not more than 2 percent per year of the outstanding principal. In 1958 this legislation was subjected to a friendly court test and approved by the Maine Supreme Court, but by the end of that year no projects had been aided yet under the plan. A similar act was passed in Rhode Island in 1958 and approved by referendum in November of that year.

Among the state financing authorities may finally be listed the Arkansas Development Finance Corporation, which, although organized as a public corporation and supported with public funds, bears a certain resemblance to the private statewide corporations discussed in the preceding section. State funds were required in this case because original attempts to organize a private corporation failed to obtain the support of the banking interests. In lieu of membership funds, therefore, the state, under 1957 legislation, accepted the obligation to purchase $5 million of interest-bearing bonds in the corporation and 50 percent of all bonds issued in excess of that amount. With this backing, the corporation succeeded in selling its full amount of $1,000,000 in common and preferred stock to members of the business community. It was further hoped that the U.S. government would purchase another $5 million in bonds through the Small Business Administration, matching the investment of the Arkansas government. The corporation is authorized to make loans to industry directly as well as indirectly through local development corporations in a manner resembling the operations of the Pennsylvania authority; officials administering the program have indicated that virtually all financing will be undertaken through local corporations. It should further be noted that in Arkansas local corporations may also directly obtain state funds under 1955 legislation which authorizes the State Board of Finance to purchase first and second mortgage bonds issued by these organizations, provided the local corporation is unable to raise sufficient capital through local subscription and the sale of first mortgage bonds to private investors.

Federal aid to labor surplus areas.[72] Federal action to influence plant location in labor surplus areas has been undertaken under a number of programs not all of which have been especially designed for this purpose. Thus the Area Development Office in the Department of Commerce is charged with assisting economic development in all communities regardless of their level of unemployment, but in practice it has concentrated on labor surplus areas. It offers technical assistance to state and local development agencies and to manufacturers seeking sites for new branch plants. In this manner it has been instrumental in bringing industry to labor surplus communities, but its budget is small ($377,000 in fiscal 1957) and the agency is unable to satisfy all requests from local groups for technical aid, including on the spot consultations.

A similar program, but more directly concerned with the alleviation of localized unemployment, is the Department of Labor's Community Employment Program. This agency also emphasizes cooperation with local development groups in designing programs that will lead to the creation of employment opportunity. It has been especially active in carrying out surveys to assess local manpower resources, adequate knowledge of which is very important to firms seeking new plant sites. The Bureau of Employment Security, which operates this program, is also responsible for the labor market classifications that identify areas where relatively heavy unemployment exists. Eligibility for special consideration in government procurement and tax amortization, discussed below, is dependent upon this classification.

72. Main sources: Levitan, *op. cit.,* and U.S. Department of Commerce, Office of Area Development, *Federal Activities Helpful to Communities* (Washington: U.S. Government Printing Office, 1958).

The Small Business Administration, an agency established in 1953, also provides a means by which the federal government can further the location of enterprise in areas where new jobs are badly needed. However, its activity is not primarily directed toward this goal. Its purpose is to provide credit to qualified small enterprises that are unable to obtain the full amount they want through the conventional channels. The agency has at its disposition a revolving fund of $305 million and has recently (1958) been authorized to channel part of its lending activity through state and local development corporations to help finance the construction of new industrial buildings that are to be rented to small enterprise. This may in the future have the effect that a larger portion of the credit it provides will be apportioned to labor surplus areas. It is of interest to note that the S.B.A. as a matter of principle refuses to make loans to firms that would transfer their business from one locality to another. The merits of such a policy with respect to relocating enterprise will be discussed in Chapter VIII.

Labor surplus areas are favored in procurement by the federal government under Defense Manpower Policy No. 4, first issued in 1952 by the Director of Defense Mobilization and subsequently modified in 1953. Under this policy the Department of Defense is directed to use its best efforts to award contracts to firms located in labor surplus areas. Where appropriate, a portion of the procurement determined by the procuring agency in each case separately is set aside to be purchased in these areas. Eligible for consideration are firms that have submitted a bid upon the non-set-aside portion of the procurement within 120 percent of the highest award made for items procured in this initial phase of the procurement process. Such firms are given a chance to reconsider their bid, and if they are willing to meet the offer made by firms located elsewhere, they may be awarded the contract. As a result, $133 million worth of orders that otherwise would have been placed elsewhere has been awarded to firms in labor surplus areas between the summer of 1952 (when the policy was inaugurated) and the end of 1956. This amounted to 2.7 percent of the total value of procurement orders placed by the Defense Department in these areas. However, in fiscal 1956 and the first half of fiscal 1957 a total of only $11 million worth of orders was placed in depressed areas under Defense Manpower Policy No. 4. In 1956 the General Services Administration started a similar set-aside policy which has resulted in the placement of $900,000 worth of orders in labor surplus areas during the first six months of its administration. Whether all this has been sufficient to offset the discrimination in federal procurement against labor surplus areas—insofar as they are low wage areas—

under the Walsh-Healey Act[73] is a question that I cannot answer, but it may be doubted.

Since November 1953 labor surplus areas have also been favored by the Office of Defense Mobilization under the policy of accelerated tax amortization (which itself dates back to 1939), designed to stimulate industrial expansion deemed necessary to meet defense requirements. The policy inaugurated in 1953 provides for a larger percentage of rapid amortization in case the new or expanded facilities are located in a labor surplus area. The amount of additional amortization is determined in each case and has ranged from 10 to 25 percent of the capital investment for buildings and equipment. By the time the measure was adopted the vast majority of 200 expansion goals had already been reached, and no accelerated amortization is provided for the mere establishment of an industry in a labor surplus area. Nevertheless, according to an estimate of the Office of Defense Mobilization, plants benefiting from this arrangement have been directly responsible for the creation of some 15,600 additional jobs in the labor surplus areas between the inception of the program in November 1953 and March 1, 1957. There can of course be no doubt that without the measure many of these plants would have been built in the same location.

Among existing programs one may finally mention the Rural Development Program, under which a number of federal agencies cooperate with organizations at the state and local level in an effort to solve the problems of low-income farm families. The idea is to develop a coordinated attack on the many facets of this problem of rural poverty, starting with a number of selected areas. One of the means by which it is thought this may be achieved is to induce industry to settle in the areas so as to create nonfarm jobs. The program was inaugurated in the beginning of 1957 with a $2 million appropriation for that year.

In addition, numerous bills making available federal funds for the rehabilitation of both urban and rural depressed areas have lately been introduced, but so far those that passed Congress have been vetoed by the president. Under these bills, loans were proposed to be used for the construction, purchase, and alteration of industrial plants and for public facilities. Some of the bills also proposed to make available outright grants to assist in the construction of public works.

73. As the reader may remember, the Walsh-Healey Public Contracts Act authorizes the Secretary of Labor to determine a minimum wage which may be in excess of that established under the Fair Labor Standards Act as well as other standards that firms must meet to be awarded federal government contracts on an industry by industry basis.

In all cases the federal agencies responsible for the administration of the appropriations were to work in close cooperation with local development groups. The extent of the federal participation in the financing of industrial projects carried out under the auspices of local development groups (for lease to private enterprise) has varied from 25 percent of the cost of the building alone under a bill introduced by the administration to 75 percent of the cost of building, machinery, and equipment under a bill introduced by Senator Paul Douglas and passed by the Senate in 1956. Provisions barring the extension of federal aid to projects resulting in the relocation of industry were included in some of the proposals.

Whether federal aid to labor surplus areas is desirable from the viewpoint of the nation or even from that of the areas themselves and if so in what form it should be given is a highly controversial subject a responsible discussion of which requires far more attention than can be given here.[74] This treatise is primarily concerned with the subsidization of industry by local communities; this section on federal aid is included only to present the briefest survey of the hitherto rather unsubstantial measures undertaken by the federal government to alleviate the problem of localized unemployment. The inclusion of a global survey of all approaches to this problem practiced in the United States seemed desirable, but it is outside our scope to consider the question of federal aid in detail. Moreover, such a discussion would raise political questions that this writer hardly feels qualified to deal with. However, a few remarks may be allowed.

The economic case for the subsidization of industry in labor surplus areas is firmly established, but I believe that an economic allocation of such subsidies is most likely to result when local communities are left free to compete with each other for industry by means of funds made available by themselves. The proponents of federal aid have argued that "the forces responsible for persistent unemployment are so strong and varied that they yield only to comprehensive measures taken jointly by private groups, state and local governments, and the Federal Government."[75] As I have indicated, however, I do not believe this to be true should the matter of subsidization at the local level be approached without prejudice and carried out with an appreciation of the gains in community income that can be obtained. And if it is agreed that the problem can be solved by local effort, it is perhaps to be preferred that we look for ways and means by which local effort can

74. Such a discussion can be found in Levitan, *op. cit.*
75. Report of the Council of Economic Advisors, 1957, cited by Levitan, *op. cit.*, p. 20.

be organized so as to accomplish this before an appeal is made to the federal government. However, it is exactly here that great difficulties exist insofar as the organization of local effort may require participation of local governments. We have seen the impediments under which at present local governments that desire to take the necessary steps operate in many states. Not without reason, representatives of municipalities have bitterly complained about this situation. Testifying before the Senate subcommittee on S.722 by Senators Douglas, Kefauver, and others (one of the bills referred to above) on behalf of the Tennessee Municipal League, H. J. Bingham stated: "I believe municipal governments, by and large, are willing to do the job needed in their communities—although at present they are severely limited in revenues and in authority by sovereign state governments. They have tried every other approach, and now they come to the federal government as their best and last hope for the necessary help."[76]

If the states are unwilling to grant to their counties and municipalities the necessary autonomy to solve their own problems, one can hardly blame the municipalities for seeking aid from the federal government. And it would take a hard-boiled attitude to argue that under such circumstances the aid should be withheld. Such aid, however, will never be sufficient, and rather than waste time in self-pity, communities should marshal whatever means are at their disposition, private or public, and tackle the problem.[77]

76. "Federal Aid for Depressed Areas," *Tennessee Town and City*, X (April, 1959), 7.

77. In an interesting article dealing with the problem of localized unemployment in Britain, Peacock and Dosser raise "the fundamental question of the social costs of a policy which seems to take it as an axiom that full employment guarantees the right of every able-bodied person of working age to a job in a particular locality, so far as possible without involving a loss of income or transfer of jobs" (Alan T. Peacock and Douglas G. M. Donner, "The New Attack on Localized Unemployment," *Lloyds Bank Review* [January, 1960], p. 28). This may be an issue when, as in Britain, the national government carries out the subsidization policy, but the right of communities to create local employment opportunity when they pay for it themselves can hardly be questioned. In addition to industrial subsidies in a variety of forms, the British government also uses a discriminatory licensing policy in its attempt to further the establishment of industry in areas with a relatively high unemployment level. Certain objections that have been raised against the approach followed in Britain and a number of other countries where similar policies have been applied under the direction of the central government are not relevant to a system of decentralizd subsidization by local communities as visualized in this work. To gain an impression of the policies followed abroad in a number of countries see also: Walter S. Buckingham, Jr., "Problems of Industrial Location in Great Britain," *The American Journal of Economics and Sociology*, XIII (April, 1954), 247-54; "Employment and Unemployment: Government Policies since 1950," *International Labour Review*, LXXIV (July, 1956), 1-22 and (August 1956), 124-45.

CHAPTER VI

An Abstract Model of Competitive Subsidization

Having discussed existing subsidization practices and the objections raised to these practices from the point of view of the individual community, we must now trace the implications of competitive subsidization of industry by communities for the economy as a whole, assuming that the practice were adopted on a large scale and carried to rational limits. In the current chapter this is done on a highly abstract level. The next chapter, which discusses the local multiplier, is in the way of an extended digression that will enable us to eliminate a certain category of restrictive assumptions. Finally, in Chapter VIII, an attempt is made to predict the effect of unimpeded competitive subsidization on the American economy (and in Appendix IV the conclusions arrived at are confronted with opinions expressed in the literature).

Listing of assumptions. The following assumptions may not constitute an exhaustive description of an economic order, but an attempt has been made to identify such conditions as are relevant to our problem. We postulate a competitive economy, except for conditions specifically indicated. Rather than to define exactly what we mean by competitiveness, however, certain aspects of this condition will be separately indicated. As will be readily apparent, there has been no striving for complete rigor or explicitness, but merely for such explicitness as will avoid ambiguity within the context of our discussion.

Thus we assume the existence of a large number of enterprises acting as income maximizers, and this assumption will be maintained throughout because it is thought a good approximation to reality. We also assume a world in which all contracts are fulfilled, honesty and foresight being sufficient to accomplish this, and one of perfect knowledge regarding existing alternatives on the part of all decision-making units participating in the economic process. For convenience of exposition we assume labor to be homogeneous throughout the economy, but it is unequally distributed relative to other production factors and is immobile between communities. Each community's labor supply is also fixed in the sense that the supply of labor is conceived to be independent of the wage rate, which makes the concept "labor force" a simple one. Workers are indifferent between occupations except that they prefer a high wage over a low wage.

Prior to the introduction of competitive subsidization there is unemployment in a number of communities, due to the imposition of a uniform nation-wide minimum wage exceeding the marginal revenue product of labor (of a fully employed labor force) in these communities and which is applicable to all occupations. These communities are designated as labor-surplus communities. There is also a large number of full employment communities, where wages are equal to or exceed the national minimum. There are no self-employed; the entrepreneurial function is seen as that of bearing the risk of the market, i.e. as that of a contractor who guarantees the market rate for productive services to those contributing land, labor, and capital in the production process and who pockets revenues that may accrue to a given combination of resources above this. Apart from the minimum wage, wages as well as other factor prices are assumed to be perfectly flexible in both the upward and downward direction. It is further assumed that the marginal revenue product of labor in every community is positive in the sense that in the absence of the national wage minimum full employment would everywhere prevail at some positive wage rate. Adjustment of production methods with respect to relative factor inputs in response to changes in relative factor prices is assumed to be instantaneous, and the substitutability of labor for other production factors under known techniques is assumed to be sufficient in a large enough number of industries to cause no conflict with the other postulates of this model. Similarly, relocation of enterprise in response to cost advantages is assumed to be costless and instantaneous. Thus it is as if at every time each enterprise starts "from scratch." Since enterprises attempt to maximize their incomes, they locate their plants where production cost per unit of output (including transportation to the market in which they sell) is lowest. The capital market is assumed to be perfect. In our economy a stable price level is maintained by means of appropriate monetary and fiscal measures. The real balance effect is assumed to be a sufficiently potent factor to guarantee the feasibility of this policy, even if there should be considerable reductions in the wage level and in labor income.

Each community has a number of enterprises more or less firmly entrenched there due to the presence of immobile resources that are particularly well suited to the production of the commodities and services turned out by these enterprises (or others just like it) and whose prices are adjustable in the downward direction.[1] But we also postulate that at any given moment each community includes a number of "marginal" enterprises (or a certain amount of "marginal" production) whose production cost within the community is only slightly less than it would be in a number of other communities. In fact we assume that at any moment within each community firms form more or less a continuum in this respect and that this spectrum also comprises firms located outside the community. Also, from the point of view of each firm, communities can at every given moment be ranked in an order of overall locational advantage, with in many cases considerable discontinuities between them. However, as the above implies, there always is a number of firms in each community to which the best alternative location is only slightly worse than the place in which they actually are located, while in the general case there also exist firms located elsewhere to which a given community is only slightly worse as a location than the place in which they are actually established.

Introducing competitive subsidization, we assume all communities —of which there is a large number—to act independently as income maximizing corporations, bidding competitively for industry if in this manner community income may be increased. For the time being, we abstract from conditions within the community that in reality may prevent it from operating that way. Also, the cost of organizing collective effort is assumed to be zero.

1. This should not be interpreted to mean that every community has within its boundaries special endowments not found elsewhere. Location itself, however, is always a unique characteristic advantageous with respect to certain markets, and comparative advantage in certain types of production may always be established by adjusting factor prices. Thus we are merely reiterating the law of comparative advantage in terms deemed expedient within the context of our discussion. For our present purpose the term "enterprise" may at times be taken to indicate the production of a certain quantity of particular goods or services, and expansion or contraction within an enterprise should be considered on par with the establishment or departure of enterprises.

Anticipating the further devolopment of our model, it may in this context also be stated that in the ideal case labor cost under a scheme of discriminatory subsidization would not only vary between firms but also between different on successive additional operations within firms, the community offering greater comparative advantages for some than for others. As to the posssibility of discrimination in this manner by the community, see the discussion in Appendix III, p. 218, on "packet deals" with individual firms.

Since at this stage it is convenient to eliminate from the analysis any "indirect" effect on community income connected with the coming of new industry, we make a set of simplifying assumptions that may be designated as "no-multiplier assumptions." First, we assume that the total produce of each enterprise in each community is "exported" to other, far-distant communities. Residents consume no goods or services produced locally and local enterprises buy no supplies produced in other local enterprises. Thus the propensity *not* to spend at home is 1 at every income level, and hence the foreign trade multiplier is 1. It should be noted that these assumptions also eliminate what in the literature on the multiplier is known as the "feedback" and the "inter-industry effect." We further assume that in each case the owners of an enterprise are domiciled outside the community in which it operates and that all local property is owned by people residing outside the community. Since we have already postulated the capital market to be perfect and labor to be immobile between communities, no further assumptions need be made about the origin of the productive agents in these categories that participate in the local production process. Under the given conditions, the sole effect of the coming of an industry upon the income of a community (i.e. the aggregate income of people residing in that community) is the direct effect on local payrolls. In the case of labor-surplus communities, the total payroll disbursed by a new industry constitutes a net addition to community income equal to the number of laborers engaged times the legal minimum wage (which in these communities determines the prevailing wage rate).

Payroll subsidies indicated. Since, as will be demonstrated, competitive subsidization under the postulated conditions would eliminate all unemployment, we must first redefine the concept of a labor surplus community. Such a community is now defined as one in which full employment can be maintained only as a result of subsidization, given conditions (including the amounts of subsidies extended by other communities) everywhere else. The income maximizing labor-surplus community in our model when subsidizing industry is literally buying payroll, for the amount by which its income is augmented as the result of the establishment of a subsidized industry is equal to the wage disbursements of that industry. It follows that every additional dollar of subsidy it is willing to extend will be offered to that enterprise which in exchange will provide the largest amount of additional payroll. Due to its diminishing locational advantage for successive enterprises, greater subsidies per dollar of payroll will have to be offered by the community as the full employment level is approached, but it will strive to obtain the given amount of subsidized payroll corresponding to the full employment level at the least total expense. In this sense there can be no question of anything but payroll subsidies.

Surplus-labor communities and only those can gain from payroll subsidies. A full employment community has no incentive to subsidize industry. Any new enterprise that could be attracted by this means would have to encroach upon the labor force of already existing enterprises, a process that would be accomplished through a bidding up of the wage level by an amount equivalent to the rise in wages that would result if in the absence of subsidies or any other change a number of workers equal to that absorbed by the new enterprise were withdrawn from the community's labor force. The same wage effect could be obtained if a nondiscriminate payroll subsidy were offered to all who employ local labor. In that case, however, there would be no transfer of workers between enterprises, since with the nondiscriminate subsidy all would still be in the same competitive position as before. The subsidy would cause an upward shift in the demand curve for local labor and, with the supply of labor—as assumed—completely inelastic, this would merely result in a rise in the wage level just offsetting the subsidy.[2] It is evident, then, that such action, which would be neutral with respect to resource allocation but which would transfer income from those who pay the subsidies to labor, could not serve the purpose of increasing community income. And the subsidization of new enterprise only would even subtract from community income, for the previously existing "marginal" enterprises that would be replaced were there by virtue of the fact that under equal competitive conditions they were able to outbid all other enterprises for the community's "last" workers. Thus the productivity of these workers in their new jobs would be less than in their previous occupations, which implies that, *given the newly established wage level resulting from the subsidies,* the community could reduce its subsidization burden *while retaining the payrolls* by transferring its subsidization offer from the newly established to the replaced enterprises.[3] But this would merely restore the latter in their old position: as in the case of nondiscriminate subsidization of all enterprise there would be no net

2. This case is discussed in James M. Buchanan and John E. Moes, "A Regional Countermeasure to National Wage Standardization," *American Economic Review,* L (June, 1960), 434-38.

3. The argument assumes the absence of any change initiating outside the community that would affect the profitability of various enterprises within it.

effect on the community's income compared to the situation existing before any subsidization was undertaken.[4] The inability of full employment communities to increase their incomes by means of subsidies to industry reflects the fact that in these communities the prices of the productive agents accurately represent their opportunity cost. There is in such communities no discrepancy between the private and social cost of employing labor and other production factors, and subsidies, far from correcting existing discrepancies, would introduce them.

But in the labor-surplus communities this is different. There, labor cost to the firm does not correspond to the community's opportunity cost of labor, which is zero as long as there is unemployment. Therefore, as long as the subsidy per additional worker employed by additional industry is less than the national minimum wage prevailing in these communities, the difference constitutes a net gain to the community. Inability of a community to establish full employment by means of subsidies *that would add to its aggregate income because of the payrolls they attract* would mean, therefore, that for the production of any kind of commodity or service the community in question is so inferior as a location that even a subsidy equivalent to the total wage bill would not cause its production cost to fall below that in the next best place. It might be objected that it is not so improbable that such communities would exist if other communities also were to engage in subsidizing industry up to the point that this would no longer contribute to their aggregate incomes, but this objection must be rejected as inconsistent with our assumptions. For competitive payroll subsidization carried to the rational limit everywhere (each community, of course, acting in the conviction that whatever it does will not alter the behavior in this respect of other communities) would at the margin have exactly the same effect as would complete wage flexibility in the downward direction throughout the economy,[5] and

4. However, see the qualification of this argument in Appendix III, p. 218.

5. This is so because to the entrepreneur it makes no difference whether his labor cost be reduced as a result of the bidding up of payroll subsidies or as the result of the bidding down of wages. And with respect to resource allocation labor cost in the marginal enterprises (or within an enterprise, at the margin), which in both cases would be the same, it is of course the decisive factor. The fact that in the case of discriminatory payroll subsidization the cost of labor is reduced below the national minimum only in those enterprises that could otherwise not be retained (or, within enterprises, only with respect to such production as could otherwise not be retained, and merely to the extent necessary to retain it) while in the case of wage flexibility all labor within a community would be available at the same cost, makes a difference only with respect to the distribution of income between labor and owners of immobile property.

we have assumed that in that case full employment would be established everywhere at some positive wage rate. It may be added at this stage that this assumption was made because it is considered a realistic proposition that in every community in the United States the marginal revenue product of labor is positive in this sense. However, the assumption is not essential to our discourse. Should the marginal revenue product of labor in a community be zero, then the point to which subsidies could be profitably carried would fall short of full employment, but both community income and employment could still be maximized by carrying subsidies to the point where at the margin they would become equal to the payroll disbursements themselves.[6]

We may conclude that, under the assumptions of our model at least, every labor-surplus community has in its striving to maximize its income an incentive to subsidize industry up to the point where full employment is reached, but full employment communities (defined as communities in which the establishment and maintenance of full employment, given conditions in other communities, requires no subsidization of industry) can obtain no gain from this type of action.

The process by which under competitive subsidization full employment is established. As competitive subsidization proceeds individual communities will find it more expensive to attract industries, and hence the increments in community income of participating communities will decline as further action is taken. (We have already seen, however, that in spite of changing outward conditions it always remains profitable to the individual community to take such action if in its absence there would be unemployment. The case is analogous to the process by which in a competitive industry profits are reduced and ultimately eliminated as the result of action by individual firms inspired by their purpose of maximizing income.) Moreover, industries that at first were firmly entrenched in the absence of subsidization will successively become marginal under the attraction of subsidization offers from other communities. Subsidies will then have to be paid in order to retain them if this is found to be more advantageous than to attract other enterprises in their place. This will also happen in some of the communities that had full employment at the outset, although, because of the assumed downward flexibility of factor prices (including wages above the national mini-

6. This statement will also be qualified later. The obvious objection is of course connected with the leisure foregone that is involved. However, at present this is taken care of since we have assumed that the local supply of labor is independent of the wage rate.

mum), not necessarily in all of those. For in these communities the existing possibility of downward adjustment of all factor prices forms a barrier against the loss of industry and the occurrence of unemployment, which may or may not suffice to maintain the full employment condition without subsidization.[7]

No assumptions have been made about changes through time of the supplies of production factors in our economy, and changes in their combinations have been assumed to be instantaneous. An accumulation of capital goods is therefore not explicitly contemplated, and the establishment of full employment in such a static model must depend entirely on changes in input combinations, also in a locational sense. In particular, there will be a redistribution of capital between communities, while more labor-intensive methods of production will be adopted in those industries where alternative techniques are available or can be developed. The adoption of such methods will be in the interest of entrepreneurs because of the fall in their labor cost. In the labor-surplus communities this fall in entrepreneurial labor cost is the result of the payroll subsidies, and in the communities where at the outset full employment existed entrepreneurial labor cost is reduced by a fall in the wage level supplemented, if necessary, by payroll subsidies. To what extent in this equilibrium payroll subsidies will determine entrepreneurial labor cost depends on the level of the national minimum wage. Conceivably it could be set at a point where in the absence of subsidies virtually all economic activity would be impossible. In that case competitive subsidization would completely supersede the "normal" working of a competitive labor market. On the other hand, the minimum wage might be effective in only a few communities. In that case full employment could be established with very little subsidization that would be highly profitable to the communities engaging in it and which would affect conditions elsewhere to only a negligible extent.

The subsidization equilibrium compared with that without subsidization and with the equilibrium that would prevail in the presence of complete wage flexibility. From the point of view of industry, the discriminatory subsidization of payrolls required by the labor-surplus communities' income maximizing policy amounts to a differential pricing of labor by these communities. The range within which labor cost to the individual firm within each subsidizing community varies extends from the marginal revenue product of labor at the lower limit

7. In either case, as a result of changing conditions elsewhere, old enterprises may be replaced by different new enterprises.

to the national minimum wage at the upper limit. Thus the minimum wage forces the rational community into the role of a discriminating seller of labor. Its power to exercise this monopolistic discrimination derives from its possession of certain unique (if only with respect to location) immobile productive resources. The overall scarcity of these resources gives rise to property rents; under a system of competitive wage subsidization coupled with a wage minimum (as compared to complete wage flexibility) these rents are in part expropriated by labor, while the efficiency of resource allocation remains unimpaired. Should the minimum wage be such as to reduce the demand for local labor to zero, the discrimination under a rational subsidization scheme would be complete and *all* property rent would accrue to labor.[8]

Summing up this part of our argument, we find that in the case of complete wage flexibility marginal labor cost, hence resource allocation in the geographical sense and otherwise, is the same as under a scheme of a national minimum wage plus competitive subsidization by communities. In the latter case there is the partial expropriation of property income[9] in communities where the minimum wage is effective, while in the communities that are not affected by the minimum wage labor income is the same as in the case of wage flexibility. It follows that aggregate labor income in the economy as a whole is greater under the minimum wage plus subsidization scheme (by an amount equal to the expropriated property income) than in the case of complete wage flexibility. With a preference for equality one might therefore claim that as regards personal income distribution the minimum wage plus subsidies scheme is to be preferred over complete wage flexibility. However, among all things that in reality are different from the assumptions of our model, the transfer problem should be emphasized in this context. We should therefore not prematurely jump to the conclusion that a national minimum wage is justified after all.

How does the competitive subsidization equilibrium compare with that which prevails in the presence of the national minimum wage but without subsidies? First and foremost, the subsidies eliminate unemployment. With respect to the efficiency of resource allocation, the adoption of competitive subsidization is equivalent to abolishing

8. For some elaboration of all this, see Appendix III, p. 218.

9. Perhaps it should be emphasized that while this choice of terminology implies that the income distribution under complete wage flexibility is taken as the norm, this is done in an ethically neutral sense comparable to the choice of the freezing point of water as the zero mark on the Celsius Scale.

the minimum wage. As to aggregate labor income, in theory it may either go up or down. This may be demonstrated by postulating two extreme cases.

In one case, the national minimum is set so high as to render all employment impossible. Should this minimum be abandoned, aggregate labor income would naturally increase, provided the marginal revenue product of labor were not everywhere zero (in which case it would remain the same). But with respect to the comparison we wish to make this is only as intermediary step: we must now introduce subsidization. Due to the expropriation of immobile local property income that this would involve, labor income would further increase.

In the other case, we postulate the marginal revenue product of labor to be zero everywhere. Without minimum wage labor income would be zero. In the absence of any subsidization, there must exist a minimum wage that would maximize aggregate labor income, which then undoubtedly would be a very large share of total national income. Thus, with a judiciously chosen minimum wage and no subsidies, labor income would be very much greater than in the case of complete wage flexibility. On the other hand, under a scheme of a minimum wage plus subsidies, labor income, as demonstrated above, exceeds labor income under wage flexibility only by a part of immobile property income. This part of immobile property income might well be less than the income that would accrue to labor without subsidies but with a minimum wage chosen for the purpose of giving labor the greatest possible aggregate income.

Thus, starting with solely a minimum wage, the introduction of a system of competitive subsidization may conceivably decrease labor income.[10] It might be added that theoretically labor could always be compensated for its losses while aggregate non-labor income would still be greater than before. This is self-evident, for it follows from the fact that the adoption of a subsidization scheme in the presence of an effective minimum wage would increase the national income. But in

10. Whether it is likely to do so in reality is another question that we are not ready to discuss yet. However, it may here be mentioned that Pigou, on the basis of a careful analysis of the problem, concludes that the establishment of a minimum wage is not likely to augment aggregate labor income (A. C. Pigou, *The Economics of Welfare* [London: Macmillan and Company, 4th ed., 1952], pp. 681-93). A reproduction or even a summary of his intricate argumentation is not possible here, and allowances should be made for differences between Great Britain at the time he wrote and the United States today. If in fact for the United States today, as seems probable, the conclusion would be justified that abolition of the minimum wage would increase labor income, then the introduction of a system of competitive subsidization in the presence of the minimum wage would benefit labor even more.

practice (to the extent that the above has practical implications) it is most unlikely that compensation would be undertaken, for this would involve the transfer of income between communities as well as within communities where no subsidization is undertaken at all. This is true because the losers among workers are concentrated in formerly full employment communities, where as a result of increased competition for industry the wage level is bound to go down when subsidization is adopted by the labor surplus communities. Workers in the labor-surplus communities who formerly were employed at the national minimum and under the new circumstances can retain their jobs only because of subsidization may also lose (if they have to pay the subsidies themselves). At the same time, gains will accrue to the formerly unemployed workers in the labor-surplus communities as well as to owners of property in the full employment communities (as a result of the general fall in the wage level). The gains of these property owners may be insufficient to compensate the workers for their losses, and besides, since the full employment communities passively undergo a process that in the aggregate is likely to be adverse to them, such compensation as would be possible internally is not likely to be contemplated. At any rate, one thing that the above points up is that the differential impact of a subsidization scheme on labor in the various communities is much more important than the effect on labor income in the aggregate.

We might continue along these lines, tracing further implications of our highly abstract and static model, investigating possibilities of compensation, etc., but this would merely be grafting quasi-realistic branches on an artificial stem. In the real world, competitive subsidization between communities would not take place under the conditions we have postulated, and it is now time to see in what way our conclusions will be affected when we replace our abstractions with assumptions bearing a closer resemblance to reality.

CHAPTER VII

The Local Multiplier

In the previous chapter a set of assumptions designated as "no multiplier assumptions" was adopted which permitted us to ignore the fact that there are indirect effects when an industry brings additional payrolls into a community. But in reality an initial increase in income of a community's residents leads to increased consumption of locally provided goods and services and hence creates additional employment. This in turn may lead to increased investment, and so on. Thus there is interaction between multiplier and accelerator, resulting in an ultimate increase in community income exceeding the difference between the payrolls and the subsidies. We must now enter into a digression to study this effect in a local setting, after which we shall return to our competitive subsidization model. The postulates of this model do not apply to the present discussion of the multiplier.

The usefulness of formal multiplier theory in analyzing the indirect effects of an autonomous change in spending at the local level. Such relevance as the theory of the multiplier has in terms of real income and employment depends upon the ability of the economic unit under consideration to supply additional quantities of those goods and services toward which incremental demand resulting from the initial rise in income will be directed.[1] This in turn depends to a large extent upon such factors as the presence of unemployed labor, the likelihood of in-migration at relatively slight wage differentials, the presence of raw materials within the economy and/or the possibility of importing these materials at non-prohibitive cost, and upon the possibility of securing capital to implement the necessary additional investments. It is clear that in a small community forming part of an

1. This has been emphasized by V. K. R. V. Rao (V. K. R. V. Rao, "Investment, Income and the Multiplier in an Under-developed Economy," *The Indian Economic Review*, I [February, 1952], 55-67), who correctly argues that in low-income underdeveloped countries, where the income-elasticity of demand for food is very great, the real multiplier effect may be largely absent because of conditions that preclude the expansion of food production to any marked degree. This is true in spite of the existence of widespread disguised unemployment in agriculture.

infinitely larger national economy these conditions are usually such that at least some "real" effect may be expected, even if it is characterized by a high employment level, but that, as in the case of a large unit (e.g. a nation), *cet. par.*, these effects will be more important when there is unemployment of labor. Again, in the case of a small community that has unemployment a lack of complementary production factors within its boundaries will seldom provide a serious technological obstacle to the occurrence of a real multiplier effect as it may in the case of a nation: because of the great mobility over short distances within a nation of capital, goods, and complementary labor, expansion of total production aided by productive agents and materials supplied from outside may proceed in a more unimpeded fashion. On the other hand, the possibility of importing a large portion of the goods and services themselves at a price lower than their local production cost is also very much greater than in the case of a nation.

Naturally, the smaller an area the less likely it is to be to a large extent self-sufficient, especially if no artificial barriers prevent specialization. Thus, leakages on account of importations of both producer and consumer goods are bound to be large when an increment in income occurs in a small community. Since a single monetary system prevails between local communities (other than between nations in the modern world), this also leads to a reduction in internal spending. One important difference, therefore, between the working of the multiplier at the local and at the national level is that in the former case a sharp rise in the price level unaccompanied by a marked expansion of production and employment is quite impossible. The two basic necessary conditions that in a nation may lead to this result— inelastic supply of total output and an increase in the money supply or velocity of circulation unrelated to the possibility of expanding the production of desired goods—are absent in the case of a small local community. This does not imply, of course, that local production, employment, and spending will all rise in the same proportion. The relation between these variables depends on the local production functions, the elasticity of supply of labor, the cost of importing commodities, etc. Since some commodities and services must of necessity be supplied locally, there will be a tendency for the local price level to increase, but this tendency is sharply limited by the low cost of importing productive agents, producer goods, and finished goods from the outside. For the same reason, there is bound to be a "real" effect, i.e. an increase in local employment and production, which in the case of a nation may not occur at all.

In the above the term "multiplier" has been used in a somewhat loose sense to indicate indirect effects of incremental spending within an economic unit. In this sense there can of course be no question as to whether such a thing as a multiplier effect exists. In formal multiplier theory, however, the term "multiplier" is used to indicate the magnitude of a finite and conceptually stable relation between a lasting "autonomous" change in spending, employment, or real income and the total ultimate change in the corresponding variable resulting from the initial change. This stability is implicit in the assumption of a stable consumption function underlying the theory, an assumption which in the case of a nation amounts to an empirical error so basic that it invalidates this theory *as a formal construct* in its application to the national scene for which it was developed. For in a nation continuous autonomous spending means a continuous increase in the quantity of money,[2] which is nevertheless as a result of the leakages subsumed in a stable consumption function supposed to have no permanent induced effect on spending. This means that the theory ignores the real balance effect, i.e. the positive relation which in reality exists between the value of asset holdings and spending. According to the theory, the relation between consumption (or spending) and income remains the same as assets accumulate in the form of idle cash balances, or at least any change in that relation is considered "exogenous." This leads to the familiar result of an increase in income as compared to the original equilibrium level equal to a multiple of the periodically repeated autonomous injections in the income stream determined by the marginal propensity to consume (or spend). The fact that in the face of an accumulation of cash balances the consumption function itself will shift upward is overlooked.[3] In other words, the formal multiplier theory implies that the marginal velocity of

2. If the expenditure considered autonomous is accomplished through dishoarding on the part of certain spending units in the economy rather than through the creation of additional money the effect of this on other spending units is still equivalent to that of autonomous expenditures involving an increase in the money supply. Therefore, and also because dishoarding on the part of certain particular spending units cannot be maintained indefinitely, this case need not be discussed separately.

3. It should perhaps be emphasized that this shift is *causally related* to the autonomous increments in spending of which the finite multiplier purports, *cet. par.*, to indicate the ultimate effect. *Cet. par.* can of course never be taken to comprise things that of necessity will change as the result of a postulated change the result of which we want to study. Nor is there any reason to believe that for small changes or in a deep depression the real balance effect would be absent. There may of course be fortuitous offsetting circumstances, as for instance when expectations are worsening, but that does not redeem the theory.

circulation is zero, an implication which can be seen even more clearly if one contemplates the effect of a onetime (or finite) autonomous increase in spending. Under the formal multiplier theory this will only temporarily lead to an increase in total spending until in the new equilibruim all the "new" money has come to rest idly in expanded cash balances, a notion which is obviously absurd.[4]

But there is nothing absurd about such a result in the case of a small local community that is part of a much larger monetary system. On the contrary, common sense tells us and analysis confirms that a one-time "autonomous" expenditure made in a community will *not* lead, *cet. par.*, to a lasting increase in its money income and that a periodically repeated increase in "autonomous" spending within that community will *not* lead to a continuous growth of that community's money income. The reason for this difference is that in the case of a small community which is part of a much larger monetary system there is in fact a real, persistent, and important leakage on account of imports, *which are paid for in the same currency that is used for "domestic" payments*. It should be realized that the difference pointed out here is not that between a "closed" and an "open" economy in the usual sense. In a national economy there can be no leakages in a monetary sense on account of importations, since the national currency does not circulate abroad. Therefore, the above criticism of the national multiplier, which amounts to saying that because of the real balance effect there are no leakages in the long run, applies to an "open" national economy as much as to a "closed" national economy. However, in the case of a small local community importations induced by an initial rise in the community's income do lead to a perpetual draining away of currency to the outside. Of this currency only a negligible fraction is likely to return to the community. The important difference then between a local and a national economy which makes the concept of a finite and conceptually stable multiplier acceptable in the former case is that a local economy is "open" in the sense that its currency circulates in an infinitely larger area outside its boundaries while a national economy is in that sense "closed."

4. The above is my summary of a type of criticism that derives from the writings of such authors as Angell and Pigou. Although in my opinion these arguments are decisive and should be common property of the profession, my impression is that in fact they have not quite made the impact one would expect. Be this as it may, their repetition in the present context seems useful to contrast the lack of applicability of the concept of a finite multiplier to the national scene with the usefulness of this concept for the analysis of the kind of local problems with which this work is concerned. In view of the pertinent criticism reviewed above, a justification of one's use of the formal multiplier concept is certainly in order.

Hence at the local level and only there can the formal multiplier theory be fruitfully applied in the guise of a "foreign trade" multiplier.[5] To my knowledge the difference in applicability of the formal multiplier theory between the national and the local scene has never been analyzed before, although the multiplier approach has been used to explain the impact of autonomous changes in spending in local communities and regions (as it is also continued to be used on the national level).

On the magnitude of local multipliers; some estimates. In the considerations following below the numerical income multiplier is in principle so conceived as to indicate the ratio of the discounted value of the total incremental income stream accruing to a community as a result of the coming of an industry and the discounted value of the wage disbursements to members of that community by the industry in question. Thus the wage disbursements by the industry are taken as the "autonomous" factor and all additional effects that may occur are subsumed under the multiplier relation.[6] For various reasons, e.g. changes in the import function (analogous to the consumption function of orthodox multiplier theory) due to changes in taste, relative prices, etc., the relation between these wage disbursements and the total incremental income accruing to members of the community derived from the presence of the industry will of course vary through time. The multiplier may nevertheless be estimated by policy makers familiar with the details of the local economy in more or less the same way as an entrepreneur estimates the returns on an investment, allowing for considerable margins of error. This is of obvious importance for communities adopting a subsidization policy: to determine the rate of returns on the subsidies such an estimate must be made.[7]

If we assume that at least municipally-sponsored subsidization action is motivated by a desire to benefit those who at the time of the action reside in the community, then for the purpose of our model we are interested in the multiplier only insofar as it affects these original

5. In the following, leakages resulting from taxation, reduction in unemployment benefits, etc., will be ignored.

6. To the present study the income multiplier is the most directly relevant, for it is concerned with the creation of local employment opportunity that will also benefit the community income-wise. However, the employment multiplier may serve as a rough indication of the income multiplier and has been estimated more often than the latter. We adopt an employment multiplier concept corresponding to that of the income multiplier defined in the text.

7. If the money is raised privately, contributing individuals, to the extent that they are acting in their self-interest, must make an estimate of how they will be personally affected.

inhabitants. This would presumably correspond to the calculus of the municipal policy makers. In a rough way this assumption is probably realistic, but it is not a precise generalization. The community may for instance also take an interest in former residents related to people still living there who are desirous to return should a suitable employment opportunity occur. On the other hand, the decision makers—i.e. the local government or those who have effective suffrage—may be less interested in the welfare of certain groups within their jurisdiction than in that of others and may more or less discount such benefits or hardships as may accrue to those who are not members of the "ruling" group. In the case of a private development corporation acting as the subsidizing agent, the group in which the decision makers take an interest—in that sense the "community"—may be even more restricted. To this problem of defining the "community" we shall have to return in our subsequent argument, but for instance the possible interest in people living outside a subsidizing political unit is mentioned here only in passing for the sake of precision. In determining the action this factor is not likely to be very important in the general case (even though the possibility of attracting skilled people desirous to return to their home town may be of great importance to an industry considering a location). At any rate, while in principle we have a functional rather than a merely geographical community concept, it will not be possible to adhere to this distinction in reporting the results of a number of attempts to estimate the local multiplier. For these studies have not been undertaken from the, for our purpose, functional viewpoint. They deal with geographical areas as such and among other discrepancies with our "ideal" they generally include the effects on income and employment of induced in-migration.

First among the factors to be considered that determine the magnitude of the multiplier is the size of the community. The smaller a community the more dependent it will be upon imports and exports, and thus the greater the leakages resulting from importations. Accordingly, the sizes of the community and of the multiplier are positively correlated, although of course no perfect correlation can be expected since some communities of a given size (measured either by area or by population) are more self-contained than others. Thus Tiebout recently found income multipliers for the Chicago suburban communities of Evanston (population 72,000) and Winnetka (population 13,000) of 1.096 and 1.054 respectively, while an estimate for Ann Arbor, Michigan (population about 40,000 excluding college students) indicated a multiplier value of approximately the same magnitude as that for Evanston.[8] This result was consistent with *a priori* notions that the larger size of Evanston would be offset by the relatively greater geographic isolation of Ann Arbor. The study of the Chicago suburbs was conducted to trace the effect on total community income of an autonomous initial increase resulting from population growth. In a primarily residential community incomes of new residents derived from outside sources are the equivalent of wages disbursed in "export" industries in communities where industrial development takes place. Thus the coming of new residents is analogous to the establishment of a new industry, although in the latter case, to the extent that expansion of community activity, direct and induced, leads to the employment of local residents that were previously un- or underemployed, the total effect on the incomes of *original* residents is of course much greater. This is true because in the case of industrial expansion the autonomous increase in spending within the geographical area in question does itself largely accrue to original residents.

The small values indicated by Tiebout's study should not surprise us. In a small community the propensity to import must of necessity be very great. If we think of retailing, for instance, a sector where the indirect effect is likely to be important, it should be remembered that the goods are imported and that only the value added by the retailing service itself constitutes an increment to local income. Moreover, many purchases, especially large ones, may be made outside the community. Similarly, there are import elements, varying in relative magnitude, in the provision of utilities, entertainment, newspapers, and practically everything else made available locally in its final form. However, in the case of industrial expansion the multiplier as defined for our purpose may be considerably larger than the values found by Tiebout. As that author explains, in his suburban residential communities both the inter-industry effect and the "feedback" (i.e. the repercussions on the income of the community in question of changes in incomes in neighboring communities resulting from the initial autonomous change) may be taken as negligible. For all practical purposes his findings represent the effect of an autonomous change in community income resulting solely from accompanying changes in consumption expenditures on the part of community residents, and his sample communities were chosen with a view to isolating this effect as much as possible. But when new industry is established it may purchase a considerable amount of its inputs within the com-

8. Charles Tiebout, "Community Income Multipliers: a Population Growth Model," *Journal of Regional Science*, II (Spring, 1960), 75-84.

munity. This may give rise to increased activity in auxiliary industries (or even lead to the establishment of such industries) and/or cause a rise in the price that may be obtained for these supplies locally.[9] There will then also be further effects resulting from increased consumer expenditures within the community by households whose incomes are favorably affected, etc. And to the extent that workers employed by the plant and households benefiting from its presence otherwise reside in adjoining communities there is an effect akin to the "feedback" if this leads to increased consumer expenditures by these households within the community in question. This may be important if the town is a center for the surrounding area to which people come for shopping, professional services, etc.[10]

A number of other estimates are consistent with Tiebout's findings in that they confirm one's expectation of considerably larger multiplier values in more extensive and self-centered areas. Thus Rutledge Vining obtained the figure 2 as suggestive of the order of magnitude of the income multiplier in the case of a ten-county area in Arkansas as well as in that of a sixteen-county area in the same state, both largely rural.[11] For the metropolitan area of Wichita, Kansas, a study of the Federal Reserve Bank of Kansas City[12] indicated "that the addition of a given number of workers to supplying outside markets may be expected to lead to an increase of approximately one and one-third times as many workers engaged in serving local area

9. Thus the establishment of a processing plant, for instance, may have repercussions on agriculture far more important than the payrolls disbursed by the plant itself. For an illustration see *supra*, p. 57-58.

10. If the "community" in the functional sense is a group of businessmen and professional people in a city that caters to an area exceeding its boundaries there may be little concern about whether the newly employed live within the city. On the other hand, a municipal government engaging in a subsidization policy may attempt to internalize the benefits that are likely to accrue to residents of adjoining political units by seeking the cooperation of the governments of these units. As our survey indicates, this is in fact a not uncommon occurrence. In such a case the "feedback" is of course also largely eliminated.

11. Rutledge Vining, "The Region as a Concept in Business-cycle Analysis," *Econometrica*, XIV (July, 1946), 201-18. Also suggestive of the correlation between the multiplier and size of the community are the ratios between domestic and export workers in various cities. Thus Flint, Michigan, in 1951 had about .5 domestic workers per export worker (which, if we ignore induced production for export and the difference that may exist between the average and the marginal propensity to import, would point to a "foreign trade" multiplier of 1.5); for the New York metropolitan area the domestic export worker ratio was 2.1 in 1940; Cincinnati in 1940 had a ratio of 1.7; in Albuquerque in 1948 it was 1; and in Rocky Mount, N.C., it varied from 1.46 in 1930 to 1.11 in 1940 and 1.48 in 1950. See F. Stuart Chapin, Jr., *Urban Land Use Planning* (New York: Harper and Brothers, 1957), p. 112.

12. "The Employment Multiplier in Wichita," *Monthly Review*, Federal Reserve Bank of Kansas City (September 30, 1952).

markets over the course of years"—hence the value of the foreign trade employment multiplier would be approximately $2\frac{1}{3}$. It should be pointed out, however, that a foreign trade multiplier derived by making estimates of the number of workers engaged in production for the domestic market (or additions to this number over a period of time) relative to the number (or additions to this number) producing for export does not quite measure the magnitude that interests us for our purpose.[13] On the conceptual level a discrepancy arises because of the inter-industry effect. To us the overall effect on employment or income within the community of an additional industry (presumably working for the export market) obtained by means of subsidization is the important magnitude. If the establishment of such an industry gives rise to the expansion of production within the area to supply the industry, the net additions to income and employment generated by this auxiliary activity should be considered part of the indirect effect and not a causative factor. The so-called "economic base" approach, however, which is illustrated by the procedure followed to derive the Wichita estimate, considers as autonomous all production for export and production for the domestic market as induced or secondary—it leaves no room for induced production for export. Induced production for export may in general be relatively unimportant when new manufacturing enterprise is established in a small region or community,[14] even though it includes such locally rendered productive services as police and fire protection, the extension of services by utility companies, etc.,[15] but it should nevertheless be recognized that the economic base approach provides at best an approximation to the magnitudes we are concerned with and that in some cases it may in that respect be quite misleading. The main advantage of this approach lies in the simple dichotomy that underlies its estimation procedure (although in practice the imputation of production to one or the other sector may meet with intricate cost accounting problems). To estimate the "true" multiplier a detailed input-output model for the local economy would be required, and the predictive value of such a model would still depend on the measure in which the local response

13. *Mutatis mutandis* this also applies to the income multiplier.

14. See Charles Tiebout, "Input-output and Foreign Trade Multiplier Models in Urban Research," *Journal of the American Institute of Planners*, XXIII, No. 3, (1957), 126-30.

15. To the extent that a subsidized industry does not pay for its share in these services their value must of course be included in the subsidy, but the part which constitutes value added locally also gives rise to local income and adds to it in the aggregate insofar as expansion of these services does not lead to a decline in other production.

of consumer and producer households may be predicted on the basis of past experience. Especially in places where the coming of an industrial enterprise is introducing an entirely new element in the community there would appear to be scant basis for confidence in this respect.[16]

The Wichita study also shows how greatly the effect of a change in the export base may vary through time in one and the same region, depending upon business conditions, the type of employment offered by the new industries, expectations, etc. Here it may be noted that, due to a complex of war-time circumstances but partly also because it was possible to use existing facilities more intensively than at the outset of the period, the expansion of the aircraft industry from 1939 to 1944 was accompanied by only a moderate expansion of employment in domestic industries. It is clear that rural communities that counteract a declining population trend by attracting new industry are in a somewhat similar position, being able to handle a considerably larger volume of local business with relatively little investment in expanded facilities and by using labor employed in rendering local services more intensively. Under such circumstances induced investment and employment may be minimal, but considerable income gains will accrue to owners of real estate in the business district, merchants, professional people, farmers who find increased local outlets for their produce, etc. Even if the community has not been declining, more intensive utilization of facilities and of labor in the service industries may be possible due to economies of scale in retailing, municipal services, utilities, etc., especially in the case of small communities.[17] And in communities

16. There is an extensive literature dealing with procedures and methodological problems that arise in estimating regional and local multipliers. In addition to the works cited above, discussions on this subject may among others be found in the following: Charles T. Stewart, "Economic Base Dynamics," Land Economics, XXXV (November, 1959), 326-36; George H. Hildebrand and Arthur Mace, Jr., "The Employment Multiplier in an Expanding Industrial Market: Los Angeles County, 1940-47," The Review of Economics and Statistics, XXXI (August, 1950), 241-49; M. C. Daly, "An Approximation to a Geographical Multiplier," The Economic Journal, L (June-September, 1940), 248-58. Two points emphasized in some of these studies may be mentioned here. One is that over any time period sufficiently long to allow adjustments in production for the local market in response to changes in the export base to be completed, responses to a host of other changes in the economy, such as changes in consumer preference, relative prices, per capita incomes, etc., affect the ratio of employment in export and local industries. Thus observed changes in production for domestic use can never be uniquely attributed to any particular change(s) in the export base. Secondly, the existing ratio of workers in domestic and export production is not necessarily a good indication of what will happen to employment (or value added) in production for the domestic market when a change occurs in the export base. In other words, the marginal ratio may not be equal to the average ratio.

with widespread un- or underemployment new construction of housing may remain a relatively small factor. Workers drawn from the farm, for instance, usually prefer to remain there and commute to their work.[18] In general it seems warranted to say that the indirect effect of industrial expansion relative to the payrolls disbursed by the new enterprises is bound to be greater when the expansion involves the establishment of additional households (through in-migration or because the area is enabled to absorb its natural population growth) than when it primarily reduces un- or underemployment or reduces population losses without causing net out-migration to cease. Thus in communities that have an interest in subsidization the multiplier is likely to be rather considerably smaller than the figures computed for areas that during the period in question experienced rapid population growth, except in special cases where the inter-industry effect and the feedback may be important.

The impact of new industry in small rural communities. Most directly relevant for our purpose are some surveys made of the impact of new industry in a number of small rural communities. A study of the U.S. Chamber of Commerce[19] summarizes the changes that took place between 1940 and 1950 in nine sample counties, eight of which were located in the Southeast and therefore probably had underemployed labor available. In each of these areas manufacturing em-

17. This may or may not lead to price reduction, depending upon such things as the pricing policy of the utility companies (or the municipality to the extent that it provides utilities), the degree and form of competition in retailing and among professional people, etc. This is a very complicated issue that would make a fascinating subject for a detailed empirical and theoretical study. Here it may only be observed that, insofar as prices would fall, part of the gain would accrue to consumers, and that this gain would not be registered as an increase in the community's money income.

18. Thus in Charlotte County, Va., where a relatively large new textile plant was constructed in 1949, the employees continued to live in the open country and the towns grew very little other than as shopping centers. No new public works had to be executed, and governmental expenditures were not affected by the presence of the plant in the first five years after its establishment. A study of this area concludes: "In general, then, it may be said that in a rural area with underemployment a new plant will not increase total taxes and total cost of government as it would in an urban community" (Bureau of Population and Economic Research, University of Virginia, *The Impact of Industry in a Southern Rural County* [Charlottesville, Va., 1956], p. 93). It might be added that in urban areas with widespread unemployment the situation would in this respect be largely similar to that in rural communities with underemployment. Where full employment prevails, however, the establishment of additional industry is likely to give rise to population inflow, necessitating investment in facilities, public and private, to accommodate these people. In that case the small (rural) community may have the advantage of increasing returns in expanding its collective services.

19. Chamber of Commerce of the United States, *What New Industrial Jobs Mean to a Community* (Washington: U.S. Chamber of Commerce, 1959).

ployment at least doubled during the observation period, with a numerical increase of at least 1,000 manufacturing employees and with manufacturing employment in 1950 amounting to at least 20 percent of total employment. The counties were not part of or adjacent to metropolitan areas, and it was felt that the expansion of manufacturing had been the dominating economic influence in each case. As the report states, a deliberate attempt was made to select the communities "in such a fashion that there is a very strong connection between the growth of industrial payroll in the particular area and changes in such other indexes as bank deposits, retail sales, etc." Nevertheless, this is of course far from the ideal of a laboratory experiment in which "everything else" is kept under control. Changes in farm income, for instance, were important in the 1940-50 period and must have favorably affected income and employment in retailing, professional services, etc., so that the observed growth in non-manufacturing employment (exclusive of the negative items referred to below) relative to manufacturing employment probably overstates the impact of the latter. On the other hand, on the non-manufacturing side the report takes account of an average decline of 31 persons employed in agriculture for every 100 persons added in manufacturing. Because of underemployment in agriculture, however, this item is not equivalent to the additions in other occupations, so that this procedure of itself tends to understate the impact of the new industries in terms of productive employment, the more so because the reduction in the number of people on farms may in part have been caused by industrialization elsewhere. The report itself cautions that "effects of increased manufacturing employment will depend upon the type of factory; nature of the labor force; nature, size, and utilization of present community facilities; and many other factors." Bearing all this in mind, the overall result of a *net* addition of 74 persons employed in non-manufacturing occupations relative to every 100 additional manufacturing jobs may be stated for what it is worth as an indication of the magnitude of induced changes in employment when an industry moves into a rural area. The breakdown of this figure is also of some interest: the greatest expansion occurred in retailing (33), followed by construction (25), professional and related services (14), transportation, communication, and other public utilities (13), etc., while the decline in agriculture mentioned above (31) was by far the largest minus factor.

A comparative study of two communities undertaken by the Area

Development Office of the U.S. Department of Commerce[20] also intends to assess the impact upon a locality's economy when new industry is established. Selected were Front Royal, Virginia, where in 1937 the American Viscose Corporation started the construction of a large textile-chemical factory, and Edmore, Michigan, where the effect was traced of the arrival of a relatively small manufacturing plant. Edmore had been an almost entirely rural town where all activity depended on the surrounding farm area and the seasonal tourist business. When the plant was established it created 285 manufacturing jobs during 1951 and 1952, but the indirect effect on employment was small. About 70 percent of the factory's labor force was recruited from among part-time farmers scattered in a wide area around the town, and out-of-town housing was available in surplus farm homes and summer houses that could be bought cheaply and converted into year-round dwellings. Thus very little housing construction was necessary, while expansion of municipal facilities was not required. In retailing the influence of the new payroll was beneficial. Remodeling and expansion of existing businesses took place and by the end of 1953 seven new retailing enterprises had been established. The result was an increase of 20 jobs in the town or an employment multiplier of 1.07.

In Front Royal the impact of the American Viscose Co. on the town was much greater, due to the sheer magnitude of the change relative to the size of the local economy at the outset. In 1935 Front Royal was a rural market town with a population of 2,425, the center of Warren County which in 1930 had a population of 8,340 (approximately the same as in 1890). The arrival of construction workers in 1937 led to an upsurge in local business, which was maintained when operations started in the plant in 1940. After successive expansions, it employed almost 4,000 workers in 1946. The number of people in the county employed in retailing rose from 286 in 1935 to 860 in 1948; the number of establishments increased from 126 in 1935 to 186 in 1939, after which no further increase took place although existing firms continued to expand frequently. The volume of retail and wholesale business as well as that of other local services increased far more than employment in these sectors. Between 1935 and 1945 there was an increase of 2,626 jobs in manufacturing, accompanied by an increase of 795 jobs in other activities—or about 30 non-manufacturing jobs for every 100 jobs in manufacturing. It may be that, as was true

20. Wesley C. Calef and Charles Daoust, *What Will New Industry Mean to My Town?* (Washington: U.S. Department of Commerce, 1955).

in Wichita, this figure is somewhat depressed as a result of war-time circumstances.

Finally, the effect of the coming of the Murray, Ohio, bicycle plant in Lawrenceburg, Tenn., may be cited.[21] As the result of the creation of 950 jobs in the bicycle plant and an additional 100 jobs at National Carbon, employment in retailing and the service trades roughly a year later, by the middle of 1957, had expanded by 412 jobs, and this expansion was expected to continue for at least two years. A building supply dealer reported 1957 gross sales up 18 percent over those of 1956, in contrast to a drop of 10 percent in most other towns in the area, brought on by the tight money market. Retail sales in a hardware store were up 10 percent over the previous year; a filling station that pumped 14,000 gallons in March 1956 was up to 23,000 gallons in April 1957; two new drug stores had opened in the city. Property values in Lawrenceburg and within a three-mile radius had risen $3.5 million; the values of small farms within ten miles of the city limits were up an estimated 10 percent; savings in Lawrence County banks increased markedly.

In concluding this chapter it may be observed that in the event of subsidization there is also an offsetting or negative multiplier, resulting from the payment of the subsidy to the owners of an enterprise re-siding outside the community. Of course a subsidization policy is rational only if the overall positive effect will prevail. And finally, it will be realized that if competitive subsidization should become general and lead to a considerable acceleration of the industrialization of a large area, the effect of this would be felt in every community. It would for instance give a great impetus to the construction industry, lead to an increased demand for farm products, local supplies of all kinds, etc. In general, the inter-industry effect would be great, in-duced investment would lead to further induced consumption, etc. The outside world would also benefit, and from this there would be an important "feedback." To the extent that the subsidies accrue to entrepreneurs and, indirectly, to property owners living within the area engaged in subsidization (say, the "South") there are no leakages on that account. The outside world (say, the "North") would benefit from an increased demand for export goods, but to the extent that the two areas compete for the location of industries this might be offset by losses. The multiplier approach is not very suitable to carry this analysis further, and we must now return to our general equilibrium model.

21. "Rx for Prosperity: Cash Register Hums; Lawrence County's Out Migration Grinds to Halt as New Plants Put Men to Work," *Tennessee Town and City*, VIII (July, 1957), 38.

CHAPTER VIII

The Probable Effects of Competitive
Subsidization Realistically Considered

Introduction of the multiplier into our static model. Now that we are prepared to account for the indirect effects on community income that the establishment of additional industry causes, we can drop some restrictive assumptions that made it possible to concentrate our attention on the direct effect, i.e. the increase in labor income resulting from wage disbursements by the new enterprises. It is no longer necessary to assume that communities produce only for export to distant markets nor that all entrepreneurs and owners of local property are "foreigners." The recipients of the subsidies as well as the owners of productive local property may or may not be members of the community: in our discourse it will in general be implied that the former are not and that the latter are. But it is not necessary to make rigorous assumptions about this.

Recognizing the multiplier, it remains true that only surplus-labor communities stand to gain from subsidies, *provided we assume that the consumption multiplier is solely related to expenditures of local residents.* But in reality communities may also subsidize industry to reap the indirect benefits that accrue to their residents as a result of expenditures by newly-employed workers *residing in adjacent areas,* and this may be a profitable policy even if there is no unemployment within the community itself. However, here we must refer again to our discussion of the concept of a community. It was indicated that within the context of our discussion a purely geographical approach may be somewhat arbitrary, although for reasons of convenience of presentation and also because of the division of a region in decision making political units comprising a given area it may be difficult to discuss the matter otherwise. From the economic point of view the important thing here is that what makes subsidization profitable is the existence of un- or underemployment in the vicinity of the enterprise; therefore, in a material sense our conclusion that only surplus-labor communities have an interest in competing for industry by means of subsidies stands unimpaired. As before, the possibility of deriving a gain from subsidizing industry rests on the inefficiency of resources allocation which unemployment implies. This is not altered when a multiplier effect is introduced: the initial source of the gain remains the same. The reader may verify for himself that but for the point discussed here the argument presented in Chapter VI (pp. 146-56) still holds. That argument is not dependent upon any of the restrictive assumptions made in that chapter.

Having introduced the multiplier, our next step is to reconsider our argument that income-maximizing communities which suffer from un- or underemployment will subsidize payrolls as such in the sense indicated in Chapter VI, i.e. that every additional dollar of subsidy a community is willing to extend will be offered to that enterprise which in exchange provides the largest amount of additional payroll. To the extent that indirect gains accruing to members of the community derive from wage disbursements by the subsidized enterprise, the proposition requires little modification. If we deviate from our assumption that labor is immobile between communities to visualize the possibility of the enterprise hiring workers from outside, we should realize that the income-maximizing community must differentiate between wages disbursed to local people and to outsiders. Suppose for instance that in both cases the indirect effect on community income is the same and is $1.- for every $2.- of payroll (so that if only local workers were hired the multiplier would be 1.5). Then the amount of subsidy the community would offer for every wage dollar paid by the industry to a worker from outside would be one-third of what it would offer for every wage dollar paid to a local worker (for wages paid to local workers are part of community income). But this is still a policy of subsidizing payrolls; the differentiation does not alter the fact that labor would in effect be supplied at rates below the national minimum. As long as we stay within the confines of a static model this conclusion remains important, for in such a model a fall in entrepreneurial *labor* cost relative to other cost elements is the crucial factor that leads to the establishment of full employment.

But the coming of a new industry may also lead to a rise in aggregate community income in ways unconnected with the wages paid by the industry. Thus we may think of the new industry purchasing supplies locally from other enterprises, and this too could give rise to an increase in community income in various ways. It is therefore even conceivable that—in the presence of un- or underemployment to be sure—an industry employing no members of the community and no workers spending a penny within the community would be subsidized. This implies that subsidies may at least in part be unrelated to the payroll disbursements of the recipient.

However, what matters is that the disbursement of wages increases community income, directly and indirectly, and that the community is therefore willing to subsidize wages—not that the community may also increase its income in other ways, including the extension of other types of industrial subsidies. It is clear that in the general case when new manufacturing enterprise is established in a community, the inter-industry effect is unimportant relative to the effects of the wage disbursements, and hence that the prevalent way in which enterprises can avail themselves of a community's subsidization offer is through their contributions to the community's income that result from their wage disbursements. The rational community that suffers from un- or underemployment will in principle offer a premium to industries that purchase local supplies and services (because indirectly this will lead to the fuller utilization of labor in the enterprises that provide these supplies and services) as well as to industries that hire local labor. One type of subsidy does not exclude the other, but simply because the scope for concentrating enterprises that represent successive stages in a production process within a small community is very limited, far more subsidies will on the whole be disbursed in the form of payroll subsidies than in other forms.[1] Thus, rational subsidization does not only imply that labor will in effect be offered at rates lower than the national minimum, but that this will be the prevailing form in which subsidies are extended. Introduction of the multiplier, then, does not impair our conclusion that competitive subsidization will lead to full employment through its effect on labor cost. The other assumptions upon which this conclusion was based, however, may not be realistic, and actual subsidization practices may

1. Moreover, for every subsidization dollar offered by a community to that enterprise which in return will cause community income to increase (in any way) by the greatest amount, the bid of an enterprise buying local supplies can be matched by that of an enterprise producing these supplies. Under the assumptions of our model (universal wage floor, no self-employed labor) the contribution the latter type of enterprise would make to the community's income would be entirely through its wage disbursements.

not fully correspond to the "ideal type" outlined above. At a later stage we shall return to this issue.

Discussion of the meaning and importance of certain assumptions made in Chapter VI. The assumption of labor being homogeneous is a convenience in presentation in that it enables us to speak of "the" wage rate, "labor," etc., and in general eliminates the need for constant qualification; this manner of speaking we shall continue to follow. The reader will realize that some types of labor are complementary rather than competitive and that while one type may be underemployed other types may be scarce. Naturally, subsidies should in principle only be extended for the creation of fully productive employment of labor that was hitherto un- or underemployed because of effective wage floors applying to that type of labor in occupations for which it is qualified.[2]

The assumptions that workers are indifferent between occupations if wages are equal and that all labor services are rendered in a wage-earning capacity are of the same nature. Similarly, it is immaterial to our argument what imperfection in the labor market causes labor to be un- or underemployed, and hence the assumption that a uniform nation-wide minimum wage law applicable to all occupations is the cause may now be dismissed. This assumption was merely introduced to eliminate the necessity for a lengthy description of the conditions prevailing in the labor market of our model. The reader is now referred to the interpretation of the actual labor market in the United States presented in Chapter I. (Later, attention will be paid to possible repercussions of local subsidization policies on the wage policies of the federal government and on the position of labor unions. Until then we take the wage floors as "given.")

By contrast, deleting the assumptions that labor is immobile between communities and that the supply of local labor is completely inelastic with respect to the wage rate does have some material significance. One of the consequences of dismissing the immobility assumption has already been discussed in the previous section of this chapter, where it was pointed out that under a rational subsidization policy the community will differentiate between wage disbursements to members and to non-members. It may further be observed that the possibility of migration widens the range of choice of the workers and is one of the dynamic forces that causes, along with others, a constant change in local labor market conditions which ideally should

2. Compare our discussion in Chapter 1 of what constitutes un- and underemployment, especially pp. 8-9.

be accompanied by a constant reconsideration of a community's subsidization policy. (Of course this is no different from the situation in which entrepreneurs are placed, and it certainly does not impair the feasibility of following a rational subsidization policy any more than constant change in a dynamic world makes it impossible to take entrepreneurial responsibility.)

If we assume that in its subsidization policy a community is in fact capable of differentiating between local and non-local labor (which does not appear unreasonable), then no further complications arise on account of the in-migration that may accompany such a policy. On the other hand, confronted with the possibility of out-migration it is difficult to attribute realism to the assumption that the supply of local labor is independent of the wage rate. That postulate is improbable anyway, and should now be replaced by a more realistic one. What concerns us here is the supply of labor to the subsidized occupations, i.e., in practice, the supply of workers to manufacturing industry. It would appear, then, that at least in rural communities suffering from underemployment in agriculture the curve would be positively inclined over the relevant range, because of a greater desire of workers to transfer from agriculture when wages in local industry are high and because of a greater inclination to seek employment in other localities when they are low. It is highly improbable that the effect of these two factors would be fully offset by a preference for leisure at higher income levels; should this preference be so strong as to lead to a reduction in total working time this would in all probability be accomplished at the expense of farm work, where returns are low, even if the individual worker had a choice in the matter. But this is not the case: with working hours in manufacturing institutionalized, the worker either has to accept the prescribed working hours or the higher income derived from manufacturing employment is not available to him at all. In this the situation is completely different from that in underdeveloped countries, where, especially on plantations, work is available on a casual basis, and where apparently workers often reduce their working time when wages are increased.

With a positively sloping supply curve of labor, the subsidization of industry so as to create full employment *at the prevailing wage rate* may conceivably interfere with an efficient spatial allocation of labor and with an efficient allocation of time between employment in subsidized industry on the one hand and other occupations (e.g. work on the farm, in the home) or leisure on the other. This is true because workers, unless they are made to pay the full difference between the wages prevailing in industry and the wage that would prevail in the community in the absence of an imposed wage floor, would receive a net labor income (wage minus subsidy paid by the worker) in excess of the marginal revenue product of labor. With a positively inclined supply curve of labor this would cause the quantity of labor supplied to the subsidized industries to be greater than it would be in the "ideal" case of complete wage flexibility. However, one should not exaggerate the importance of this issue. After all, if a choice has to be made between two types of imperfection, one that we may call overemployment in the local economy of a subsidizing community and another consisting of underemployment, the former alternative should, in my opinion at least, certainly be preferred. For the latter condition, which now exists, causes poverty, frustration, and discontent, while the former is only an implied deviation from a theoretical "optimal" condition that cannot be completely realized in practice. Furthermore, the argument presented here to the effect that subsidization may lead to this distortion leaves out of consideration other factors, in the general case undoubtedly stronger, that work in the opposite direction. These factors are discussed in a later section of this chapter dealing with the circumstances that may prevent a community from fully acting as an income maximizing corporation. For various reasons, then, the difficulty that arises on account of the positive slope of the supply curve of labor is largely academic.

Our assumption that the marginal revenue product of labor is positive has already been discussed,[3] and, as stated above, our assumption that enterprises attempt to maximize their incomes will be retained. However, we need not adhere to the notion that they do this with perfect knowledge of existing alternatives or that subsidizing communities have such knowledge. Certainly in reality there will never exist such a thing as a perfect market in payrolls. The absence of such perfection increases the discreteness in the ranking with respect to locational advantage of firms by communities and of communities by firms: in reality a community can consider only a limited number of prospects at a time, while firms desirous to move or expand production in a new locality may also find their choice limited to a relatively small number of communities with differences in net advantage between them that may be cancelled by subsidies. This leads to a bargaining process between communities and enterprises. With a differentiated "product" and imperfect knowledge of this product (for a firm can find out what a community is really like only after

3. *Supra*, pp. 151-52.

establishing itself there, and vice versa), there is also considerable room for salesmanship, as evidenced in the promotional literature, red carpet treatment of visiting company executives, etc.

"Frictions" that prevent ready relocation of enterprise and adjustment of production processes in response to a reduction in labor cost; irreducibility of wage rates in full employment communities. In a static model such as the above the achievement of full employment depends upon the adjustability of production methods to relative factor prices and upon the ready relocation of enterprises between communities. We have, therefore, assumed these conditions to exist to an extent that on this account no difficulties would arise. In reality there is only a limited number of techniques available for each production process at any given time, and, in a changing world, developing and experimenting with new ones when an enterprise moves from one location to another where labor cost in due time will also rise (which is not the same thing as saying that regional *differentials* will be eliminated) is usually not a paying proposition.[4] Moreover, both adjustment of production methods and relocation are impeded because of the existence of capital goods, some fixed and others expensive to dismantle and reassemble elsewhere, that have a long productive life. Enterprises must also take into consideration the likely preference of those on their staff who would be required to move along with a plant for staying where they are. These people may have to be given extra incentives to induce them to move. In addition there is the cost of training a new labor force, of having to build up new local connections, etc., all of which adds up to an in most cases very considerable cost of relocating. For these reasons, outright relocation of a plant is actually a relatively rare occurrence. Some industries, of course, can move more easily than others, but on the whole the great majority of plants that newly establish themselves in a community are new enterprises or branch plants of existing concerns that represent net additions to capacity rather than relocation.[5]

4. In accordance with this, Hoover and Ratchford note that in the same type of industry capital equipment does not greatly vary between North and South (Calvin B. Hoover and B. U. Ratchford, *Economic Resources and Policies of the South* (New York: Macmillan Company, 1951), p. 66. This is true in spite of the fact that in most industries there is a considerable interregional discrepancy in wage rates.

5. Thus Robock writes: "Recent industrial growth in the Southeast resulted almost completely from new additions to industry capacity rather than from northern plants pulling up stakes and moving South. As was pointed out in the Committee of the South study, 'relocations have made a relatively minor contribution to the postwar wave of industrialization in the South.'

"The question of relocations is frequently raised as a political issue in connection

In the real world application of competitive subsidization this great initial advantage of the community in which an existing plant is established is probably a good thing. In our static model we have implicitly assumed the existence of a first line of defense against the migration of plants out of the full employment communities in that wages were taken to be flexible in the downward direction until the legal minimum was reached. In reality, however, wages never adjust smoothly in the downward direction. Therefore, in the case of effective outside competition for *existing* industry such as the general adoption of a subsidization policy by surplus-labor communities would cause if relocation were not expensive, the full employment communities would immediately have to join the ranks of subsidizing communities or suffer unemployment themselves. This would then presumably lead to the adoption of more labor-intensive production methods everywhere and the establishment of full employment throughout the nation. It is clear that this is not realistic. As indicated above, there would be no ready adjustment of production methods and therefore full employment could not be established through the redistribution of existing industry within an acceptable time-span.

Thus, in the real world, once there is unemployment, it may be very hard to establish full employment other than through economic growth. This is true not only because the "too high" wages that

with the industrialization of the Tennessee Valley. Yet studies which go back to 1940 reveal only eight cases of plants relocating in the Valley region out of a total increase of several thousand new establishments over this period. These eight relocations involved less than 600 employees and none were from New England.

"Even in the case of the textile industry, where a regional shift to the Southeast has been under way for at least 50 years, recent growth has been due mainly to the expansion of more efficient operations in the South and a closing down *by different firms* [italics mine] of less efficient operations in other regions. Despite the impression given by the unusual publicity accorded those rare cases of moving a plant lock-stock-and-barrel from one region to another, only an insignificant amount of industrial expansion in the Southeast has been due to other than a new increase in industry capacity.

"The general conclusion that 'outright relocation of establishments is relatively uncommon' was reached in 1942 in a major study by the National Resources Planning Board. All available evidence since that time further supports this statement. Yet, flailing away at the invisible straw man of relocation to the South continues to be a favorite pastime, as evidenced by a recent article in the *Harvard Business Review*" (Stefan H. Robock, "Industrialization and Economic Progress in the Southeast," *Southern Economic Journal*, XX [April, 1954], 319-20). See also Glenn E. McLaughlin and Stefan Robock, *Why Industry Moves South*, Report No. 3, National Planning Association (Washington: Committee on the South, N.P.A., 1949), pp. 19, 122, and Harold M. Groves, "The Effect of Tax Differentials and Tax Exemptions upon the Relocation of Business," *Proceedings of the Thirty-first Annual Conference on Taxation* (Columbia, S.C.: National Tax Association, 1939), p. 558.

cause the unemployment are not readily amenable to reduction (this could theoretically be remedied by means of payroll subsidies) but also because production methods are not easily changed in the sense of becoming more labor intensive. It should be noted that there is not likely to be symmetry between the readiness with which production methods may adjust to a relative increase and a decrease in labor cost. Labor intensive methods are in the general case technologically less advanced than capital intensive methods, and their adoption is therefore likely to be resisted by technicians who consider them "backward." Competitive subsidization in the absence of growth would therefore contribute very little to the economy at large. It might cause some relocation of industry but probably not much, considering that communities threatened with the loss of industry could retaliate in kind and in doing so would have the advantage of being the original location. The main effect would be to impose upon communities a certain burden of subsidization without any noticeable reduction of unemployment.

Since very little can be expected from relocation and adjustment of production methods within existing industry, our case comes to rest on the advantages of competitive subsidization in directing *additions* to our productive apparatus, i.e. new investments, to those locations in the nation where the marginal productivity of capital is greatest, given the preferences of the labor force with respect to its spatial distribution.

The relevance of our frictionless static model to the real world. The development of a frictionless static model is nevertheless a useful step in evaluating the welfare implications of a given policy. By doing so we bring within our reach a body of economic theory to which the particular issue at hand can be readily related. Furthermore, although the assumptions are very abstract, the link with reality is not lacking. Paradoxically, this link between an approach which in its formal assumptions implicitly ignores dynamic change and reality is strongest when the reality is one of vigorous growth. What in a static frictionless model such as ours is accomplished instantaneously by means of the *transfer* of production factors (the total supply of which is taken as given) from one industry or locality to another and by arranging these factors in different combinations will in the reality of a growing economy be accomplished over a period of time largely *through the effect on incremental investment* of the policy variable under consideration. It is true that the introduction of dynamic considerations may also have an entirely different bearing on a problem, one that may contradict or qualify conclusions based on static assumptions, but as far as I can see the importance of growth for our problem is that it makes it possible to drop our "no friction" assumptions without having to change our conclusions materially, provided we allow time for the adjustments to take place. Naturally this is a greatly simplified picture the details of which need to be filled in. This will be done in the course of the subsequent discussion, which must first be directed toward some remaining assumptions of our model.

Local communities as income maximizing corporations. It is obvious that democracy within a community prevents it from fully acting as a business corporation in the matter of maximizing its income. This would require the pursuit of a single-minded purpose under authoritarian leadership, as in a business corporation. Since a local political unit serves individuals who can influence its action but who are primarily concerned with their own incomes rather than that of the community as a whole, the local government is faced with a situation in which it must reconcile interests that may be conflicting. This introduces the problem of political bargaining, which under existing rules and in the presence of restraints imposed by higher authorities need not lead to optimal solutions.[6] It is therefore by no means certain that a favorable decision can be obtained in the political process when an opportunity exists for increasing a community's collective income such as a business corporation would not hesitate to seize. As I have argued in Chapters III and IV, chances to rally broad support for such a decision may be best when a deliberate effort is made to apply the benefit principle, i.e. to distribute the burden of taxation as much as possible among those who stand to gain from the measure for which the funds are required, and to use these funds also to compensate prospective losers. It was also indicated, however, that there exist many impediments to such a procedure, in the law and otherwise. Some of these will always remain, even if local political units should be given much greater autonomy than they now possess, for they are inherent in the political process. In the case of subsidization these factors have not always precluded its virtually

6. The word "optimal" should here be interpreted in a limited sense, because the rules and restraints that determine the outcome of the political process may (although they need not) be rational in a more basic way, i.e. when considering the aggregate of decisions in the long run and also the cost of bargaining itself under different rules. For an incisive discussion of this issue the reader may again be referred to J. M. Buchanan and Gordon Tullock's forthcoming book.

unanimous support by the community, but that is because the prospective gains were large and clearly perceptible. Should they be less, yet still large by business standards, the community might withhold its support. If this be true, and for several reasons to be discussed below it seems likely that it is, it means that the theoretical maximum subsidy which a community can afford on the assumption that it attempts to maximize its collective income can hardly even be approximated.[7]

The first reason why in this a community might not act as a business corporation is that the lack of perfect foresight, especially also with respect to the distribution of gains and losses among individuals, is bound to be a matter of much greater moment in the political sphere than it is in business. This would primarily be a question of disagreeing about the quantitative aspects of the proposed measure and of being unwilling to take risks. Much more important also than in business, in the political process, is the matter of less than perfect insight. This pertains to the degree of understanding of the issues involved. Business leaders are specialists in income maximizing, and in the market there is a process of natural selection that tends to eliminate incompetent leadership or the enterprises themselves whose leaders do not skillfully play the game of income maximizing, certainly in this country, where competition is vigorous. Political units, however, cannot be eliminated in this manner, and, since they are not singularly devoted to the game of income maximizing, success in furthering the material welfare of the community as a whole is but

7. If we assume that the negative or offsetting multiplier corresponding to the payment of a subsidy to owners of an enterprise residing outside the community is as large as the positive multiplier corresponding to the disbursement of additional wages, that no wages are disbursed to non-members of the community, and that the presence of a subsidized enterprise benefits the community solely through the direct and indirect effects of its wage disbursements, then the maximum subsidy a community could theoretically afford is a yearly sum equal to the wage disbursements of the enterprise or its capitalized equivalent. If we take into consideration the indirect effect on community income of wages paid to non-members of the community brought in by the enterprise from the outside, the maximum comes to exceed the sum-total of wages paid to members of the community. Thus if wages paid to these outsiders give rise to an increase in community income of one third the amount they receive in wages, say a sum of $300,000 (wages being $900,000), the community would break even when paying for this an amount of $225,000 and would gain if it paid less than this amount. (For the payment of $225,000 to people residing outside the community would reduce community income by that amount plus one-third or $300,000.) Should there also be an interindustry effect, the theoretical maximum would be further increased. It hardly needs saying that, starting from a given position, it may not be necessary for a community to pay this maximum in order to attract an industry. On the whole, a considerable buyer's surplus would naturally exist.

one among many other things that determine the staying power of political leadership. Also, political power is not infrequently distributed in such a way that furthering the material welfare (and other interests) of certain groups is more important than that of the community as a whole.

In the absence of a ready check on incompetence, prejudice against certain methods by which a community may benefit materially may play an important role. As our survey of subsidization practices indicates, prejudice against the outright subsidization of industry has in fact often prevented communities from taking action where all other obstacles had been cleared. It alone explains the failure of many development corporations, which are not impeded by political difficulties, to accomplish their avowed purpose of attracting industry.

Another impediment, to a large extent probably irreducible, is of a psychological nature. It is unlikely that it would ever be feasible to collect from formerly un- or underemployed workers or their relatives upon whose income they would otherwise be dependent more than a small fraction of the income gain that employment in a subsidized industry means to them. As we have seen, payroll deductions have been used in a number of instances, but by no means universally. Of course, when subsidies are small relative to the overall gain, even a small payroll deduction may fully pay for labor's share in the gain. But to the extent that my observation is correct, it also means that communities cannot possibly push subsidies to a level approaching the theoretical maximum. That this is true when the financing is undertaken by private development corporations that are dependent upon voluntary contributions is self-evident. Indeed, in many cases, also when the local tax power is used, the contributions may mainly come from people who benefit only indirectly. Since the implementation of a subsidization scheme will almost invariably depend upon their support, it may be expected that these indirect gains rather than the total gains in community income will be weighted against the subsidy.[8] For all of these reasons it may be concluded that in the general case the greatest subsidy that we can expect to materialize in reality will be small relative to the total gain in community income that may be reasonably anticipated, even assuming that prejudice against the practice can be largely overcome.

8. In terms of the numerical example given in footnote 7 this would mean that when an enterprise disburses $900,000 in wages *to members of the community*, this would have the same effect as if the wages were disbursed to non-members. The maximum subsidy the community might agree to pay would, *on this account alone*, be reduced from the theoretical maximum of $900,000 to $225,000.

This, of course, is implicitly taken for granted in any discussion of what will happen if the practice of subsidizing industry should be widely adopted within limits dictated by the self-interest of the individuals that constitute a community.

Subsidies small relative to the gains in community income may suffice to bring a community close to full employment. The above does not preclude maximizing behavior in other respects (i.e. in awarding subsidies when there is a choice between prospects) and precludes the actual maximization of community income only insofar as at a certain stage it would become necessary for a community to offer subsidies that are large relative to the gains from creating jobs for additional unemployed workers. If for a moment we consider unemployment solely to represent that state of affairs in which normally competent workers are completely idle, then the circumstance that subsidies cannot be pushed to the theoretical maximum might have little bearing on the problem. For if this were the only type of unemployment, no community might have to pay subsidies large relative to the gains that could be derived from absorbing its last workers in the production process, even if all other communities suffering from unemployment also were to follow a subsidization policy. The gain from absorbing the last worker would be approximately equal to the marginal revenue product of labor in the community, and the subsidy necessary to accomplish this would be equal to the difference between the prevailing wage rate and the marginal revenue product of labor. The ratio between the latter and the former magnitude might well be small in the great majority of American communities, so that, in spite of the factors that prevent communities from pushing subsidization to the theoretical maximum, full employment might be established. If this were true—and I believe it to be so—competitive subsidization can in fact virtually eliminate open unemployment of competent workers, provided of course that the real minimum wage is not drastically increased.

The point that relatively small subsidies are in practice likely to accomplish a great deal in this respect will be further argued below. Here it may be emphasized that in the postulated case there is a fundamental difference between the situation facing an income maximizing enterprise and that in which a similar community finds itself. To the extent at least that production techniques permit continuity an enterprise cannot maximize its income without actually equating marginal cost and marginal revenue of its variable inputs, carrying its outlays on each input to the point of indifference. Thus the "last" worker contributes no more to the enterprise than the total cost (including possible repercussions on the wages of other workers) of hiring him. In the case of a community striving to maximize its income by means of subsidies, however, there would be a sharp discontinuity at the point of full employment. Just prior to this point the difference between the income gains resulting from the employment of additional workers and the subsidization outlays might be quite large, and beyond the full employment point it would suddenly become negative. With the marginal revenue product of labor positive, income maximizing would therefore not require that subsidies be carried to a point where the last dollar spent would yield a return of just that amount. That would be true only if the marginal revenue product of labor were zero.

The above is true on the assumption that unemployment consists solely of competent workers being completely idle. But workers differ in quality, and because of this there is naturally a problem in specifying the "point" of full employment. However, this qualification is not of very great practical importance. Especially in a rural society the not-so-competent may in most cases prefer to remain on the farm or in minor jobs not subject to wage regulations that they are able to perform, and, while in theory it may be impossible to draw a sharp distinction between unemployment and inherent unemployability, the community itself will at a certain point be satisfied that there is full employment among those considered normally competent. In other words, the people whose absorption in manufacturing industry would require relatively heavy subsidization outlays, such as to make the subsidization of their wages impracticable if not outright disadvantageous, in the general case would constitute a small minority whose non-employment is not likely to be interpreted as unemployment. Yet strictly speaking some un- or underemployment will on this score persist under a subsidization scheme, for it may be assumed that if wage setting in the subsidized enterprises were not subject to a floor some of these people would find jobs there at low wages which would nevertheless improve their position.

A more important qualification derives from the fact that there is underemployment as well as outright unemployment. Where underemployment means that an insufficient amount of productive work is divided among a relatively large number of people, as may be the case on farms, the situation is approximately equivalent to that of outright unemployment with respect to the problem under discussion. The idleness resulting from this condition is more of a curse than a blessing, and when some of the superfluous labor is drawn to industry farm output need not go down. However, as the process continues the labor situation on farms becomes tighter, and further transfers of labor will then lead to a reduction in income derived from farming. This reduction may at first be very small relative to the industrial payrolls, but as more workers transfer from the farm the marginal revenue product of labor in farming increases. Therefore the gains from successive transfers diminish and the subsidies necessary to accomplish these transfers become larger relative to the gains. They are likely to be discontinued, therefore, at a point prior to the theoretical optimum at which community income would be maximized. As a qualification to this qualification it may be stated that worker preference for the accustomed occupation would probably prevent an equalization of the marginal revenue product of labor in agriculture and in industry anyway, i.e. if no wage floors imposed from the outside should exist. It should nevertheless be recognized that, on account of the limitations indicated in the previous section, it may not prove feasible to wipe out *under*employment completely by means of subsidization. But a subsidization policy can certainly make important strides in that direction.

It may here be made explicit that subsidization, in order to increase the productivity of the economy as a whole, need not be "complete" in the sense that every community carries the policy to its rational extreme or in the sense that communities follow more or less the same pace in this respect. Sometimes a partial move towards a condition which, if reached, is better than an existing condition may make things worse rather than better. Thus the elimination of trade barriers between a restricted number of countries, because of the element of discrimination such a move introduces, may conceivably tend to decrease world income. Similarly, it is conceivable that relatively heavy subsidization outlays in some communities that are well-organized for this purpose may attract industries that otherwise would have been established in communities where their net-contribution to the national product would be even greater. While this may occur in individual instances, it is most unlikely that this effect will prevail in the aggregate. Since full employment communities have no incentive to subsidize industry and since the incentive to become organized for this purpose is greatest in those communities where the prospective gains through the absorption of un- or underemployed labor are largest, the net effect of subsidization, regardless of the precise extent to which it is carried in the various individual cases, will undoubtedly be to draw more industry to the surplus labor communities than otherwise would be the case. Thus, while the effect of subsidization may not always be to bring an enterprise to that locality where its contribution to the national product would be greatest, it will in the great majority of cases be to bring enterprises to localities where their contributions are greater than in the localities where they would otherwise have been established.

Effect of the general adoption of a subsidization policy by surplus labor communities on the possibility to attract additional industry in a given community. That practically any community suffering from unemployment or widespread underemployment can at present greatly increase local employment opportunity by means of attracting industry through subsidization at little expense relative to the income gain, given the present level of subsidization activity elsewhere, is something about which I have absolutely no doubt. Another way of saying the same thing is that the rate of returns on additional subsidies would under present conditions almost universally be very high. Evidence already presented in this treatise strongly suggests that this is so, and additional quantitative data presented in Appendix V confirm this point.

This condition is not hard to explain. As we have seen, the special incentives offered are currently very feeble, and it should therefore in the general case take only a little more for a community to outdo its rivals in attracting a so-called footloose industry, to which labor cost rather than nearness to markets or sources of raw materials not generally available is the most important consideration. To such an industry, labor in one community, provided it is not greatly inferior in quality, is a close substitute for that in others. Therefore, the cross-elasticity of demand on the part of such industries for a given community's labor with respect to labor in other communities is in the general case large. Thus a slight reduction in a community's labor cost such as a modest subsidy can afford may be expected to have a relatively large employment effect on account of its attraction to footloose industries seeking a location for additional plant capacity.[9] And of course the gains are very large in every case of a community that has unemployment or a large degree of underemployment. The situation is analogous to that in which a high price is set in the market

9. The word "footloose" may suggest an industry that has no roots, hence easily moves from one location to another. But this is not the proper meaning of the word, and the condition itself is typical of no industry except perhaps hot dog stands.

for a commodity the sale of which is dominated by a cartel in such a manner as to cause over-capacity in the participating enterprises. Any small enterprise in this market can derive gains determined by the extent of its over-capacity by breaking away from the cartel and selling its produce at a slightly lower price. Similarly, by means of subsidizing wages a small community can "sell" such labor as is not already employed at a slightly lower price than that prevailing in the market and achieve great income gains in the process. In other words, the marginal revenue product of labor in a community is in part determined by the price of labor maintained elsewhere, and, because of the possibility to attract capital from the outside, is not likely to be very far below that price. This, again, is confirmed by the fact, stressed in Chapter III, that those communities which have done "what it takes" to attract industry have found that it took relatively little in view of the circumstance that very few other communities have been prepared to act likewise.

But while it is evident that breaking away from the general pattern leads on to fortune, the question that mainly concerns us here is what effect the general adoption of a subsidization policy would have. We may visualize a series of demand curves for a community's labor where each one represents the demand schedule at a different given level of subsidization elsewhere, i.e. under different assumptions regarding the price of labor in other communities insofar as communities would have to hold out subsidies in order to establish full employment. At a high subsidization level elsewhere the demand curve for our community's labor would be situated farther to the left than at a low level.[10] The curves would exhibit the traditional negative slope, due to the existence of immobile resources within the geographical area that comprises the community. To each demand curve would correspond a different price of labor consistent with full employment, determined by the intersection of that curve with the local supply curve of labor. Thus it can be seen that this price, the marginal revenue product of labor, is positively related to the price of labor elsewhere and that it becomes increasingly difficult for a community to attract new industry and to establish full employment as

10. This would be due to the substitutability of one community's labor for that of others. The effect of this would in part be offset by that of the higher real income in the nation at large and in neighboring areas in particular which the general adoption of more intensive subsidization would bring about. It appears unlikely, however, that with respect to the majority of communities the income effect would prevail over the substitution effect over the relevant range under present conditions. With respect to some communities, however, this might be true, for instance tourist centers.

subsidization activity elsewhere becomes more important. However, this process would inevitably come to a halt at the point where full employment is established in all other communities, and in practice, for reasons indicated above, earlier. It should therefore be stressed that the competition from other communities which a particular subsidizing community may experience is not necessarily a factor that would greatly impede that community's efforts to create employment opportunity. Even if somehow all other communities could in time reduce their labor cost to a point where full employment would prevail, the marginal revenue product of labor might remain large enough to permit of considerable gains relative to the subsidies required to absorb that particular community's last normally competent and fully idle workers. The question here is, to what extent are present industrial wage levels out of line with the wage levels that would establish full employment within a reasonable time or would have done so had they prevailed in the past.[11] My personal feeling is that current industrial wages are not too much out of line, for otherwise un- and underemployment would prevail on a far larger scale. For after all, relative to the national economy and its annual growth prolonged or "structural" un- and underemployment are not very large. The problem is to wipe out in the shortest possible time pockets of poverty that now disgrace the American economy. It is of course true that the problem is widespread in many predominantly rural areas, especially in the South and also in some declining industrial and mining regions, but even in these areas many communities have been able

---

11. Time must be allowed if we think in terms of additional industry being directed toward the un- and underemployment areas rather than in terms of instantaneous relocation. This makes the whole problem somewhat indefinite. Should wages instantaneously become completely flexibile, they might at first fall to zero, since more industry would not be immediately available. Similarly, if subsidies could be pushed to the theoretical limit and all communities would simultaneously adopt a subsidization policy, competition would at first in fact push the subsidies up to the limit, leaving hardly any gain, since there would in the very short run be little industry to be divided. But it is of course foolish to assume that competitive subsidization would be adopted instantaneously. All we can say with certainty is that the reduction of labor cost resulting from the competition between communities desirous to attract industry by means of subsidies will draw more industry to these communities than otherwise would be true, and this is sufficient to build a strong case in favor of the adoption of a subsidization policy by communities that suffer from un- and underemployment. For the rest, we can only offer some general reflections as to the extent that this may cure unemployment "within a reasonable time." One might of course develop a growth model with specific assumptions that would make the effect of subsidization on employment quantitatively determinate at various points in time, but since the conditions that in reality will determine this effect cannot be manipulated or predicted with reasonable accuracy this would merely be a rather useless intellectual exercise.

to attract new industrial plants without or with only very feeble subsidies. It is hard to see why these communities and others very much like them that have hitherto not been successful should not be able to attract a larger share of the nation's expanding industrial potential so as to eliminate most un- and underemployment, say within a decade, if their labor cost should be reduced by a relatively small amount.

Subsidies and relocation. The above tends to show that subsidies given freely without prejudice by communities competing for industry are likely to remain small relative to the gains derived from them for two separate reasons. First, because of the way a community operates it will be *impossible* to obtain funds for subsidies that are large relative to the prospective gains. Secondly, relatively small subsidies will in general be *sufficient* to achieve near-full employment. From this it may be concluded that competitive subsidization is not likely to jolt the existing industrial pattern in a serious manner. *Moderate subsidies, sufficient to cause the location of new plants in the areas where jobs are needed and where their net-contribution to the national product is greatest, will seldom be sufficient to cause a change in location of existing enterprise.* This is an important conclusion, for while in a large, expanding city the loss of an enterprise is not a serious problem, it may cause grave difficulties in relatively small, stagnating communities. In a free enterprise economy plant mobility can of course not be entirely prevented and the possibility of its occurrence in extreme cases constitutes a useful check on excessive wage demands and other abuse, but there would be some justification for regarding with suspicion the introduction of measures tending to greatly increase this mobility.

Should competitive subsidization become a potent force in the economy, instances of plants relocating and receiving subsidies in their new location would nevertheless undoubtedly occur. For even without subsidization there is always some plant relocation, and in marginal cases the possibility of obtaining a subsidy in a new location would of course make some difference. In individual cases it would be difficult to establish whether the subsidy had caused the relocation or whether without it the plant would also have moved (possibly to a different community), but this would certainly not deter the opponents of subsidization, representatives of injured communities, etc., from raising a great outcry against the practice, taking causation for granted. This might arouse public opinion, lead to repressive legislation, and jeopardize the whole practice, although in spite of incidental disturbances that it may in fact create the good would on the whole far outweigh the harm (the main effect being to direct more *additional* enterprise to places where jobs are most badly needed). Undoubtedly for this reason, the Puerto Rican government excludes relocating industry from its tax exemption program. Similarly, the Small Business Administration refuses to make loans to relocating industry, while several of the bills proposing federal participation in the financing of industry establishing itself in surplus labor areas contained provisions designed to prevent the extension of aid to enterprises removing their operations from other communities.[12] These are wise measures, from the economic but especially from the political point of view. It is true that relocations are sometimes executed gradually, so that what at first appears to be an expansion may turn out to have been the beginning of a transfer, the decision perhaps having been made after the entrepreneur had been able to evaluate the suitability of a new location from experience. This may at times cause difficulties, but certainly a well-designed law could cope with these. It is to be recommended that subsidizing communities follow a similar policy of refusing to subsidize relocating enterprises, and legislation might be enacted by the states restricting subsidization (open and implicit) involving local governments so as to exclude relocating enterprises.

Even as it is, agitation against the subsidization practice on the ground that it leads to relocation of industry is rampant, in spite of the rather obvious truth that the feeble inducements now in vogue can hardly be an important factor among the totality of circumstances that may cause (part of) an enterprise to be moved to another community. A careful reading of the literature dealing with this subject shows how unsubstantiated these charges are. This may be illustrated by the following discussion of an American Federation of Labor report entitled: *Subsidized Industrial Migration; the Luring of Plants to New Locations.*[13] This work constitutes the most elaborate attempt I have encountered to marshal evidence in support of the thesis that subsidies extended by southern communities frequently cause the uprooting of plants in other parts of the country. Its conspicuous failure to do so is therefore the more telling.

The report presents no statistical material on relocation but merely a number of "typical examples of plant transfer induced by subsidiza-

12. Compare *supra*, pp. 142, 144.

13. *Subsidized Industrial Migration; the Luring of Plants to New Locations*, Recommendations for legislative action by the Subcommittee on Migration and Subsidization of Industry, National Legislative Committee, American Federation of Labor (Washington: American Federation of Labor, 1955).

tion." It may be worth our while to look briefly into each case. The first example, that of Baxter Laboratories, Inc., concerns a BAWI promotion, featuring the usual ten year local tax exemption and self-liquidating bond issue to finance the construction of the new plant—hardly any subsidization to speak of therefore. The report itself shows awareness of the fact that the existing wage differentials between the old and the new location must have been a far more important factor, for it emphasizes these differentials and presents them in tabular form within the context of the argument. Second comes the case of the Hat Corporation of America, of which it is merely stated that in the new locations (to which only a small part of the operations were transferred) the company occupied buildings leased by development corporations. Since no rental terms are mentioned, one cannot determine how much (if any) implied subsidization was involved. In the next "typical" example, that of the Mid-City Uniform Cap Co., Inc., the firm in question was awarded a government contract for the production of navy caps in Puerto Rico, where as yet it had no establishment. Steps undertaken by the United Hatters, Cap and Millinery Workers Union, A. F. of L., instigated a government investigation of the circumstances under which the contract had been awarded, which led to the discovery of irregularities and the consequent blacklisting of the firm from bidding on any future government contracts. Moreover, at the time the report was written the government of Puerto Rico (which, as mentioned, follows a policy of not extending tax concessions in the case of relocation) was in the process of deciding whether to withhold its tax exemption privileges. So here we have a case that did not even materialize. The fourth case quoted also concerns a BAWI promotion in which wage differentials and the apparent desire of the firm to escape the union are emphasized, and in the fifth example, that of Textron American, Inc., subsidies are not even mentioned—probably there were not any. We are merely told that the firm closed its New England mills and concentrated its operations in the South. The same is true of the sixth and last case, that of Burlington Industries, one of the nation's largest textile manufacturers. In addition to these examples which the report discusses in some detail, a list is presented of more than 40 cases of industrial migration that occurred in recent years, with no information on subsidies in many instances but with lower wages and a public opinion hostile to unionization in the new location conspicuous throughout. In the view of the report these latter factors do not constitute good reasons for industrial migration either.

The logic of subsidization in the form of providing industrial buildings below cost. Inasmuch as subsidization may be expected to be mainly instrumental in securing for the surplus labor areas a larger share of additional investments than these areas would otherwise be able to attract, its extension in the form of a payroll subsidy or what amounts to that is not as essential as our original static analysis made it appear. However, as we have seen in the first section of this chapter, in the general case the rational community will still find it in its interest to secure as much payroll per subsidization dollar spent as possible. This concern on the part of the subsidizing community may be expected to work systematically in favor of industries in which labor cost constitutes a high percentage of total cost. And it may be stressed here that a subsidy is in effect a payroll subsidy as long as its total value is adjusted to the payroll the recipient will bring in, whether it be given in the form of tax exemption, low rental of a building, or any other form. It is obviously immaterial whether the community pays you $1 for every $10 of payroll you disburse or whether you get a $1 tax or rent reduction in exchange for every $10 of wages you pay. Conversely, a subsidy would be a capital subsidy if the amount made available were in fact to depend on the value of the industry's investment in the community, even if it were stated as an amount per worker employed or dollar of payroll disbursed.

Communities may not always make their subsidies dependent upon payrolls in any precise or explicit manner, but with production methods more or less given this is largely a matter of arithmetic. Any sensible decision regarding the extension of subsidies must be based upon a fair knowledge of the payrolls that can reasonably be expected to accrue to the community, and it may be taken for granted that in the general case this will be the community's decisive consideration.[14] Besides, disbursement of a given sum in wages to local residents within a specified period often is included in the contract as the main obligation of the subsidized enterprise. But even without specific stipulations of this nature the community can roughly act so as to maximize the amount of payroll per dollar of subsidy.

Nevertheless, in view of changing circumstances the most logical

14. Thus Ernest J. Hopkins (*Mississippi's BAWI Plan, an experiment in industrial subsidization* [Atlanta: Research Department, Federal Reserve Bank of Atlanta, 1944], p. 48) mentions that the city of Natchez refused to act on a request of the Armstrong Tire and Rubber Co. to provide funds for the construction of a tire warehouse on the grounds that a warehouse does not employ a large labor force and that, as figured on a ratio of bond issue to prospective payroll, the investment would not be remunerative to the city.

procedure from a community's standpoint would be to pay the subsidy periodically and to make it vary directly with the payroll dispensed by the recipient. This would also greatly simplify the financing problem as compared to subsidization in a form that necessitates capital outlay, such as the financing of a building. One reason that the latter method is often adopted is of course exactly the fact that for various reasons discussed in earlier chapters it often is more feasible and cheaper for a community to raise capital funds than for the enterprise. But in addition to this there is another important reason why enterprises may prefer subsidization in a form that enables them to reduce their investment in immobile equipment to a minimum.

This reason is that relocation is expensive. Therefore, once an enterprise is established a community has a certain monopoly power over it. It could presumably reduce the subsidies (without which the plant would never have been located) or stop payment altogether without causing the plant to move to another location. Given the uncertain legal status of subsidization, it may be impossible to obtain contractual security of future payments—the legality of the contract may be questioned, etc.[15] The position of the community is of course greatly strengthened when the enterprise has made a large investment in a factory building. For an enterprise to make such an investment in a community where it would not locate without a subsidy is like walking into a baited trap. In such a community the value of the building to whoever occupies it depends to a large extent on the prospect of future subsidies. Should the subsidies be discontinued, the owner would suffer a loss equal to their capitalized value and would probably be unable to recover his investment plus a reasonable return. However, as the production value of the plant would remain above zero, operations would continue undiminished, so that the community would not suffer a reduction in payroll. The plant would never have been built if such a contingency were foreseen, but once it is there it does not pay to abandon it. Entrepreneurs of course do foresee the possibility of such a contingency and therefore insist, as far as possible, on receiving the subsidy in capitalized form or to operate a plant owned by the community (in which case a low rent or free occupancy is the indicated form in which to give the subsidy).

It might be thought that this puts the risk on the community, but

15. Compare the case of New London, Wisconsin, discussed in Appendix V, p. 229. This is an example in which the municipality was the victim of dishonesty. To avoid having to consider problems like this the assumption was made that all contracts are fulfilled, honesty and foresight being sufficient to accomplish this.

that is not at all true. If the original enterprise should abandon the building, for instance because it has gone bankrupt as a result of mismanagement, the community can rent it to someone else. As long as the plant has any value at all to an entrepreneur it can bring in a payroll. This does not depend on any particular enterprise and is true even if the community should not have retained title, in which case the original owner is likely to sell it to the highest bidder at a price below replacement value.[16] It is clear, therefore, that in a situation where the profitability of an investment depends on subsidization the community should make the investment. To the community such a building is a lasting asset, whereas if an enterprise should make the investment the community can expropriate it by discontinuing the subsidy. In case a free building is not a strong enough inducement, the community can also supply machinery that is very expensive to move, provided this equipment is not too specifically geared to any particular enterprise's peculiarities. (This also applies to the building.) Additional subsidies should of course be given on a current basis;[17]

16. However, it would seem best for a community to retain title to a building it constructs, for then it can immediately take steps to secure occupation in the event it is vacated.

17. These may well be necessary. In 1952 the average amount of capital investment per production worker in manufacturing, according to an estimate of the National Industrial Conference Board, was about $10,000. However, the amount varied widely between industries, ranging from about $3,000 in apparel to $60,000 in petroleum. On the average about a quarter of the total amount would go in land and buildings; a third was required for equipment and machinery; and the rest for inventory, working capital, etc. (Source: Sar A. Levitan, *Federal Assistance to Labor Surplus Areas,* a report prepared at the request of the chairman of the Committee on Banking and Currency, U.S. House of Representatives, 85th Cong., 1st Sess. [Washington: U.S. Government Printing Office, 1957], p. 34). If we consider the case of an apparel factory, assuming a $2,500 average annual wage and an investment of say $750 per worker (a quarter of $3,000) in land and buildings, it is clear that the value of site and factory may amount to only a very small fraction of the capitalized value of the payroll this factory would bring into the community, leaving indirect benefits out of consideration. Thus, even if equipment and machinery would also be donated the community might be able to recoup its investment in less than half a year in the form of additional income accruing to its residents. Since 1952 investment per worker in the various industries has of course increased, but so have wages and the relation between the two has of course not greatly changed. Thus a community suffering from unemployment would be foolish not to supply an industry that has a relatively low investment per worker with more than a free site and factory if more would be required to attract one. In addition to providing fixed equipment free of cost, this may be done in the form of tax exemption, free utilities, periodic cash donations, etc. It may be added in passing that, while a community ought to investigate a prospect carefully as to its standing in the business world, treatment of employees, etc., it hardly pays to drag on negotiations in order to get an industry at the lowest possible subsidy, for even a few weeks delay on that account may cause a loss in income foregone quite out of proportion to any possible saving.

the only cash donation that a community can reasonably give in capitalized form is a contribution toward construction cost (or a sum of money not exceeding the cost of construction and perhaps equipment of a building on condition that the building be constructed), for otherwise it has no guarantee of payroll delivery.

Possible effects of subsidization on the wage level. One final question may be raised. So far we have taken the wage level that makes subsidization necessary if there is to be full employment as "given." But is it not to be feared that, when the community stands ready to subsidize wages whenever these are too high to be compatible with full employment, this will eliminate all incentive on the part of management to resist demands for higher wages and all restraints on the part of organized labor in making these demands? This depends entirely on how the policy is executed and in what type of environment. First of all, unions are not always the cause of wages being too high for full employment. Especially as regards the rural communities in the South, the federal wage minimum must be held responsible at least as much (and in addition there is the more deep-seated factor, discussed in Chapter I, of the relation between wages and labor productivity). It is difficult to foresee what effect, if any, the general adoption of a subsidization policy by communities would have on the minimum wage. It might inspire those now demanding further increases to do so with more determination than ever when they see the hoped-for result of their policy thwarted,[18] but it would probably also evoke greater resistance. All one can say with certainty is that, should these increases materialize, the need for offsetting measures will become all the more urgent.

With respect to labor unions, I do not believe that their chances for effective wage-boosting action will be enhanced in an environment of communities organized in an effort to create employment opportunity by means of subsidizing industry. People actually paying for the privilege of securing jobs will not tolerate action that would increase the sacrifices demanded of them, would push the necessary subsidization level closer to the feasible maximum, and might jeopardize their program. Instead, they will do all they can to keep the subsidies within reasonable limits.[19] It is the general experience that

18. To the extent that the concern of the proponents of minimum-wage legislation really is the "sweated" worker, however, the solution offered in this book should be ideal to them—or so one would expect.

19. As with the national debt, it is essential to keep the transfer problem within reasonable limits. But unlike the national debt, people are close enough to the problem to realize this.

in communities with such a stake in industry, public opinion is decidedly pro-management. As Clinton Hoch observes: "Where the man on the street has a financial interest in the success of the operation, labor relations problems are less frequent, tax assessments and municipal utility rates tend to be lower, and excellent cooperation can be anticipated in the matter of street maintenance, water and sewer line construction, etc."[20]

In this connection a stipulation in the contract between the city of Grenada, Mississippi, and Grenada Industries, Inc. (a branch of Real Silk Hosiery Mills, Inc., of Indianapolis, brought in under the BAWI plan in 1937) is of interest. It reads as follows:

The Second Party [Grenada Industries] pledges itself . . . that it will not require membership in any organization, religious, fraternal, or otherwise, as a prerequisite to the employment of said Second Party. Second Party agrees that it will not enter into any contract with any group of employees unless and until said contract shall first have been submitted to First Party [the municipality] for its approval.[21]

This agreement, in effect, prohibited the union shop and required city approval of any contract negotiated by a union. The clauses it contains deserve the attention of subsidizing communities that wish to safeguard their interest not only against arbitrary wage setting by local unions but especially against outside union pressure on wages exercised through an enterprise that has factories in other localities. When a labor dispute did arise in the Grenada plant, it was arbitrated by a local committee chosen by the workers with the consent of management. The recommendations of this committee were accepted by both parties.[22]

Summary of positive findings. Considering the implications of competitive subsidization, it was found that the subsidization practice can only increase community income in the presence of un- or underemployment within or in the vicinity of the subsidizing community. Consequently only communities suffering from lack of employment opportunity can be expected to engage in the practice. The basic reason for this is that the possibility of deriving a gain from subsidizing industry rests on the inefficiency of resource allocation which

20. L. Clinton Hoch, "The Location Decision," a paper presented before the Semi-Annual Conference, Production Executives Division, The National Association of Shirt, Pajama and Sportswear Manufacturers, New York, June 20, 1957, p. 15 (mimeographed).

21. Cited in Hopkins, *Mississippi's BAWI Plan,* p. 41.

22. *Ibid.*

unemployment implies. It was shown that in the general case the subsidies will be related to the wages a new firm may be expected to disburse, so that in that sense they may be considered payroll subsidies. This is not altered by the fact that in the interest of the recipient subsidization frequently takes the form of the community making a factory available below cost. Such an investment within the community has the power of bringing in a payroll without further outlay independently of the success or failure of any particular occupant and is therefore also fully justified from the point of view of the community.

In the real world there is of course nothing resembling a frictionless process whereby enterprises can be relocated under the impulse of labor cost differentials created by payroll subsidies. Similarly lacking in realism is the notion that production processes are readily adjustable so as to accommodate more workers when labor cost declines. But in a growing economy these are not necessary conditions for a generalized policy of subsidization at the local level to succeed. The adoption and vigorous pursuit of such a policy by communities lacking employment opportunity within limits dictated by their self-interest would help attract new *additions* to the nation's industrial apparatus to the areas suffering from un- and underemployment without markedly disturbing the location pattern of existing industry. This is true because relocating an existing enterprise is very expensive, so that by and large the "lure" of financial inducements held out by labor surplus communities is felt much more strongly by entrepreneurs faced with incremental investment decisions than by those already established in a particular location. Primarily for political reasons it is nevertheless recommended that, following Puerto Rico, no subsidies be granted to relocating enterprises. In practice, the real contribution in the general interest which competitive subsidization can make is in shaping the spatial growth pattern of the nation's industry.

There are several reasons why in the general case the greatest subsidy we can expect to materialize will be small relative to the total gain in community income that may be reasonably anticipated. On the other hand, such a relatively small effort may be sufficient to eliminate open unemployment and to reduce underemployment to small proportions. That practically any individual community can do this given the present level of subsidization activity elsewhere can hardly be doubted. But it was also argued that if the adoption of a determined policy to create work opportunity by unemployment communities should become general, subsidization would remain highly profitable at or near the full employment margin. Besides, regardless of the overall extent to which subsidization is carried, the practice contributes to the solution of the unemployment problem and tends to increase the productivity of the economy as a whole.

It may finally be remarked that one need not oppose minimum wage legislation and the wage policies of national labor organizations to be in favor of local subsidies to industry in areas of substantial un- and underemployment. If legal wage floors and union rates are seen as socially desirable, then payroll subsidies should be perfectly acceptable as a necessary complement in the same way that rationing is a necessary complement to the setting of price ceilings on essential commodities in times of scarcity. For the subsidies make it possible to have the desired wage rates and a high level of employment as well. Similarly, if wages are irreducible for other reasons, payroll subsidies can expand employment opportunity. The idea that it may be feasible to stimulate local communities to competitive activity in this respect so as not to overburden the central government's budget and unduly expand its sphere of activity might be worth looking into in under-developed countries as well.

Note on the North-South Wage Differential

Professor Bronfenbrenner has accused some writers of presenting their views "as matters of common notoriety, without rebutting or even mentioning the views of others."[1] There may be a dilemma here, however, in that avoiding to expose oneself to this reproach may mean dragging up an old controversy that has never yet been solved but is hackneyed all the same. In the present case I feel that the latter procedure is the lesser evil. For after all, the notion that even now in an efficiency sense Southern wages in many sectors are "too high" and that only evil can come from artificial attempts to raise them still more is a cornerstone of the analysis presented in this treatise, in which the subsidization of industry is seen as a measure to offset the effect of excessive wages on entrepreneurial labor cost. Thus it would indeed be somewhat cavalier to proceed without paying due attention to the views of a large number[2] of distinguished economists who have argued that the Southern wage level is hardly adequate and that the strengthening of union power as well as an increase in the minimum wage level could be useful (or at least might not be harmful) to Southern economic development. Moreover, delving into this controversy I have found, somewhat to my surprise in view of the extensive literature, that some important angles have been rather neglected. This is true, for instance, with respect to the theory of monopsonistic wage determination in its application to the Southern setting and also with respect to the "purchasing power argument" as used to defend existing minimum wage legislation.

The purchasing power argument. This argument states in essence that an overall wage increase in the presence of unemployment may reduce rather than increase unemployment, due to the fact that wages do not only constitute a cost element but also the most important com-

---

1. M. Bronfenbrenner, "The Incidence of Collective Bargaining Once More," *Southern Economic Journal,* XXIV (April, 1958), 400.

2. Indeed the great majority, I think, of those who have expressed themselves on the subject take a view opposite to mine in many important respects.

ponent of aggregate purchasing power. If we make certain assumptions regarding the propensities to spend of various groups in the population, it can be shown that an overall increase in the wage level may alleviate the unemployment problem and a wage reduction aggravate it. In the case of a general wage reduction individual firms would be faced not only with a fall in their cost schedule but also with a fall in demand, and the latter effect may conceivably prevail over the former. According to this theory, any facile conclusion that a fall in the wage level would lead to increased employment is the result of applying a method appropriate for partial analysis to a macro-situation in which the impounding in "ceteris paribus" of the demand schedule is unwarranted—a glaring example of the fallacy of composition. And of course, to the extent that a conclusion regarding this problem should in fact be based upon such reasoning the criticism is valid.

One could question the reasonableness of the assumptions that are necessary for a general wage reduction to have the effect of decreasing employment, but for the sake of the argument we shall accept them. It is of more interest to note that under static assumptions and given the distribution of the means of production the real wage level compatible with full-employment in long-run equilibrium is uniquely determined. Therefore, other than through its possible effect on expectations,[3] an increase in money wages can have a positive effect only insofar as this sets in motion a chain of events leading to a new equilibrium under which real wages are reduced as a result of a more than proportionate rise in the price level. Aggregate demand, of course, can be much more easily managed directly by means of a deliberate monetary and fiscal policy; in the presence of such a policy, aimed at preventing deflation, the purchasing power argument becomes virtually irrelevant. Besides, the purpose of minimum wage legislation and union bargaining is to increase real wages, not merely money wages.[4]

3. In a deep depression there may simply be a general underevaluation of the marginal revenue product of labor due to widespread unwarranted pessimism, so that with a return of confidence the employment situation can be permanently improved without a reduction in the real wage level. It may be observed that any approach which ignores the substitution possibilities between capital and labor and which has people blinded by the money veil does not constitute a long-run equilibrium approach.

4. In a dynamic model one could still derive the conclusion that in the long run an overall increase in real wages would have a favorable effect upon employment. Such a conclusion would have to be based upon assumptions which imply that as a result of the wage increase the process of capital formation would proceed more rapidly than without the increase. Since the propensity to save among wage-earners is hardly higher than among other groups, it would take some tortuous reasoning to argue this case.

While the purchasing power argument is dubious, to say the least, when it concerns a *general* rise in the wage level, it is still another matter to use it in defense of the kind of wage legislation that we have in this country under the Fair Labor Standards Act. In a typical example, Hamberg gives us a good insight into the mental process by which this step is taken. After stating that we must distinguish between the effect of a legal minimum wage as applied to a single industry or sector of the economy on the one hand and that of such an increase as applied to the economy as a whole on the other, he writes: "In view of the fact that minimum wage laws have now reached the national level, it is even more pertinent to examine the effects of a general advance in wage rates."[5] Thus he equates the application of a minimum wage on a national scale with a general rise in the wage level.

Granted that a legal minimum wage tends to have certain indirect effects in the industries immediately concerned and perhaps also on other industries, the identification of the impact of a nation-wide minimum wage with an overall increase in the wage level is still completely unwarranted. This is true because there exist great differentials between the wages of different types of workers within and between industries, between those of workers doing similar work in different industries, between wages in rural and urban areas, and between wages in different regions of the country. It follows that the impact of a national wage minimum, *at whatever level it is set,* must vary greatly between regions, industries, occupations, etc. Moreover, it is common knowledge that invariably at the levels set in reality (and given the exceptions) only a relatively small portion of the labor force has been directly affected at all.[6] In most regions of the country and in most occupations the effect on the wage level has been negligible, so that for all practical purposes the expression "national" in this context is only an empty phrase. Similarly the effect has been negligible with respect to the bulk of the labor force in many "high-wage" industries, regardless of their location. No doubt this is and will always be so because any attempt to impose a truly comprehensive minimum wage would be disastrous, but here it is sufficient merely to pin down a fact. Given this fact, it is clearly unwarranted to argue that the increase in the purchasing power of workers whose wages are

5. D. Hamberg, "Minimum Wages and the Level of Employment," *Southern Economic Journal,* XV (January, 1949), 322.

6. However, this varies greatly between regions. Compare the figures presented in Chapter I, footnote 12, p. 12.

increased might lead to a shift in the demand schedules facing the firms in question sufficient to offset the rise of their cost schedules. Only to a slightly greater extent than in the case of a wage increase in a single enterprise or industry will the increased purchasing power of the workers who benefit from the law be directed toward the products of the industries in which they are employed. The essential aspect of a national minimum wage is that its effect is partial and discriminatory. Therefore, to analyze these effects, the methods and conclusions of partial analysis are more nearly applicable than the aggregative approach of macro-economics.

The monopsony argument. Another point Hamberg discusses with beautiful clarity is "the condition of oligopsony that prevails through most of the labor market," a condition which, according to this author, is inherent in modern production technology.[7] He argues that obviously little competition prevails in many local labor markets, while labor mobility is insufficient to permit competition among firms in different localities. On this basis he derives the conclusion that a legal minimum wage may result in employers raising the number of workers hired.[8]

Like the purchasing power argument in its application to minimum wage legislation, the monopsony argument (or oligopsony—according to Hamberg the result is the same since in an oligopsonistic situation employers tend to act in concert) similarly applied can be questioned at different stages. First, one can raise a question as to whether the absence of competition in the labor market is really as prevalent as Hamberg alleges. I certainly believe that effective (although not perfect) competition for labor is the rule rather than the exception. In the first place, in large cities employers are of course sufficiently numerous to rule out, in the majority of occupations, any important discretionary wage-setting power on the part of individual employers or combinations of employers. Secondly, there is a great deal of mobility from low-wage areas to high-wage areas *when employment opportunity for newcomers exists in the latter.*[9] And third, with

7. *Ibid.*, p. 333.   8. *Ibid.*, p. 336.

9. Thus, while studies carried out in Europe and America during the depressed conditions preceding World War II created the impression, among labor economists, "that economic theory made assumptions about the labour market [regarding labor mobility] which were not realistic," the decade 1940-50 revealed "an internal flexibility in the American labour force which corresponds roughly with the theoretical model of a labour market within which workers move in response to differences in 'net advantage' " (Charles A. Myers, "Labour Market Theory and Empirical Research," *The Theory of Wage Determination,* ed. John T. Dunlop [London: Macmillan and Co., 1957], pp. 318, 325).

modern transportation facilities, workers in rural areas often commute to work over very large distances, so that labor markets are not restricted to any one small locality.[10]

However, to the second and third objection Hamberg has an answer: "In many cases, movement would merely mean going from one oligopsonistic area to another."[11]   But this reasoning is simply fallacious. If there is movement from one oligopsonistic (or monopsonistic) area to another, there is competition between these areas, and if there is competition, there is no monopsony. With similar logic Hamberg could have argued that it does not matter whether a locality has just one employer or a great many: with respect to the hiring in his own enterprise each employer has a monopsonistic position, and the movement of workers from one to the other merely means going from one monopsonistic market to another.

FIGURE I

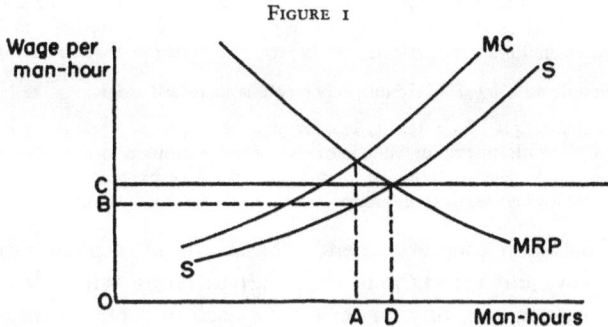

The conventional monopsony model indicates that the monopsonist sets a wage OB, employing the quantity OA of man-hours supplied at that rate. Introduction of a minimum wage OC leads to an expansion of the labor force to OD.

Defendants of minimum wage legislation who use the monopsony argument are prone to reproach their opponents that the latter base their conclusions on the assumption of pure competition. Hamberg for instance, having demonstrated that "a minimum wage . . . legally set at a level above that at which the employer was previously hiring labor oligopsonistically . . . will result in raising both the wage and the number of workers hired," writes: "Thus, once again, we have come to conclusions completely opposed to those reached under the unrealistic assumption of pure competition."[12] These writers forget,

10. Thus the chairman of the Arkansas Industrial Development Commission points out that in his state it is quite common for workers "to drive 20, 30, even 40 miles to their place of work" (Winthrop Rockefeller, "Development of Rural Areas through Industrialization," *The Arkansas Economist*, II [Fall, 1959], 5).

11. Hamberg, *op. cit.*, p. 333.   12. *Ibid.*

FIGURE 2   FIGURE 3

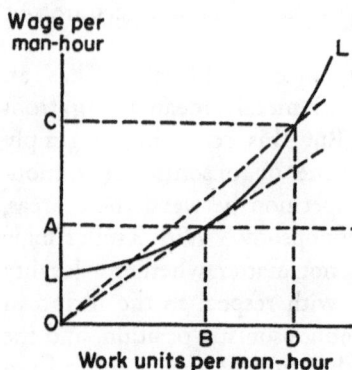
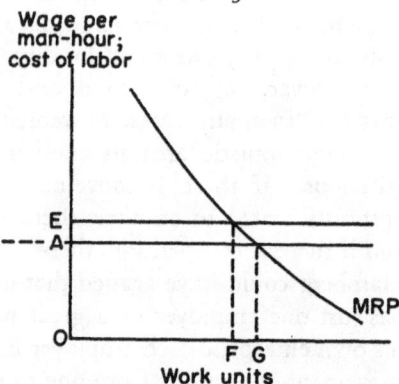

The curve LL represents the relation between the amount of work units forthcoming per man-hour and the wage rate. The employer (whom we may assume to be a monopsonist, although it makes no difference) sets a wage OA which minimizes the cost of a work unit, defined as the quantity of work performed in a man-hour at wage OA. This is indicated in Figure 2. It can also be seen in Figure 2 that some higher wage OC, corresponding to a legal minimum, labor cost is increased from $\dfrac{OA}{OB}$ to $\dfrac{OC}{OD} = OE$ (indicated in Figure 3). As a result, employment in terms of work units is decreased from OG to OF, while unemployment in terms of work units is decreased from OG to OF, while unemployment in terms of man-hours increases by more than that amount (because at the higher legal wage more work units are forthcoming per man-hour).

however, that their own argument is based on an implicit assumption of full employment throughout. For the reasoning which leads to the conclusion that monopsony power can be used to suppress wages below the competitive equilibrium level assumes an upward sloping supply curve of labor and the establishment of a wage level that clears the market.[13] The increase in employment that would allegedly result from the establishment of a minimum wage comes about solely because the higher wage elicits a larger voluntary supply of labor than that forthcoming at the wage previously paid by the monopsonist; there is no question of a reduction in involuntary unemployment, since this condition is not assumed to exist in the first place. However, under the conditions typically prevailing in labor markets where the minimum wage is likely to be effective, this assumption of full employment is as unrealistic as that of pure competition. Such labor markets are usually characterized by widespread disguised or open unemployment (this abundance of labor being the primary cause of the low wage level). As Chapter II indicates, this certainly is true in those regions of the United States where the minimum wage is an

13. See the graph in *ibid.*, p. 335.

effective determinant of the wage level in some industries. Thus the usual monopsony model, while valid if we accept the underlying assumptions, is irrelevant in the situation to which it is applied when used to argue that a legal minimum wage may have a beneficial effect upon the employment situation. As we have seen, when there is un- or underemployment the principle of wage determination is entirely different from that postulated in the usual monopsony model: each individual employer sets a wage at that point which minimizes his labor cost.[14] There is then no reason to distinguish between monopsony and competition, for, given these wages, labor is in excess supply: any employer can reduce the wages in his enterprise and still obtain any amount of labor he can use, *his reason for not doing so being that this would increase labor cost.* Thus at actually prevailing wage rates in the various enterprises the supply of labor is perfectly elastic.[15] There simply is no relation between the wage rate and the quantity of labor demanded by either the individual entrepreneur or all entrepreneurs together, and in the absence of such a relation there is no room for the exercise of monopsony power.[16] The introduction of a minimum wage when there is unemployment merely means that

14. *Supra,* pp. 5-6.

15. This may be illustrated by a description of a labor market characterized by surplus labor, found in B. M. Wofford and T. A. Kelly, *Mississippi Workers* (University, Alabama: The University of Alabama Press, 1955), p. 45, which clearly brings out this point:

"In the period following World War II, business activity in general in Tupelo [in the northeast part of Mississippi, population 11,527 in 1950] was quite high. Unemployment, even during the reconversion period, presented no particular problem." Yet: "Ample labor was to be found to meet all demands. . . . The apparent contradiction of little unemployment and an adequate labor supply is to be explained by the fact that much of the growth in Tupelo's industrial labor force resuled from transfers from lower-paid occupations, especially in the rural areas nearby. It was estimated that 70 percent of the industrial labor force in Tupelo lived outside the city, mostly on small farms. Thus the tight housing situation . . . was not a serious deterrent to the recruitment of industrial workers for plants in the city."

Similarly, when the Pathfinder Coach Division of Superior Coaches, Inc., located in Kosciusko, near the geographical center of Mississippi, embarrassment was experienced because of the inability of the company to give employment to all those who wished to be employed, despite the fact that the number of registered unemployed at that time was low after the recovery from the nation-wide recession in 1949.

16. One might venture to speculate that an intuitive appreciation of the implications of the presence of surplus labor for the wage determination process is responsible for Hamberg's assertion, criticized above, that the movement of laborers from one oligopsonistic labor market to another will not lead to a bidding up of the wage level. Naturally, when labor is in abundant supply, this effect would not obtain. Martin Bronfenbrenner, in his article "Potential Monopsony in Labor Markets," *Industrial and Labor Relations Review,* IX (July, 1956), 577-88, explicitly says that monopsonistic employers usually set "disequilibrium" rates higher than those that would clear the market (p. 579).

employers come to be faced with a horizontal supply curve of labor at a higher level, employment will tend to be reduced, and the unemployment problem is aggravated.[17] The difference between the conventional monopsony approach and the approach outlined above is illustrated in Figures I-III, pp. 203-204.

Wage rates and labor cost. The argument used in the previous section to demonstrate the inadequacy of the monopsony argument as applied to markets characterized by a labor surplus is closely related to one used by some authors *in favor* of high wages. The positive relation between wages and labor productivity is emphasized, and it is accordingly argued, to use the often-quoted words of perhaps the foremost spokesmen for this group, that "it is no longer necessary [for the South] to base promotional efforts on low wage rates, as many of the Southern development groups are realizing."[18] McLaughlin and Robock admit that "search for a certain wage rate advantage will now and then be the main interest of a producer,"[19] but they emphasize labor cost savings that may occur aside from wage differentials "because of lower turnover, less absenteeism, and high productivity."[20] My answer is that entrepreneurs are aware of all this, and that the wage rate they establish *when not interfered with* is the rate that minimizes labor cost.[21] But that does not eliminate the North-South differential, for the fact is that in the South it is possible to secure a good class of labor with a cooperative attitude *at wages significantly lower than those prevailing in other regions.* Thus I do not find in the existence of a positive relation between wages and labor productivity a reason to defend an artificial narrowing of the existing differential.

A few words may be added here about Bronfenbrenner's discussion of this argument,[22] which he considers one of the two major argu-

17. With respect to collective bargaining it is not possible to arrive at an equally definite rejection of the monopsony argument, because union power may often have been asserted in markets characterized by virtually full employment (although not necessarily by oligopsony or monopsony). See, however, Bronfenbrenner's discussion of Lloyd Reynold's notion that collective bargaining has brought the wage structure closer to the competitive norm (Martin Bronfenbrenner, "The Incidence of Collective Bargaining Once More," *Southern Economic Journal,* XXIV [April, 1958], 398-406), particularly pp. 404-06.

18. Glenn E. McLaughlin and Stefan Robock, *Why Industry Moves South,* Report No. 3, National Planning Association (Washington: Committee on the South, N.P.A., 1949), p. 120.

19. *Ibid.* In fact they give so many instances in which this was true that one feels that in their conclusions these authors greatly underplay this part of their findings, as for instance where they state to have discovered that "anything but 'cheap' labor was important in attracting industry to the South" (p. 7).

20. *Ibid.*   21. *Supra,* pp. 5-6.

ments in favor of the contention that minimum wage legislation will increase rather than decrease employment in the occupations that it covers (the other being the purchasing power argument). Bronfenbrenner's theoretical construction is logical, although to my mind far-fetched as a defense of minimum wage legislation; the author himself makes it clear that he is not convinced that the relation he postulates exists in reality. The relation between wages and labor productivity, then, Bronfenbrenner looks upon as a purely physical one, and when real wages are raised productivity does not go up immediately, but only after a considerable period—years rather than months or weeks. In such a situation the beneficial effect on labor productivity may not accrue to the individual employer who raises the wage at all—it becomes largely an external effect, and at least in the beginning labor cost as a result of a legal wage minimum would rise. This would have a detrimental effect on employment, which, Bronfenbrenner argues, could be offset by a temporary subsidy.

I just do not believe that this is a true description of American reality. The American labor force, even in the low-income areas, is physically quite capable of performing efficiently in factories at wages employers see fit to pay in the absence of any interference. To the extent that some individuals are diseased, mentally or physically, this cannot be remedied by a moderate increase in the wage level such as a legal minimum wage can provide. Of course Bronfenbrenner's article was written almost two decades ago, but at least nowadays there would not be, on the ground indicated by Bronfenbrenner, any call for an increase of the present $1 minimum (which should not be interpreted to imply that I consider the current minimum justifiable). As indicated above, the wage-productivity relation in this country is primarily a psychological one, and the effect is immediate and internal to the enterprise. Hence it is taken note of and incorporated in entrepreneurial wage policy. Even if the relation were primarily physical, I do not think that it would become manifest after years only. As things are, there is on the farms an underemployed labor force consisting primarily of able-bodied men and women waiting for a chance to work in industry, and who, as experience indicates, make excellent industrial workers.[23]

However, I wish to use this occasion to point out that if one accepts

22. M. Bronfenbrenner, "Minimum Wages, Unemployability, and Relief: a Theoretical Note," *Southern Economic Journal*, X (July, 1943), 52-59.

23. This is not to say that a higher level of living that could be attained with higher wages might not somewhat improve the physical condition of these people in the long run but that it is highly questionable that this would lead to an increase in labor productivity sufficient to offset the effect of the wage increase on labor cost.

Bronfenbrenner's reasoning as applicable to American reality or if for any reason one disagrees with me in my evaluation of minimum wage legislation and collective bargaining, the positive proposals made in this work should not be rejected for that reason. On the contrary, if on the one hand one starts from the premise that wages higher than those set freely in the market are a social necessity, and recognizes on the other that, at least temporarily, attempts to raise the wage-scale to the desired level may have undesired side-effects on employment opportunity, a workable subsidization scheme should be an ideal solution.

Labor cost and managerial efficiency. The argument in the previous section is based on a reaction to a raising of the wage level emanating from the labor force itself. Everything else equal, it says, laborers will work harder and better when wages are raised, and this improvement in performance will be so great that, over the relevant range, labor cost will fall as wages rise. This argument must be distinguished from another "labor productivity" argument, which contends that when a wage increase is imposed management may be shocked into greater efficiency leading to greater output per worker, thereby offsetting the cost increase resulting from the higher wage rate. When all is said and done, this seems to be the main point upon which Lester's case in favor of eliminating the North-South wage differential rests. Summing up an article which itself summarizes the result of extensive research on this problem, this author asks: "How would continued reduction or complete elimination of existing South-North wage differentials affect industrial development in the South?" And he answers:

> Reduction or elimination of remaining South-North wage differentials could help to improve living standards in the South. Answers of southern business executives to questions regarding the adjustments they would make to marked reductions in South-North differentials indicate that much can be done through better management, product development, and sales effort to offset the effect of relative wage increases. In addition to stimulating industrial efficiency by encouraging improvements in management and labor, relatively higher wage scales for some southern firms and industries would tend to improve the South's barter terms of trade with the rest of the country, especially in the case of articles produced only in the South and protected by lack of competitive substitutes.[24]

Leaving the second point out of consideration (Lester's own qualification is sufficient reason for this procedure, and besides, it is hardly

24. Richard A. Lester, Southern Wage Differentials: Developments, Analysis, and Implications," *Southern Economic Journal*, XIII (April, 1947), 393-94.

consistent with the first), Lester's whole affirmative case comes to rest on the wage-induced improvement in managerial efficiency.[25]

It does appear plausible that when business conditions are made worse there may be a mild improvement in managerial efficiency, but I do not consider this a good reason for making conditions worse. The question is how much we can expect along this line in the general case. And here it would appear relevant to point out that, at least to the extent that firms are subject to competition, conditions are usually difficult enough for the relatively poorly managed firm (i.e. the firm in which there would be considerable room for improvement) without such extra complications as would result from a wage increase. When business conditions are too easy, efficiency may certainly slacken and production decline, but when they are too difficult only the strongest survive and production also declines, in spite of further gains in efficiency that may be made. Somewhere in the middle there must be an optimum; personally I am inclined to think that it is likely to be approached when the price level is stable and active competition in commodity and factor markets (excluding artificial wage boosts) is maintained. Moreover, efficiency gains may at least in part take the form of labor-saving measures so that the unemployment problem can be aggravated even if output falls little or not at all. In the case at hand it would be quite natural if managerial ingenuity should turn in that direction.

What clinches the case against this argument, however, is that clearly it only applies to existing enterprise. It has no bearing on the fact that as a choice for a new location the area in which the (relative) wage increase becomes effective loses in attractiveness.[26] In a region that aspires to rapid economic growth (which alone can cure the underemployment that exists in the South today and raise the level of living in the long run),[27] this should be decisive.

Critique of the "orthodox" position. The position of those who

25. Of course in addition Lester has a great deal to say in connection with what he considers spurious arguments in favor of the differential.

26. For a similar opinion see Calvin B. Hoover and B. U. Ratchford, *Economic Resources and Policies of the South* (New York: The Macmillan Company, 1951), pp. 409-10. See also the discussion on the reliability of questionnaires as means to find out about the incentive-value to manufacturers of the North-South wage differential (p. 410).

27. We deliberately avoid the notion that there should be some compelling force which in the long run would cause the wage differential between the South and the rest of the country to disappear. One can conceive of equilibrium with a considerable differential still existing as the result of people's preference for one place over another where wages may be higher. It is a misunderstanding to think that "classical" economic theory teaches that such a differential is incompatible with long-run equilibrium, and this misunderstanding underlies much of the writing on this subject.

hold that the wage differential should not be tampered with is based on standard economic theory and has been expounded for a long time with great lucidity and irresistible logic by various authors.[28]   There is no need to restate it here: where the eloquence of writers such as Simons and Van Sickle has failed, I have no hope to convince.   However, since Lester is by many considered the outstanding opponent of the view that attributes to the wage differential an essential role in the economic development of the South, it may be of some interest to examine his direct rebuttal of this view.   We have already seen that this author's main argument on the affirmative side of his own position has no bearing on the problem of attracting new industry. Apparently Lester realizes this for, having stated it,[29] he continues:

> Some economists believe that North-South wage differentials are neces-
> sary in order to attract labor away from the South and to attract capital
> investment to the South.   Wage levels in the South approximately equal
> to wage scales paid by competitors in the North—a situation widely prev-
> alent nowadays—are considered "wage distortions."   The same reasoning
> has not, however, been applied to commodity prices; uniform prices be-
> tween the North and the South—characteristic of most trade-marked
> commodities—are not called "price distortions."   The widespread ex-
> istence of geographic price uniformity has been an important factor in the
> demand for geographic wage uniformity.   The two are obviously related.[30]

That wage differentials should be necessary to attract labor away from the South is highly questionable, and I do not think that the "orthodox" economists attacked in the paragraph quoted here believe this.   To the extent that wage standardization reduces employment opportunity in the South migration is stimulated by it.   Apart from this, however, the opening sentence does represent the essence of the "orthodox" position.   This position Lester finds inconsistent because it opposes wage uniformity but not price uniformity, although the two are related.

28. For instance, Henry C. Simons, *Economic Policy for a Free Society* (Chicago: University of Chicago Press, 1948), pp. 135-38; John V. Van Sickle, *Planning for the South* (Nashville: Vanderbilt University Press, 1943), pp. 181-95. An exposition second to none of the advantages in a wage differential for a region's economic development can also be found in Seymour E. Harris *et al., New England Textiles and the New England Economy,* Report by the New England Governors' Textile Committee to the Conference of New England Governors (Cambridge, Mass., March, 1958), pp. I-22 to I-25.   The authors of this document, however, find in the competitive advantage to the South of the relatively low southern wage level, which they themselves so clearly indicate, a reason to recommend that the differential be abolished, so as to protect industry in New England and further its expansion at the expense of the South.

29. Cited above, p. 208.   30. Lester, *op. cit.,* p. 394.

Insofar as price uniformity is the result of the so-called "fair trad-ing" practice (to which Lester probably refers when he mentions trade-marked commodities, for branding alone without this practice is not sufficient to cause price uniformity), this is of course a "distortion" too and has often been designated as such. However, the situation would not be very much different if there were no such distortion. Apart from relatively small differences on account of transportation cost and the local cost of retailing, price uniformity in commodity markets is the natural result of free trade, and hence an economic phenomenon fully consistent with the optimality conditions of the market. That prices are more uniform than wages is simply the result of the fact that commodities are more mobile than labor. Basically, therefore, price uniformity is not a "distortion," Lester's suggestion to the con-trary notwithstanding. Moreover, there is no compelling economic force that relates price uniformity to wage uniformity, and certainly no welfare principle that prescribes such a relation. Lester might as well have argued that there would be no "distortion" if equal wage rates were set for janitors and doctors, since they have to pay the same price for bread. To say that people's relative incomes should be regulated by the relative prices they must pay is to discard all economic reasoning. Of course economic reasoning often *is* totally discarded when wages are regulated under collective bargaining or by the state, and because of this there may conceivably even be such a queer thing as a relation of the kind Lester has in mind between interregional price uniformity and wage uniformity (to the extent that demands for equal wages are granted and granted in recognition of the argument that there ought to be such a relation).[31] But this does not make the demands reasonable or giving in to them in the interest of the South, as this author seems to imply.

The statistical argument. And finally (I think this more or less completes the list) there is the argument that low wages may not be so important for economic expansion as is sometimes alleged since within the South the states and industries with higher than average wages have expanded more rapidly than the states and industries with less than average wages. All I have to say about this is that the case could be stated in much stronger form, for instance by pointing to the fact that economic expansion in the United States, always a high-wage country, has on the whole been much more rapid than elsewhere. Perhaps it may even be hoped that when stated in this form a ques-tion about the implied causality will arise.

31. It is my conviction that the extent to which this is true is negligible.

Evaluation of the North-South wage differential by interested groups outside the South. There is no reason to question the sincerity of the belief expressed by the authors whose work has been discussed above that elimination of the North-South wage differential by means of minimum wage legislation, the encouragement of collective bargaining, and similar measures is or may be in the best interest of Southern economic development. Presumably, therefore, they will find but little comfort in the fact that the type of policy defended by them is identical with that recommended by others who do not at all profess to argue from the point of view of the interest of the South but rather from that of other regions which feel themselves in competition with the South for industry. This difference in evaluation of the role and importance of the wage differential has been noted by De Vyver, who writes: "Recently the state of Massachusetts has become interested in why its textile industry is losing ground to the South. The report of a special commission issued May 12, 1950, considers wage differentials as one of the important factors involved in the removal of the industry from that state."[32] This commission recommended among other things repeal of the Taft-Hartley law, so that Southern industry might be organized more easily and competition would become "more even."[33]

Quite recently all this has been brought in clear focus again by another New England textile report, that of the New England Governors' Textile Committee.[34] I have already mentioned[35] that in it can be found one of the most forceful and convincing explanations of how the industrialization of a rural area suffering from underemployment in agriculture (the Southern Piedmont) is furthered by a relatively low wage level, and of the benefits that this process may bring upon such an area. I must resist the temptation to reproduce this glowing account here. Of even greater interest in the present context is the connection between it and the policies advocated by the committee, about which the report is perfectly candid. Quoting its own March 1957 report, it says:

In 1955, our Committee worked with the New England Congressional Delegation, providing material . . . that helped bring about a one dollar minimum. The Committee also has urged increases of minima under the Walsh-Healey Act, which sets the minimum wages by industries for work under government contracts. The Committee intends to continue to strive for higher minima and for strict enforcement, because the minima tend

32. Frank T. De Vyver, "Labor Factors in Industrial Development of the South," *Southern Economic Journal,* XVIII (October, 1951), 190.

33. *Ibid.*   34. Seymour E. Harris *et al., op. cit.*   35. *Supra,* p. 210, footnote 28.

to raise wages in regions where they are abnormally low, as they are in much of the South. *Higher minimum wages mean a better competitive position for New England.*[36] [Italics mine.]

Elsewhere the report states that at a certain time the wage differential in some branch of the textile industry "was 31 cents against New England."[37] Its authors further argue that an increase in the national wage minimum is now more necessary than ever, since rising opposition in the South against trade unionism has exploded any hopes that regional differences in wage scales would rapidly be reduced as a result of organization of the Southern labor force.[38] Apart from such stratagems as habitually referring to the payment of wages below the national "norm" as "exploitation" of labor, the report exhibits remarkably little preoccupation with justifying its recommendations in any other way than that they would help New England.

Similarly, organized labor is greatly concerned about industry being attracted, by wage differentials and "substandard labor laws," toward areas in which hitherto unionism has been unable to make much headway.[39] It appears that among those who for whatever reason would rather *not* see the South in the strong competitive position which its industrialization requires, there is virtual agreement that the wage differential should be eliminated. And from their point of view they are absolutely right.

Empirical studies. Numerous studies have been made that attempt to assess the effect on employment of the minimum wage empirically. The usefulness of these studies is limited because they can at best only indicate the effect in the short run, which of course is not likely to be great. With given plant and equipment, there usually is little room for variation of labor input, and enterprises will continue to operate as long as they can cover variable cost. In the long run, on the other hand, wage minima such as have been successively established in this country are not sufficiently high to lead to an overall reduction in economic activity, but merely slow down growth and distort resource allocation. Accordingly, no great overall effects were found,

36. *Ibid.*, p. I-25.   37. *Ibid.*, p. I-29.   38. *Ibid.*, p. I-34.

39. See for instance: *Subsidized Industrial Migration; the Luring of Plants to New Locations,* Recommendations for legislative action by the Subcommittee on Migration and Subsidization of Industry, National Legislative Committee, American Federation of Labor (Washington: American Federation of Labor, 1955), especially pp. 9, 35-41. One typical phrase in this document goes: "The oppressive features added to the labor relations law by the Taft-Hartley Act and the long delay of the Congress in raising the minimum wage to an adequate level have provided a new incentive to unscrupulous employers, particularly in the South, to seek competitive advantages on the basis of low wages and non-union conditions of work" (p. 36).

although the inquiries do indicate some reduction in employment in the areas and industries primarily affected. However, as Van Sickle says, the imposition of an uneconomically high wage-scale "works out its results only over a considerable period of time and shows up in the number of new plants that were never established. While the federal government has made enormous strides in its statistical techniques and in the coverage of economic activities, this statistic is still lacking."[40] In the more intelligent discussions of the empirical investigations, the various difficulties that make it virtually impossible to draw any definite conclusions other than on the basis of economic analysis are usually emphasized. In other cases, however, authors have been inclined to see in the fact that mass-unemployment does not usually follow the introduction or increase of a minimum wage proof of the innocuous character of the measure. Since the literature provides a fully satisfactory coverage of the subject, a more detailed discussion is not necessary here.[41]

40. John V. Van Sickle, "Industrialization and the South," *Southern Economic Journal*, XV (April, 1949), 421.

41. One statement that neatly summarizes the nature of the difficulties referred to may be cited: "The United States Department of Labor studied the effects of the 75 cents minimum imposed in 1950. It concluded that the wage increase had no appreciable effect upon employment which remained stable, and that industry displayed a high degree of adjustment to the increased minimum wage. . . . The Department of Labor studies were, however, not conclusive. They were based upon only a few months' experience and the Korean war started within 5 months after the 75 cents minimum became effective. The war spurred economic activity and was accompanied by a more than 10 percent rise in prices during about an 8-month period" (U.S. Congress, Senate Committee on Banking and Currency, *Selected Materials on the Economy of the South*, 84th Cong., 2nd Sess. [Washington: U.S. Government Printing Office, 1956], p. 28).

For further discussions of the subject see for instance: Hoover and Ratchford, *op. cit.*, pp. 416-17; Van Sickle, *Planning for the South*, pp. 181-91; Walter E. Boles, Jr., "Some Aspects of the Fair Labor Standards Act," *Southern Economic Journal*, VI (April, 1940), 490-511; H. M. Douty, "Minimum Wage Regulation in the Seamless Hosiery Industry," *Southern Economic Journal*, VIII (October, 1941), 176-90; Van Sickle, "Industrialization and the South," *Southern Economic Journal*, XV (April, 1949), 412-24; John M. Peterson, "Employment Effects of Minimum Wages," *Journal of Political Economy*, LXV (October, 1957), 412-30; Robert J. Myers and Odis C. Clark, "Effects of a Minimum Wage in the Cotton-garment Industry, 1939-41," *Monthly Labor Review*, LIV (February, 1942), 319-37; Harry S. Kantor, "Two Decades of the Fair Labor Standards Act," *Monthly Labor Review*, LXXXI (October, 1958), 1097-1106; U.S. Department of Labor, *Results of the Minimum-Wage Increase of 1950* (Washington: U.S. Government Printing Office, 1954); U.S. Department of Labor, *Studies of the Economic Effects of the $1.00 Minimum Wage* (Washington: U.S. Government Printing Office, 1957); George Macesich and Charles T. Stewart, Jr., "Recent Department of Labor Studies of Minimum Wage Effects," *Southern Economic Journal*, XXVI (April, 1960), 281-90.

APPENDIX II

Note on the Louisiana Tax Exemption Program

This is a note on Professor Ross' cost-benefit analysis of the Louisiana tax exemption program, referred to in Chapter IV, footnote 69 (p. 110). His article concludes that "the cost of the program in terms of lost revenue is out of proportion to the direct results obtained."[1] If we take the figures upon which this conclusion is based for granted this is true in one sense but not in another.

The total cost of the ten-year exemptions (including those granted by the special taxing districts, municipalities, and parishes, which are the major part) contracted between December 1946 and June 1950 Ross estimates at $51,417,848.40, say $50 million. Since this is to represent the revenue foregone as a result of the program, only taxes on those investments that would supposedly also have come in the absence of the program should have been included. This would have reduced the figure by about 7 percent, but Ross fails to make this adjustment. However, we shall retain the $50 million figure. This sum Ross compares with the estimated $25 million worth of investments which the state would have lost in the absence of the inducement (about 7 percent of the exempted total; compare Chapter IV, footnote 69, p. 110) and this leads him to the conclusion cited above. This conclusion is correct in the sense that if the state and the local units had collected $50 million taxes on new investments over the initial ten-year period (which presumably they could have), this money might conceivably have been used to make about twice the total investment attracted by the exemption program, creating twice as many jobs, etc.

However, if we assume that the revenue foregone under the program would, if collected, not have been used for productive investment

1. William D. Ross, "Tax Exemption in Louisiana as a Device for Encouraging Industrial Development," *The Southwestern Social Science Quarterly*, XXXIV (June, 1953), p. 22.

in the state,[2] we reach a different conclusion. Unfortunately it is a rather tentative one because Ross does not provide us with the information we need to follow the line of argument upon which it is based, but we can estimate the relevant order of magnitude. What we should like to know is the size of the payrolls brought into the state by the 7 percent supposedly induced by the tax exemptions to establish themselves in Louisiana.

In 1948 (we take the middle year of the 1946-50 period in which the investments were made), the amount of capital invested per production worker was estimated at about $9,000; the average weekly pay of male production workers was $60.98 and of female workers $41.86.[3] To make a rough calculation, let us assume that this relation between investment and payrolls holds for the enterprises in question, i.e. a ratio of investment per worker to annual payroll of between 3:1 and 4:1. Then the $25 million in new investment attracted by the exemptions (purchased at a cost of $50 million in revenue foregone over the ten-year life of the exemptions) would have yielded an annual payroll (production workers only) of about $7 million, or about $70 million in the ten-year exemption period alone. In addition, of course, there are others than production workers who received wages as a result of the investment; there are indirect (multiplier) effects which for an area as large as Louisiana must be considerable; the payrolls continue when after ten years the exemptions cease. On the other hand, some of the workers absorbed in industry as a result of the investments (many undoubtedly transferred from existing industrial enterprises, creating employment opportunity there for workers from the low-income occupations) probably contributed a little in agriculture, etc. However, this kind of calculus shows that the state may well have gained considerably more income-wise than it lost, even though only about 7 percent of the exemptions may have been effective.

Naturally this conclusion is based on the assumed payroll-investment relation in the enterprises attracted by the exemption. Enterprises to which the exemption meant most and to which therefore the

2. This is more realistic, for the state would then probably have collected a smaller amount in other taxes and spent more on public works, etc. Part of the tax savings might have been used for private investment in the state, but the major part would have been spent in other ways. This case may therefore be taken to represent by approximation what would have happened in the absence of a tax exemption program.

3. Source: *The Economic Almanac, 1958* (New York: The National Industrial Conference Board, 1958), p. 216. The exact investment figure given is $8,815.

state's program made a crucial difference may well have been exactly those with a more unfavorable ratio. This reflection indicates that the state program may be adversely discriminatory. Yet even with all the objections that can be raised against them it is hard to condemn state tax exemption programs outright under the present conditions. This note merely aims at bringing some relevant considerations to bear on the problem.

Note on Chapter VI

It was indicated in Chapter VI, p. 146, that the establishment of a minimum wage high enough to reduce the demand for labor in a locality to zero coupled with a completely discriminatory subsidization policy would be equivalent to the expropriation in favor of labor of all immobile local property used in the production process. This is so because the discriminatory selling of labor such a policy amounts to would, as compared to a situation of complete wage flexibility, convert a buyer's surplus into a seller's surplus. The buyer's surplus normally being passed on to property owners as the result of competition for local property by entrepreneurs, the incidence of a change from a system of wage competition to one in which the community acts as a discriminating monopolist in the labor market would entirely fall upon the property owners. This can perhaps best be seen if we look upon entrepreneurs as agents of property owners, buying labor in the local market. For the purpose of visualizing income distribution effects this approach is fully justified, for in competitive equilibrium entrepreneurial income itself is zero in any case. It should be noted that the above is true if labor pays the subsidies itself, in which case the income of the factor labor is equal to entrepreneurial labor cost (= wages minus subsidies).

Although Chapter VI is concerned with a highly abstract model, a point may be made here that retains its validity within the context of the more realistic approach followed in Chapter VIII. In his chapter on discriminating monopoly in *The Economics of Welfare*, Pigou discusses the conditions under which perfect discrimination (discrimination "of the first degree" under which no buyers' surplus is left to the buyers) may conceivably be established. He indicates that this may be done by detailed separate bargaining with every separate buyer. In the case at hand, labor would then have to be sold to the various entrepreneurs in packets of a determinate size rather than per unit, the price of each packet being fixed so as to make it worth the entrepreneur's while, but only just worth his while, to purchase it. Pigou, thinking of the sale of consumer goods, declares that the cost and trouble involved in this method would invariable be prohibitive and concludes that therefore in reality rougher methods would have to be followed.[1] However, but for an in reality existing element of bilateral monopoly due to imperfect knowledge, this objection to perfect discrimination does not exist in the case of the subsidizing community, which at any rate has to conclude packet deals and bargain with each prospect individually. Thus the subsidization of industry by labor-surplus communities may be seen as an application of the type of action visualized by Pigou, or at least subsidization policies can in principle be applied in that manner.

In Chapter VI it was assumed that immobile local property is owned by "foreigners." This assumption was made solely for the sake of convenience with a view to the elimination of multiplier effects and is in no way essential to our basic conclusions. However, since it was made, precision requires that our conclusion to the effect that only labor-surplus communities can increase their aggregate incomes by means of subsidizing industry be qualified. With local property owned by outsiders, it is naturally in the interest of the individual community striving to maximize the aggregate income accruing to its residents to expropriate all of this property. If the community had the power to set local wage floors in excess of the national minimum wage, this could be achieved by setting a local minimum such that there would be no demand for labor and then following a subsidization policy in accordance with the principles of our model. Furthermore, in theory at least, the same effect could be reached without a wage floor, simply by giving each enterprise the subsidy that would be necessary to secure continued full employment in the least costly manner *if* a wage floor should exist that without any subsidies would be prohibitive of all employment. This would also work in full employment communities. The scheme would lead to a bidding up of the wage rate to the level of the hypothetical wage floor, causing the expropriation of all property bound to the locality. Total subsidies would have to be equal only to the difference between the increase in wage disbursements and the total value of property rents; hence the community would increase its aggregate income. For rather obvious reasons, among which I shall only mention the fact that local property is not generally owned by outsiders, this qualifica-

1. A. C. Pigou, *The Economics of Welfare* (London: Macmillan and Company, 4th ed., 1952), pp. 279-80.

tion has no importance in reality.[2] Subsidization in response to a previously existing effective wage floor is a completely different matter, for there partial "expropriation" (relative to what property incomes would be under a hypothetical condition of complete wage flexibility) is an accomplished fact, and subsidies carried to the full employment point and no further are more likely to benefit the average property owner than to harm him. The difference is underlined by the circumstance that local property owners are frequently counted among the supporters of industrial subsidies, in the justified hope of an increase in real estate values.

2. However, organized workers as such could of course do the same thing. This might be something for labor unions to consider. Simply by handing out money to unsuspecting entrepreneurs they might greatly increase the share of labor in the national income, avoiding all conflict while doing so.

Opinions on Competitive Subsidization
Expressed in the Literature

Having discussed the probable effect of competitive subsidization on a larger scale and in a more intensive manner than that which is currently practiced, we may contrast our conclusions with a number of typical statements in the literature that also primarily pertain to the effect of competitive subsidization as seen from the viewpoint of the economy as a whole. These opinions, we find, are generally not based on analysis. Rather, it is taken for granted that when communities compete with each other for industry, this must necessarily lead to either a cancellation of benefits when all engage in this game equally vigorously (with presumably only the financial burden imposed on the citizens of subsidizing communities and the resulting neglect of municipal services, etc., as the net effect) or else will lead to a distortion of resource allocation. But for a very few exceptions the idea that the practice may serve to offset imperfections in the market instead of constituting unwarranted interference with a perfect allocation mechanism seems never to occur to the authors expressing themselves on the subject. Particularly revealing is the attitude expressed by economists as well as others toward competition, as if merely using this word is indicating an evil so obvious that elaboration is unnecessary. The terms in which competition is denounced implicitly apply to competition between enterprises as much as to that between communities. The general contention is that one community's gain constitutes another's loss, with no benefit to society at large. This is exactly how free competition between enterprises was viewed in the Middle Ages (and by many also today!). From a wide selection of examples a few are presented to illustrate this, while some related points brought forward by the authors in question are also mentioned.

Thus Harold M. Groves writes:

Is it sound policy for states and municipalities to grant tax exemptions? Certainly something will depend here upon the universality of the exemption program. If one merchant keeps his store open on Sunday while others are closed he can make money by so doing. But if all merchants follow the same policy none of them are benefited. Similarly, if only one municipality were to offer special tax advantages, it could attract, perhaps, a considerable number of desirable industries, but when the favors are universalized they cease to be effective. Of course, one municipality can outdo another in its inducements. The question then arises as to when and where will the competition in subsidies stop?[1]

It may be observed that while the merchants as a group might not benefit, the public would, and that the same argument could be used with respect to price maintenance agreements, which presumably should on that ground be encouraged. As to one municipality outdoing another, we have seen that communities in which there is unemployment will be able to gain more industry than they otherwise would, outdoing the others, so that capital will be directed where its social productivity is greatest. And while Groves and others seem to suggest that there is no limit to this type of competition except perhaps the common ruin of the contending parties,[2] our analysis indicates definite limits and suggests that subsidization will under no circumstances be carried beyond the level required to establish and maintain full employment. Groves, however, concludes:

From the social point of view it can be said categorically that tax concessions and other special inducements extended to industries by specific municipalities and states are very undesirable. Concessions and inducements might conceivably be supported by the infant industry argument but industry has had no trouble in getting started in this country where the territory was well adapted to its growth. Exemption tends to provoke retaliation and further exemption in an unending cycle. Migration of industry is likely to leave much human disaster in its trail since labor

1. Harold M. Groves, "Effects of Tax Exemptions and Tax Differentials on the Location of Business," *Proceedings of the Thirty-first Annual Conference on Taxation* (Columbia, S. C.: National Tax Association, 1939), pp. 564-65.

2. This is expressed in plain language in the following statement, which fully concurs with that of Groves: "Local bounties to encourage settlement of business enterprises are suspect. The gain of the community which thus attracts an enterprise may be offset by the loss of whatever other community would otherwise have had it. *Suicidal rivalry in such bounty-granting is a logical outcome of the practice.* The country may benefit little, and the taxpayers of one set of communities have bought the distress of another" (Italics mine) (William J. Schultz and C. Lowell Harriss, *American Public Finance* [Englewood Cliffs, N.J.: Prentice-Hall, Inc., 1959], p. 81).

cannot in many cases follow the factory. Finally, exemptions to particular property owners are demoralizing to those who continue to pay taxes.[3]

Since other authors have also suggested the infant industry argument as a possible justification for subsidies, although on the whole not with great conviction, it may be useful to say explicitly that the argument presented in this book is not of that type at all. Regarding the migration of industry, I do not deny that this may cause difficult problems in the localities left behind. However, it is impossible to prevent industrial relocation while still maintaining the essential features of a free enterprise economy, and, specifically with respect to the present argument, I have argued that competitive subsidization is unlikely to have an important effect on plant mobility. That the relocation of existing industry is not now an important factor in our economy is recognized by Groves himself: "The newspaper headlines usually suggest that the relocation of industry is a matter of its moving from high pressure to low pressure areas. However, it is generally agreed among students of the matter that actual migration of going plants is only one, and probably a minor one, of the ways in which industrial development takes place."[4] Competitive subsidization will not materially alter this picture because subsidies necessary to bring the economy close to full employment within a reasonable time period are not likely to become large relative to relocation cost, and also because communities threatened with the loss of an industry are, if need be, in a favorable competitive position to retain the industry due to their initial advantage over all rivals. However, as also indicated, there is much to be said in favor of restricting competition between communities by means of subsidies to the wooing of new industry if means can be found to accomplish this. (If not, in this writer's opinion, the advantages of unrestrained competition far outweigh the disadvantages.) Perhaps states, in imitation of the Commonwealth of Puerto Rico, could prohibit the extension of special inducements to any relocating industry. Should this be done, the only legitimate, although grossly exaggerated, objection to the industrial subsidization practice would be eliminated.

A number of authors who have made a thorough study of the subsidization practice express some bewilderment at the apparent contradiction between the favorable results they observe and their notion that in the light of economic theory the practice deserves nothing but condemnation. "Especially in the case of communities with a large

3. Groves, *op. cit.,* pp. 566-67.   4. *Ibid.,* p. 557.

amount of unemployment," Knight writes, "it appears that subsidies, if kept within proper limits, may serve a useful purpose. It is clear, however, that subsidies, not limited in amount or duration or by the incorporation of self-liquidating provisions, may easily lead to the waste of public or semi-public funds, or to unfair and uneconomic competition with nonsubsidized firms and nonsubsidizing communities."[5] And again: "Has the effect of subsidization been to distort the geographic distribution of industry from its most economical pattern, or by overcoming the immobility of capital and thus offsetting the immobility of labor, or by giving effect to social costs not reflected in the existing price structure, to facilitate the distribution of industry in accordance with fundamental economic factors and socially desirable objectives?" For a moment this author seems to turn to the right track when in a footnote he says: "These costs [social costs not reflected in the existing price structure] are most apparent in the industry-losing cities where they take the form of at least temporary unemployment and more permanent loss of individual and community property values as the city becomes to some degree a 'ghost town.'" However, he then goes on in the text: "This issue may partially be resolved in terms of the familiar infant-industry argument, for it will be generally conceded that indefinitely continuing of repeated subsidies are [sic] clearly inconsistent with the economic principles set forth above. . . . As a practical consideration supporting this proposition it may be observed that subsidization, unlimited in duration or amount, would leave the way open for unlimited competition in subsidization among communities and, as a result, each city would be almost certain to lose."[6] Thus, in spite of his infant-industry argument, on the ground of which feeble and temporary, and preferably self-liquidating concessions may at times be justifiable, Knight remains basically opposed to the practice: "the basic principles, both of economics and law, are opposed to such programs and reflect the basic philosophy that a worthwhile industrial enterprise should be able to pay its own costs without public assistance."[7] It is competition between communities that is most likely to lead to a violation of these "basic economic principles," and in his almost instinctive horror of competition, which he shares with most other authors on the subject, Knight asserts: "It does seem apparent, however, that some central

5. W. D. Knight, *Subsidization of Industry in Forty Selected Cities in Wisconsin 1930-1946* ("Wisconsin Commerce Studies," Vol. I, No. 2 [Madison: The University of Wisconsin, 1947]), pp. 197-98.

6. *Ibid.*, p. 5.   7. *Ibid.*, pp. 19, 20.

agency, political or nonpolitical, should perform a supervisory, or at least advisory, function in connection with the activities of local communities to further sound industrial development and to prevent excesses and unsound practices. One of the most interesting and meritorious parts of the Mississippi BAWI plan . . . was the investigatory and supervisory function of the State Industrial Commission which had the power to pass upon each community promotion before it took effect."

This opinion is echoed by Hopkins, who also begins by saying that economic theory condemns the subsidization practice. In Mississippi, as elsewhere, community rivalry "threatened economic chaos under pressure of emergency and showed the need of some centralizing structure."[8] Hopkins does not say what this economic chaos consisted of, but one can imagine that it may have been an occasional instance of two or more communities bidding for the same enterprise. (Perhaps also it is merely a sense for having things done in an orderly fashion, by a respectable board of central planners rather than by the forces of self-interest and rivalry, which must "obviously" lead to chaos, that makes these authors turn so violently against the very notion of competition.) At any rate *"The BAWI, as practiced in Mississippi, demonstrated the superior results of a two-level approach to developmental problems.* Local energy and community self-interest were combined, in the BAWI setup, with the more neutral judgment and greater factfinding ability of a central state agency"[9] (italics in the original). As we have seen in Chapter III, what BAWI really did, certainly in the early period to which Hopkins' comment refers, was to stifle local initiative completely in all but a very few cases, in which, under this bureaucratic regime, communities were given permission to do what they deemed in their interest. To show the remarkable similarity in thinking between prominent authors on our subject we may still add a quotation from Lowry. Having stated that "the principle of subsidy does not bear up well against theoretical argument," this author goes on to say that temporary encouragement, if necessary, of industries that promise to become self-supporting soon may be beneficial and finally raises among others the question: "How can excessive competition for industries between communities, states,

8. Ernest J. Hopkins, *Mississippi's BAWI Plan, an experiment in industrial subsidization* (Atlanta: Research Department, Federal Reserve Bank of Atlanta, 1944), p. 63.

9. *Ibid.* It should be recognized that in other places Hopkins shows some appreciation of arguments to the effect that BAWI may have been too restrictive and that an agency without mandatory power over the communities might have been preferable.

and regions be controlled?"[10] Like the others, Lowry takes it as self-evident that competition is undesirable, will be "excessive," and should be controlled.

A few other typical opinions may be mentioned in passing. An article by Milton Derber in *The Municipality*[11] is a veritable catalogue of objections to the practice, but unfortunately not much more. Early in his argument the author states that, in spite of great outcry against the practice, there has not appeared a scientific study which could convincingly challenge the belief of many municipal leaders that subsidization of industry may decrease unemployment and generally improve the economic status of the community. The reader who after this promising beginning hopes to find an analysis, however, is disappointed. Derber merely repeats the standard "objections," listing the following: a sound industry needs no subsidy; the company may not be interested in the bonus "but in ulterior motives such as a chance to exploit labor or to break away from a strong union"; maybe the industry will not succeed; the increased income for the community may not be greater than the increased cost (this point is vague but seems to be based mostly on narrow municipal budget considerations); one group may benefit at the expense of others; "undesirable competition may and does usually result, with only the companies benefiting at the expense of the general public"; subsidization is short-sighted, for a subsidized firm can be lured away again by an offer from elsewhere. Infant industries may perhaps be helped temporarily to get on their feet, and a community might consider coming to the rescue of an old established industry facing emergency difficulties, but neither type of aid should be stretched too far. "The greatest evil is that a vicious circle is created: the more intense the competition, the more reckless become the communities and the more vulnerable, while the lower become the standards of employment. Concrete illustration of this unfortunate fact is found wherever the subsidy problem exists."

Similarly, in an American Society of Planning Officials newsletter the policy of issuing municipal bonds to finance industry is called "shortsighted";[12] Sanders A. Kahn, in an article entitled "Stop Giving

10. Robert E. Lowry, "Municipal Subsidies to Industries in Tennessee," *Southern Economic Journal*, VII (January, 1944), 328-29.

11. Milton Derber, "Municipal Subsidy of Private Industry," *The Municipality*, XXXII (June, 1937).

12. "Bargains for Industry," *A.S.P.O. Newsletter* (a publication of the American Society of Planning Officials), XVIII (August, 1952), 57.

Away America,"[13] notes that the practice is most prevalent among small communities, "which can least afford the expense," and proclaims that such participation of the community in business amounts to socialism; Walter calls an advertisement of a small Georgia town offering free rent and tax exemption for ten years "an example of the give-away type of program which advertises mainly poverty of resources and ideas";[14] and even Van Sickle states: "The competitive bidding of her [the South's] towns for industrial suitors renders difficult the enactment of the social controls that should guide industrialization."[15]

And so it goes. I know of only two papers dealing with the industrial promotion efforts of local communities in this country in which reference is made to external economies in the presence of downward wage inflexibility to justify the subsidization practice—and neither of these has even been printed. Thus Davis, having pointed out that "the community development corporation has been most widely used in economically retrogressing communities in which unemployment was increasing disproportionately," writes:

The very nature of our business system makes impossible the centering of all gains and losses in one firm or business establishment to the extent that wise decisions from the community's point of view will always be made. This . . . can mean that business activities may not be initiated, or that established business operations may be discontinued, solely because a balancing of but part of the gains and costs arising from any particular business operation gives a result at variance from the result obtained by balancing the total gains and costs to the community in question. Here is where the community development corporation steps in, and from the advantage of its position it is enabled to weigh these gains and costs in the light of changes in property values, payrolls, governmental payments, and similar changes which may accrue to the community. To the community development corporation the results obtained may present a sharp contrast to those apparent to the single business institution.[16]

Similar insight is shown by Lefeber, who argues: "Barring a decrease in labor prices as impracticable on humanitarian and political grounds,

13. Sanders A. Kahn, "Stop Giving Away America," *The American City*, LXVI (May, 1951), 106-07.

14. Mabel Walker, *Business Enterprise and the City* (Princeton, N.J.: Tax Institute, Inc., 1957), p. 58.

15. John V. Van Sickle, *Planning for the South* (Nashville: Vanderbilt University Press, 1943), p. 103.

16. Gordon F. Davis, *The Community Development Corporation in Kansas* (sponsored by the Kansas Industrial Development Commission), Bureau of Business Research, School of Business, University of Kansas (Lawrence, Kansas, 1954), pp. 5-6.

other means have to be found to increase the return on capital to an appropriate level."[17] Subsidization of industry may therefore fulfill an important role in speeding up the development process, since it tends to correct the imbalance between the factor allocation in industry and in agriculture. Even this paper is at times ambiguous, however, in that it repeatedly emphasizes that "economic development in the South is a healthy, natural phenomenon" and that the subsidies are sound in that they further a development which in all likelihood would take place anyway, albeit at a somewhat slower pace. But I do not believe that it is Lefeber's intention to assert that a subsidization policy is well-advised only if it is reasonably sure that in its absence the same effect would in the long run also be reached.

17. Louis Lefeber, *Policies of State and Local Governments to Promote Local Industrialization in the South of the United States,* Center for International Studies, Massachusetts Institute of Technology, Italy Project, D155-38 (Cambridge, Mass., December 29, 1955), pp. 1-2 (mimeographed).

Rates of Returns on Subsidies

On several occasions data have been presented in this work which suggest the generally very high returns that communities suffering from un- or underemployment have been able to obtain on investments in subsidies to industry. This appendix includes a number of computations that will show this more clearly. They may be preceded by a few preliminary remarks on the nature of this type of "investment."

If it were not for practical difficulties in the political process and the particular way in which the returns necessarily accrue to certain individuals, labor surplus communities could in fact form the kind of businesslike corporations that we have assumed they are in the first abstract phase of our model. What the opponents of subsidization who have argued that the practice is not in the general interest should do is to demonstrate why this would be different from other enterprises tapping highly profitable investment opportunities that may exist in the economy. Usually we claim that capital should be allowed to flow into such investment outlets, so as to bring about equal marginal returns to capital in its various usages. Since none of these corporations would be able to dominate the market, it is hard to see why competition between them could not be relied upon to safeguard the public interest. And even if only a few of them were to be formed, this would still be a step in the right direction, with results all the more interesting to those who take the step.

There have recently been some interesting attempts to estimate rates of return on certain types of investment, such as in research and in education, that hitherto have been made in an intuitive fashion. An example is Zvi Griliches' calculation of the social rate of return on hybrid-corn research, as a modest step in the direction of determining whether more or fewer resources should be allocated to (different types of) research in general.[1] It was concluded that as of 1955 at

1. Zvi Griliches, "Research Costs and Social Returns: Hybrid Corn and Related Innovations," *Journal of Political Economy*, LXVI (October, 1958), 419-31. See also Gary S. Becker, "Underinvestment in College Education?" *American Economic Review*, L (May, 1960), 346-54.

least 700 percent per year was being earned on this investment. The calculations to be presented below indicate that up to now the returns accruing to communities engaging in the subsidization of industry have been of a similar order of magnitude and at times have even been much greater.

In a sense these rates also represent social returns and in another sense it is perhaps better to avoid putting the matter that way. This is because for our problem there exist two levels of society: the local community and the nation as a whole. From the point of view of a community, scarce funds are allocated for the purpose of subsidizing industry in the expectation that in this usage they will yield higher returns (in the form of community income) than in other usages. In this sense it is certainly useful to look upon subsidization as an investment. From the point of view of the nation one can liken subsidization to the discovery of a new production process that would suddenly give a high value to a hitherto worthless mineral deposit. Un- or underemployed labor can be made productive (i.e., given value) by means of subsidization in just that way. In that light the subsidies themselves do not constitute investments, but they are instrumental in procuring highly remunerative investment opportunities, which, like other innovations, may have further stimulating repercussions on the economy. The revival of hitherto stagnating towns is, for instance, likely to awaken local initiative, which may lead to capital formation.

To determine the immediate gain in national income caused by the adoption of subsidization by individual communities we should draw a distinction between two cases. In the event that subsidization is instrumental in bringing an industry that would otherwise have been established in a full employment community to a labor surplus community, the net gain to the nation is equal to or larger than that of the community in question.[2] In many cases such a directing of activities to a "more optimal" location is what the subsidy will in fact accomplish, and it is obvious that any minor payment which brings about the absorption of previously unproductive workers yields very

2. The national gain may be larger than that of the community as a result of competition between surplus labor communities. This may drive up the subsidy to an amount beyond the point just necessary to compensate the enterprise for the difference in production cost beween the full employment community where it would have established itself in the absence of subsidization and production cost in the surplus labor community to which it is attracted by the subsidy.

high returns.[3] In an unknown number of other cases, however, the industry would have been established in a labor surplus community anyway. From the national point of view the effect of subsidization in these cases may be considered approximately neutral.[4] The subsidy is then not itself a loss or a misallocation of capital funds but merely a transfer payment.

But this is not the whole effect of subsidization on the national dividend. Indeed, its main effect in the long run may well be that of reducing forced migration. To that extent the gains would be largely nonmaterial. Also, because of this, there need be no great concern on the part of Northern labor that the attraction of industry to the South will cause the Northern wage level to rise less rapidly than it otherwise would. For the migration of Southern workers to the North for lack of employment opportunity at home also tends to keep Northern wages lower than they would be in the absence of this phenomenon, and since the establishment of industry in the South tends to cancel the migration of workers to the North, its wage reducing tendency is offset by a wage increasing tendency.

Turning now to the returns on investment in subsidies that local communities may obtain, a few words must be said about the calculation procedure. To make exact calculations we would need an accurate estimate of the income multiplier in each case. We could then distinguish a positive multiplier effect initiated by the payrolls and a negative multiplier effect initiated by the subsidies. In the case of underemployment the absorption of workers in manufacturing may in addition cause some income loss in the occupations from which the workers are drawn, e.g. agriculture, and of this too we would need an estimate. If we indicate the income multiplier as k, the annual value of the payrolls as p, that of the income losses in agriculture, etc., as l, the annual value of the subsidy as s_a, the capitalized value of the subsidy as s_c, and the rate of returns on the subsidy expressed in percentages as r, then $r = \dfrac{k\{p - (s_a + l)\}}{s_c} \cdot 100$, in

which $k\{p - (s_a + l)\}$ represents the annual income gain resulting

3. Also, it should be emphasized, these dividends accrue to the least affluent people and communities in our society.

4. Actually this is probably an understatement. The net contribution of an enterprise to the national product is not the same in all surplus labor communities. Perfect competition between these communities would secure the most favorable location for an enterprise in each case, and while we may not expect such perfection in practice, real world competition between surplus labor communities will probably on the whole tend to have a favorable effect.

from the subsidy.[5] However, since we have no specific information for the cases to be discussed on k and l, while any transformation of s_c to s_a or vice versa on the basis of an assumed interest rate would also be arbitrary, we shall take p to represent the annual income gain. Naturally the deletion of $s_a + l$ tends to overstate r, while ignoring k has the opposite effect. Given the very low marginal revenue product of labor in agriculture in most rural southern communities, l tends on the whole to be very small relative to p and of course is zero in the case of open unemployment; that in the cases to be discussed s_a is small, not to say negligible, relative to p will become very evident. Since our data mostly pertain to rather small communities, neglecting to consider the indirect effects of the payrolls does not appear too serious either, the more so because the error on this account tends to understate r. On the whole our procedure may lead to a fairly close approximation of r in the case of small rural communities suffering from underemployment and is certain to yield a conservative estimate in the case of larger urban communities where the problem is unemployment rather than underemployment and where the multiplier effect may be important.

We may begin with a so-called "disastrous" case, that of the Menzies Shoe Company in New London, Wisconsin, often quoted in the literature to warn against the dangers of subsidization in general.[6] In 1927 the company started operations in this city, having received a $100,000 bonus from the city government, against which it had agreed to construct a plant and to pay $1 million in wages to city residents over a ten-year period. The company provided a surety bond of $100,000 to guarantee performance of the agreement, with the understanding that the liability under the bond was to be reduced proportionately as the $1 million in wages were being paid. In addition the company was to receive free water for five years.

As subsidies go, this was a drastic one, the anticipated rate of returns in terms of payroll being somewhat less than 100 percent per annum (because of the free water supply). However, the company

5. Actually this formula defines the net returns or profits and not the gross returns on the investment. To obtain a gross returns concept the numerator should be taken $\left\{ p - (s_a + l) \text{ as } k \right\} + s_a$. Since in practice s_a is a factor of second order magnitude altogether, it makes little difference whether we introduce this refinement.

6. See for instance Harold M. Groves, "Is There an Economic Justification for Municipal Incentives to New Industries?," *The Municipality*, XL (January, 1945), 3. For a full description of the New London experience see W. D. Knight, *Subsidization of Industry in Forty Selected Cities in Wisconsin 1930-1946* ("Wisconsin Commerce Studies," Vol. I, No. 2 [Madison: The University of Wisconsin, 1947]), pp. 22-23.

ceased operating the plant in 1930, having disbursed a total of only $134,089 in wages. The balance of the liability on the bond was $86,591, but the city was unable to recover this sum. The Wisconsin Supreme Court ruled that the subsidy was illegal because it had been paid out of public funds and that it was against public policy to enforce the bond under these circumstances, even though the defense of the bonding company involved in the dispute was "a dishonest one." The city had no other recourse, since title to the plant had been vested in the company from the outset (although the bonus exceeded the construction cost). The mortgagee later sold the plant to a local firm, but the president of this company stated that the availability of the plant had been of no appreciable assistance to the expansion of his firm. In conclusion Knight states: "The only return of any kind received on the community's expenditure, therefore, seems to have been the tax revenue realized from the building—revenue which averaged about $1,000 a year. With this relatively minor qualification the shoe company promotion must be regarded as an absolute failure, and the funds expended by the city a complete loss."[7]

This is a strange conclusion indeed in view of the fact that the expected return was in the form of wages and that over a period of less than four years the company had disbursed $134,089 in this form. Certainly with this sum alone the community had received a normal return on its investment; the fact that it did not receive much more than a normal return was due to deliberate fraud and the city's failure to obtain security that would stand up in court. The lesson we may draw from this episode is that, in view of the uncertain attitude of the courts in some states with respect to the matter of subsidization, communities should observe certain rules of business conduct. If the city had retained title to the building and had paid any additional subsidies on a current basis, the contingency could not have arisen.[8]

7. Knight, op. cit., p. 23.

8. Another case that has been used over and over again to demonstrate how onerous subsidization may be concerns a transaction that did not even materialize. I am referring to a proposition made during the depression to the city of Augusta, Georgia, by an enterprise in a neighboring state. This case is cited here to show the lack of any criterion on the part of those who stand ready with their condemnation of the subsidization practice. Under the proposal, the city would fix up an old factory building according to the specifications of the enterprise, extend railroad siding to the premises, furnish free water for ten years, pay 50 percent of the cost of training employees, and pay moving expenses to an amount not exceeding $5,000. The industry was to be given free occupancy of the building for a period of ten years or until a sum of $1,500,000 would have been disbursed in wages, at which time the industry was to receive full title free of charge. Without being presented with any estimate of the total value of these concessions (which, as in all other cases, would probably

How atypical this case is may be clearly shown by contrasting it with a table presented by Knight[9] in which this author summarizes the results of his investigation of the subsidization practice in 40 Wisconsin cities, involving 130 firms. The total "gross" value of subsidies extended to these firms over the period 1930-1946 was $3,310,040, against which an estimated average *annual* payroll was obtained of $23,788,000. Included in the "gross subsidies" is a category "advance of capital," representing funds advanced by subsidizing agents "and subsequently repaid or compensated."[10] The total amount in this category is $1,051,175. According to Knight, it contains little or no net subsidy, but perhaps we should allow a small amount for interest foregone—say $51,175. Subtracting the rest ($1,000,000) from the gross sum of $3,310,040, we arrive at a total "net" subsidy of $2,310,040, or less than 10 percent of the average annual payroll. If we are to go by these figures, the rate of returns on the average subsidy in Knight's large sample has been in the vicinity of 1,000 percent per annum. Perhaps, however, we ought to take into consideration that in a number of these communities during the war full employment might have been established without special measures and that the subsidies were in part given at a time when the purchasing power of the dollar was greater than when some of the wage payments were made. Even so, an average real return of 500 percent per year in terms of payroll alone for at least the decade of the thirties does not seem exaggerated.[11]

---

have compared very favorably with the annual payroll that could reasonably be anticipated), we are asked to be horrified by the presumptiousness of this proposal, apparently for no other reason than that it contains a number of different items. See Harold M. Groves, "Is There an Economic Justification for Municipal Incentives to New Industries?" *The Municipality*, XL (January, 1945), 4, citing Thomas L. Stokes, "Carpetbaggers of Industry," pp. 38-39. Reprinted from the New York *World Telegram* and other Scripps-Howard papers.

9. Knight, *op. cit.*, p. 179.

10. *Ibid.*, pp. 174-75 (Table 41, footnote 4, and Table 42, footnote 4).

11. Knight presents two tables which indicate that in 56 cases, or nearly half the total of 116 promotions, the net subsidy (i.e., the cash value of the subsidy) amounted to less than 5 percent of the annual payroll and that in 20 cases this ratio exceeded 35 percent. In terms of payroll and employment created the latter cases were quite insignificant, involving only 200 workers out of a total of 13,040. Defining a successful promotion as one that produces a large payroll relative to the net subsidy involved (a criterion of success that as a rule of thumb may be considered quite acceptable), Knight labels the 35 percent and over category "unsuccessful." This is very strange, implying as it does that an investment must be considered a failure if it fails to yield a return of at least 300 percent per annum. (It should be added that among the 20 firms in question 18 had discontinued their operations in the subsidizing communities at the time of Knight's reporting. However, in at least 12 cases they had been succeeded by other firms without any substantial additional subsidy, so that

Of course all this supposes a causal relation between the subsidy and the establishment of a plant in a particular community, and due to imperfect knowledge this relation may not always exist. It should be admitted that when subsidies are generally very low there may be justifiable doubt in individual cases—yet we also know that many industries even then hardly ever consider a community not willing to make some concessions. While this uncertainty may subtract something from the validity of the computations in the eyes of logical purists,[12] one feels that if subsidies are so low that their decisive importance may be reasonably questioned, communities that have long been characterized by un- or underemployment should scarcely take the chance of continuing to suffer this condition for failure to supply these small concessions.

In a similarly rough fashion, Hopkins has calculated the aggregate result of the 12 BAWI promotions carried out during the first period of the plan's operation. In a four and one-half year period falling within the years 1939-43 a sum total of $43,539,361 in wages was disbursed by the subsidized plants. Against this stands the sale of a total of $980,500 in public bonds, the unknown cost of additional municipal services, and the operating cost of the State Industrial Commission ($77,250). By far the greater part of the bond proceeds represents outright subidization. Presumably making an estimate of the unknown variables, Hopkins arrives at a 36 to 1 ratio of " 'returns' to total 'investment' " in four and one-half year's time or an average return per annum of 800 percent. Perhaps of greater interest is the

the payrolls remained. And certainly in all cases without exception the payrolls disbursed amounted to substantially more than the community's investment.)

12. This attitude is well illustrated by the following passage: "A subsidy is an inducement, not an investment, and the causative effect of that inducement can never, in the nature of things, be satisfactorily proved" (Ernest J. Hopkins, *Mississippi's BAWI plan, an experiment in industrial subsidization* [Atlanta: Research Department, Federal Reserve Bank of Atlanta, 1944], p. 56). This is mere fruitless skepticism, for in life and in science there are many things we must take for granted without being able to prove them in Hopkins' sense. Several basic propositions in economics are of this nature, for instance the proposition that demand curves are usually negatively inclined. Every businessman knows this, or at least acts accordingly, yet we could always argue that when we reduce prices and are then able to sell more it is because of a sudden change in taste, for instance, or another incidental circumstance. Even statistical proof would be hard to give: it might well be impossible to obtain a sample that could be considered random in a rigorously scientific sense. Perhaps an indirect statistical proof might be devised in cases like this: if there is among people practically concerned a group ·denying that there is satisfactory evidence concerning a postulated causal relation, the results obtained by this group could conceivably be contrasted with that of those who affirm their belief in the relation, provided actions are not manifestly contrary to expressed opinions.

fact that in the year 1939 alone, when some of the subsidized plants were not even in operation or were just starting, wage payments totalled $1,407,574. (During the first half of 1943 wages in the subsidized plants totalled $13,372,527.)[13]

Among the cases included in the above summary we may look at one considered "extreme" in a little more detail, namely the subsidization of the Armstrong Tire and Rubber Company by the city of Natchez.[14] Involving the largest bond issue under the old BAWI, the State Industrial Commission had its misgivings about this project, pointing out that the $300,000 issue was to bring in a stipulated $300,000 annual payroll or a ratio of one to one, whereas in all previous subsidization propositions the ratio of prospective payroll to bond issue had been considerably higher. Still not a bad prospect, one would say, as returns on other types of investment go. One wonders whether the city could have done better by putting up schools or playgrounds or by improving its garbage collection.

The money (except for a $10,000 location fee paid by the city) was used for the construction of a factory, which, under the original contract, was to be rented to the company at an annual rent of $600 for five years. At the end of that time title would be transferred to the company, provided it had disbursed $1 million in wages. If not, transfer would be postponed until it had done so. This, of course, practically amounted to a gift of the building contingent on the payment of the stipulated wages. As Hopkins puts it: "The weakness of Natchez' bargaining position [the city desperately needed employment] was apparent in the rental terms of the contract."

At the end of 1938, when operations were beginning, the rental arrangement was amended. A 50-year lease was provided, the city retaining the property. In this way the company was able to avoid the payment of property taxes—an extra subsidy. The company, on the other hand, agreed to pay a $3,600 annual rent, starting after an initial five-year period of free occupancy. The city was also obligated to provide pavement to the site and do some grading work at a total cost estimated between $35,000 and $50,000. From the beginning of 1939 up to June 30, 1943, the plant disbursed in payroll more than nine times the face value of the bonds.[15]

13. *Ibid.*, pp. 55-56.
14. *Ibid.*, pp. 46-48.
15. As things turned out, the ratio of average annual payroll to bonds in the 12 enterprises varied from 1.5 to 1 at the lower limit to 73.2 to 1 at the upper limit beween January 1, 1939, and June 30, 1943, or for that part of this period during which the plant was in operation (*ibid.*, p. 57).

As our last example may be cited the case of Herrin, Illinois, related by Victor Roterus.[16] This is a town located in the soft-coal region in the southern part of the state with a long history of unemployment. The population is around 9,300. Since 1942, five new industries have come to the town. In 1956 these firms together averaged between 2,900 and 3,000 employees each month; every one of these industries was attracted by means of subsidization. The details may be omitted here and only the global results stated. Roterus computes that the price per head of the population for an annual combined payroll of about $7,150,000 (the 1956 figure) amounted to a $12 donation on the extension of a $72 (low interest) loan. This implies a direct return on investment (in the form of payroll alone) of almost 6,000 percent per annum if we consider only the donations, while the return is still more than 900 percent if donations and loans are taken together and the entire sum is considered a donation. Clearly the actual return has been closer to 6,000 percent and probably a good deal more than that because of the multiplier.

To these examples others could be added. Together with the cases quoted earlier, however, I feel that those cited suffice to convey my point. It is that under the circumstances that have hitherto prevailed and that prevail today, subsidies so small that they are dwarfed by the returns can make the difference between eked-out misery and prosperity. The order of magnitude of the returns is such that it does not matter that for lack of precise data our computations are a bit rough and that in some cases even the causation may be questionable. As to the profitability of subsidization when employment opportunity is needed there can be no question.

16. Victor Roterus, "Community Industrial Development—a Nationwide Survey," in U.S. Congress, Senate Committee on Banking and Currency, *Development Corporations and Authorities*, 86th Cong., 1st Sess. (Washington: U.S. Government Printing Office, 1959), pp. 128-29.

Bibliography

PUBLIC DOCUMENTS

Black, Robert E. "Localities Organize for Industry," *Report of the Commission to Study Industrial Development in Virginia to the Governor and the General Assembly of Virginia.* Commonwealth of Virginia, Senate Document No. 10. Richmond: Division of Purchases and Printing, 1957.

Calef, Wesley C. and Daoust, Charles. *What Will New Industry Mean to My Town?* Washington: U. S. Department of Commerce. 1955.

Citizen Saving and Loan Association vs. Topeka. U.S. 655 (1874).

Fjelstad, Ralph S. "Local Development Corporations in Minnestota," in *Development Corporations and Authorities,* 86th Cong., 1st Sess. Washington: U.S. Government Printing Office, 1959.

Kentucky, Department of Economic Development. *The Local Industrial Development Corporation.* Frankfort, Ky., 1959(?).

Levitan, Sar A. *Federal Assistance to Labor Surplus Areas.* A report prepared at the request of the Chairman of the Committee on Banking and Currency, U.S. House of Representatives, 85th Cong., 1st Sess. Washington: U.S. Government Printing Office, 1957.

Louisiana. *Constitution,* as amended by Act. 401 of 1946, Article X, Section 4, Paragraph X.

Mississippi. *Balancing Agriculture With Industry.* Seventh Report to the Legislature by the Mississippi Agricultural and Industrial Board, Biennium 1956-58.

New York. *Report of the Joint Legislative Committee on Commerce and Economic Development.* Legislative Document No. 28. Albany: Williams Press, Inc., 1954.

Roterus, Victor. "Community Industrial Development—a Nationwide Survey," in *Development Corporations and Authorities,* 86th Cong., 1st Sess. Washington: U.S. Government Printing Office, 1959.

Shils, Edward B. "State Development Credit Corporations and Authorities and Problems of Financing Small Business," in *Development Corporations and Authorities,* 86th Cong., 1st Sess. Washington: U.S. Government Printing Office, 1959.

South Carolina, State Development Board. *Industrial Data on South Carolina.* Columbia, S.C., 1959.

U.S. Congress, Joint Committee on the Economic Report. *Underemployment of Rural Families.* 82nd Cong., 1st Sess. Washington: U.S. Government Printing Office, 1951.

U.S. Congress, Subcommittee on Low-Income Families, Joint Committee on the Economic Report. *Hearings, Low-Income Families.* 84th Cong., 1st Sess. Washington: U.S. Government Printing Office, 1955.

————. *Characteristics of the Low-Income Population and Related Federal Programs.* 84th Cong., 1st Sess. Washington: U.S. Government Printing Office, 1955.

U.S. Department of Agriculture, Bureau of Agricultural Economics and Department of Labor, Bureau of Employment Security. *Unemployment and Partial Unemployment of Hired Farm Workers in Four Areas.* Washington, April, 1953.

U.S. Department of Commerce, Office of Area Development. *Communities with Locally Financed Industrial Development Organizations.* Washington: U.S. Government Printing Office, 1958.

————. *Federal Activities Helpful to Communities.* Washington: U.S. Government Printing Office, 1958.

U.S. Department of Labor. *Factory Workers' Earnings.* Bulletin No. 1179. Washington, 1955.

————. *Results of the Minimum-Wage Increase of 1950.* Washington: U.S. Government Printing Office, 1954.

————. *Studies of the Economic Effects of the $1.00 Minimum Wage.* Washington: U.S. Government Printing Office, 1957.

U.S. Senate, Committee on Banking and Currency. *Development Corporations and Authorities.* 86th Cong., 1st Sess. Washington: U.S. Government Printing Office, 1959.

————. *Selected Materials on the Economy of the South.* 84th Cong., 2nd Sess. Washington: U.S. Government Printing Office, 1956.

Virginia. *Report of the Commission to Study Industrial Development in Virginia to the Governor and the General Assembly of Virginia,* Senate Document No. 10. Richmond: Division of Purchase and Printing, 1957.

Virginia, Department of Conservation and Development, Division of Planning and Economic Development. *Virginia's Southwest Triangle, Past and Present.* Richmond, May, 1956.

Virginia, Department of Conservation and Development, The Advisory Council on the Virginia Economy. *Labor Resources and Labor Income in Virginia,* Vol. II: *Labor Income and Per Capita Income.* Richmond, July, 1953.

Virginia, Fiscal Study Committee, Advisory Council on the Virginia Economy. *A Report on Virginia's Economy.* Richmond, November, 1957.

Virginia, Subcommittee on Finances, Industrial Development Study Commission. *Should a State-wide Industrial Development Credit Corporation Be Organized in Virginia?* Richmond, May, 1957.

BOOKS

Backman, Jules. *Wage Determination: An Analysis of Wage Criteria.* Princeton, N.H.: D. Van Nostrand Co., Inc., 1959.

Chapin, F. Stuart, Jr. *Urban Land Use Planning.* New York: Harper and Brothers, 1957.

Davis, Gordon F. *The Community Development Corporation in Kansas.* Sponsored by the Kansas Industrial Development Commission. Bureau of Business Research, School of Business, University of Kansas, 1954.

Floyd, Joe S., Jr. *Effects of Taxation on Industrial Location.* Chapel Hill: The University of North Carolina Press, 1952.

Ford, Paul Leicester (ed). *The Writings of Thomas Jefferson,* Vol. VII. New York: G. P. Putnam Sons, 1896.

Hoover, Calvin B., and Ratchford, B. U. *Economic Resources and Policies of the South.* New York: Macmillan Company, 1951.

Herring, Harriet L. *Southern Industry and Regional Development.* Chapel Hill: The University of North Carolina Press, 1940.

Knight, W. D. *Subsidization of Industry in Forty Selected Cities in Wisconsin, 1930-1946.* ("Wisconsin Commerce Studies," Vol. 1, No. 2.) Madison: The University of Wisconsin, 1947.

Myers, Charles A. "Labour Market Theory and Empirical Research," *The Theory of Wage Determination,* ed. John T. Dunlop. London: Macmillan & Co., 1957.

National Industrial Conference Board. *The Economic Almanac, 1958.* New York, 1958.

Pigou, A. C. *The Economics of Welfare.* 4th ed.; London: Macmillan & Co., 1952.

Schultz, William J., and Harriss, C. Lowell. *American Public Finance.* Englewood Cliffs, N.J.: Prentice-Hall, Inc., 1959.

Simmons, Henry C. *Economic Policy for a Free Society.* Chicago: University of Chicago Press, 1948.

Taylor, Milton C. *Industrial Tax-Exemption in Puerto Rico.* Madison: The University of Wisconsin Press, 1957.

Thompson, Lorin A. "Urbanization, Occupational Shift and Economic Progress," *The Urban South,* ed. Robert B. Vance and Nicholas J. Demarath. Chapel Hill: The University of North Carolina Press, 1954.

Van Sickle, John V. *Planning for the South.* Nashville: Vanderbilt University Press, 1943.

Walker, Mabel. *Business Enterprise and the City.* Princeton, N.J.: Tax Institute, Inc., 1957.

Wofford, B. M., and Kelly, T. A. *Mississippi Workers.* University, Alabama: The University of Alabama Press, 1955.

ARTICLES AND PERIODICALS

"A Look Ahead," *Tennessee Town and City,* X (January, 1959), 5.

American Society of Planning Officials. "Bargains for Industry," *A.S.P.O. Newsletter,* XVIII (August, 1952), 57.

Bachmura, Frank T. "Man-land Equalization through Migration," *American Economic Review,* XLIX (December, 1959), 1004-17.

Backman, Jules. "Why Wages Are Lower in Retailing," *Southern Economic Journal,* XXII (January, 1957), 295-305.

Baum, E. L., and Heady, Earl O. "Some Effects of Selected Policy Programs on Agricultural Labor Mobility in the South," *Southern Economic Journal,* XXV (January, 1959), 327-37.

Becker, Gary S. "Underinvestment in College Education?" *American Economic Review,* L (May, 1960), 346-54.

Boles, Walter E., Jr. "Some Aspects of the Fair Labor Standards Act," *Southern Economic Journal,* VI (April, 1940), 490-511.

Brandt, Harry. "Another Look at Development Corporations," *Monthly Review,* Federal Reserve Bank of Atlanta (September 30, 1954), pp. 3-5.

Braunhut, Herman Jay. "Farm Labor Wage Rates in the South," *Southern Economic Journal,* XVI (October, 1949), 189-96.

Brewster, John M. "Long Run Prospects of Southern Agriculture," *Southern Economic Journal,* XXVI (October, 1959), 134-40.

Bronfenbrenner, Martin. "Minimum Wages, Unemployability, and Relief: a Theoretical Note," *Southern Economic Journal,* X (July, 1943), 52-59.

————. "Potential Monopsony in Labor Markets," *Industrial and Labor Relations Review,* IX (July, 1956), 577-88.

————. "The Incidence of Collective Bargaining Once More," *Southern Economic Journal,* XXIV (April, 1958), 398-406.

Buchanan, J. M. "Note on the Differential Controversy," *Southern Economic Journal,* XVII (July, 1950), 59-60.

———— and Moes, John E. "A Regional Countermeasure to National Wage Standardization," *American Economic Review,* L (June, 1960), 434-38.

Buckingham, Walter S., Jr. "Problems of Industrial Location in Great Britain," *The American Journal of Economics and Sociology,* XIII (April, 1954), 247-54.

" 'Buy Industry' or 'You May Not Get it' says Lafayette Mayor Who Learned the Hard Way," *Tennessee Town and City,* VIII (July, 1957), 6, 46.

Carlebach, William D. "State and Local Government Responsibility for Economic Development," *Tax Policy,* XXIV (January, 1957), 16-21.

Chamberlain, Edward H. "Can Union Power Be Curbed," *Atlantic Monthly* (June, 1959), pp. 46-50.

Daly, M. C. "An Approximation to a Geographical Multiplier," *The Economic Journal*, L (June-September, 1940), 248-58.

Derber, Milton. "Municipal Subsidy of Private Industry," *The Municipality*, XXXII (June, 1937), 125.

"Development Credit Corporations, a Stimulant for Economic Growth," *New England Business Review* (June, 1958), pp. 1-4.

De Vyver, Frank T. "Labor Factors in Industrial Development of the South," *Southern Economic Journal*, XVIII (October, 1951), 189-205.

Donovan, C. H. "The Spread of Development Corporations," *Monthly Review*, Federal Reserve Bank of Atlanta, XXXI (October 31, 1946), 105-09.

Douty, H. M. "Development of Trade-Unionism in the South," *Monthly Labor Review*, LXIII (October, 1946), 555-82.

———. "Minimum Wage Regulation in the Seamless Hosiery Industry," *Southern Economic Journal*, VIII (October, 1941), 176-90.

"Employment and Unemployment: Government Policies Since 1950," *International Labour Review*, LXXIV (July, 1956), 1-22 and (August, 1956), 124-45.

"Federal Aid for Depressed Areas," *Tennessee Town and City*, X (April, 1959), 6-7, 21.

Fulton, Maurice. "Plant Location—1965," *Harvard Business Review*, XXXIII (March-April, 1955), 42.

Galax Gazette, (Galax, Va.), September 3, 1959.

Gitlow, A. L. "Wages and the Allocation of Employment," *Southern Economic Journal*, XXI (July, 1954), 62-83.

Goldberg, Melvin J. "Industry Fights Back on State and Local Taxes," *Dun's Review*, LXXI (April, 1958), 33 ff.

Griliches, Zvi. "Research Cost and Social Returns: Hybrid Corn and Related Innovations," *Journal of Political Economy*, LXVI (October, 1958), 419-31.

Groves, Harold M. "The Effect of Tax Differentials and Tax Exemption upon the Relocation of Industry," *Proceedings of the Thirty-first Annual Conference on Taxation*. Columbia, S.C.: National Tax Association, 1939, pp. 557-68.

———. "Is There an Economic Justification for Municipal Incentives to New Industries?" *The Municipality*, XL (January, 1945), 3.

Hamberg, D. "Minimum Wages and the Level of Employment," *Southern Economic Journal*, XV (January, 1949), 321-36.

Harrod, R. F. "Full Employment and Security of Livelihood," *Economic Journal*, LIII (December, 1943), 321-42.

Heady, Earl O., and Baker, C. B. "Resource Adjustments to Equate Productivities in Agriculture," *Southern Economic Journal*, XXI (July, 1954), 36-52.

Heer, Clarence. "State and Local Finance in the Postwar Plans of the South," *Southern Economic Journal*, XI (January, 1945), 246-54.

Hildebrand, George H. "Economics by Negotiation," *American Economic Review*, XLIX (May, 1959), 398-411.

―――― and Mace, Arthur, Jr. "The Employment Multiplier in an Expanding Industrial Market: Los Angeles County, 1940-47," *The Review of Economics and Statistics*, XXXI (August, 1950), 241-49.

Kahn, Sanders A. "Stop Giving Away America," *The American City*, LXVI (May, 1951), 106-7.

Kantor, Harry S. "Two Decades of the Fair Labor Standards Act," *Monthly Labor Review*, LXXXI (October, 1958), 1097-1106.

Lester, Richard A. "Southern Wage Differentials: Developments, Analysis, and Implications," *Southern Economic Journal*, XIII (April, 1947), 386-94.

Lewis, H. Gregg. "The Labor-monopoly Problem: a Positive Program," *Journal of Political Economy*, LIX (August, 1951), 277-87.

Logsdon, C. S. "Some Comments upon the Effectiveness of State and Local Area Development Programs," *Southern Economic Journal*, XV (January, 1949), 303-10.

Lowry, Robert E. "City Subsidies to Industry Wane," *National Municipal Review*, XXXIV (March, 1945), 112-15.

―――― . "Municipal Subsidies to Industries in Tennessee," *Southern Economic Journal*, VII (January, 1941), 317-29.

Macesich, George, and Stewart, Charles T., Jr. "Recent Department of Labor Studies of Minimum Wage Effects," *Southern Economic Journal*, XXVI (April, 1960), 281-90.

Machlup, Fritz. "Relations between Economic Theory and Economic Policy: A Discussion," Proceedings of Seventy-second Meeting, *American Economic Review*, L (May, 1960), 49-52.

"Migration at All Time High, Three State Comparison," *Tennessee Town and City*, VIII (July, 1957), 21.

Muehlner, Felix, and Richardson, James G. "Financing New Manufacturing Plants in Florida," *Engineering Progress at the University of Florida*, X, No. 10 (October, 1956).

"Municipal Inducements to Private Industry," *Minnesota Law Review*, XL (May, 1956), 691.

"Municipal-Industrial Bonds," *Monthly Review*, Federal Reserve Bank of Richmond (September, 1953), p. 6.

Myers, Robert J., and Clark, Odis C. "Effects of a Minimum Wage in the Cotton-garment Industry, 1939-41," *Monthly Labor Review*, LIV (February, 1942), 319-37.

"Needed: Investment Capital," *Tennessee Town and City,* VIII (December, 1957), 12.

"Needed: New Municipal Revenues," *Tennessee Town and City,* X (January, 1959), 25.

Parker, William. "Operation Bootstrap," *Burroughs Clearing House,* XLI (June, 1957), 37-39, 92.

Peacock, Alan T., and Donner, Douglas G. M. "The New Attack on Localized Unemployment," *Lloyds Bank Review* (January, 1960), p. 28.

Peterson, John M. "Employment Effecting Minimum Wages," *Journal of Political Economy,* LXV (October, 1957), 412-30.

Pollock, William. "The Southern Sales Pitch," *I.U.D. Digest,* (Winter, 1960), p. 26.

Rao, V. K. R. V. "Investment, Income and the Multiplier in an Underdeveloped Economy," *The Indian Economic Review,* I (February, 1952), 55-67.

Ratchford, B. U. "Patterns of Economic Development," *Southern Economic Journal,* XX (January, 1954), 217-30.

Rees, Albert. "Wage Determination and Unvoluntary Unemployment," *Journal of Political Economy,* LIX (April, 1951), 143-53.

Robinson, Joan. "Disguised Unemployment," *Economic Journal,* XLVI (June, 1936), 225-37.

Robock, Stefan H. "Industrialization and Economic Progress in the Southeast," *Southern Economic Journal,* XX (April, 1954), 307-27.

Rockefeller, Winthrop. "Development of Rural Areas through Industrialization," *The Arkansas Economist,* II (Fall, 1959), 5.

Ross, William D. "Tax Exemption in Louisiana as a Device for Encouraging Industrial Development," *The Southwestern Social Science Quarterly* XXXIV (June, 1953), 14-22.

"Rx for Prosperity: Cash Register Hums; Lawrence County's Out Migration Grinds to Halt as New Plants Put Men to Work," *Tennessee Town and City,* VIII (July, 1957), 38.

Scheer, Julian. "Labor: Ready, Willing, and Able," *New York Times,* November 17, 1957, section 10, p. 9.

Snell, Seward B. "Tax Exemptions to Encourage Industry," *Taxes,* XXIX (May, 1951), 383-87.

Somers, Gerald C. "Labor Recruitment in a Depressed Rural Area," *Monthly Labor Review,* LXXXI (October, 1958), 1113-20.

———. "Labor Supply for Manufacturing in a Coal Area," *Monthly Labor Review,* LXXVII (December, 1954), 1327-30.

"Speculative Industrial Building," *New England Business Review* (November, 1959), pp. 1-4.

Stewart, Charles T. "Economic Base Dynamics," *Land Economics,* XXXV (November, 1959), 326-36.

Tanzer, Lester. "Dixie Dilemma; Bond Buyers Frown on Public Money

246   BIBLIOGRAPHY

Lure for Southern Plants," *Barron's*, XXXII (August 18, 1952), 15-16.
Tennessee Town and City, July, 1957, January, 1959, and April, 1959.
Tiebout, Charles. "Community Income Multipliers: a Population Growth Model," *Journal of Regional Science*, II (Spring, 1960), 75-84.
———. "Input-output and Foreign Trade Multiplier Models in Urban Research," *Journal of the American Institute of Planners*, XXIII, No. 3 (1957), 126-30.
Troy, Leo. "The Growth of Union Membership in the South, 1939-1953," *Southern Economic Journal*, XXIV (April, 1958), 407-20.
Van Sickle, John V. "Industrialization and the South," *Southern Economic Journal*, XV (April, 1949), 412-24.
Vining, Rutledge. "The Region as a Concept in Business-cycle Analysis," *Econometrica*, XIV (July, 1946), pp. 201-18.
"What Does Industry Expect in an Community," *Virginia Economic Review*, IV (April, 1951), 3.
Whitlach, George I. "Qualified Towns Planned for Progress and New Industry," *Tennessee Town and City*, VIII (July, 1957), 27.
Wolkstein, Harry W. "Recent Problems and Developments in Property Tax Exemptions," *Proceedings of the Forty-fourth Annual Conference on Taxation*, Dallas, Texas, November 26-29, 1951 (Sacramento, Calif: National Tax Association, 1952), pp. 167-190.

PAMPHLETS, REPORTS, AND STUDIES

Alabama Business Research Council and the School of Commerce and Business Administration, University of Alabama. *Alabama Goes Industry Hunting*. University, Alabama, 1957.
American Federation of Labor. *Subsidized Industrial Migration; the Luring of Plants to New Locations*. Recommendations for legislative action by the Subcommittee on Migration and Subsidization of Industry, National Legislative Committee, American Federation of Labor. Washington: American Federation of Labor, 1955.
Andrews, Robert A. *Community Industrial Financing Plans in Operation*. Stanford, November, 1950. (Mimeographed.)
Chamber of Commerce of the United States. *What New Industrial Jobs Mean to a Community*. Washington: U.S. Chamber of Commerce, 1959.
Gilmore, Donald R. *Developing the "Little" Economies*. Committee for Economic Development: Supplementary Paper No. 10, April, 1960.
Harris, E. Seymour, *et al*. *New England Textiles and the New England Economy*. A Report by the New England Governor's Textile Committee to the Conference of New England Governors. Cambridge, Mass., March, 1958.
Hoch, L. Clinton. "The Location Decision." Paper presented before the Semi-Annual Conference, Production Executives Division, The Na-

tional Association of Shirt, Pajama and Sportswear Manufacturers, New York, June 20, 1957, pp. 5-6. (Mimeographed.)

Hopkins, Ernest J. *The Louisville Industrial Foundation, A Study in community capitalization of local industries.* Atlanta: Research Department, Federal Reserve Bank of Atlanta, 1945.

————. *Mississippi's BAWI Plan, an experiment in industrial subsidization.* Atlanta: Research Department, Federal Reserve Bank of Atlanta, 1944.

Hutchinson, Robert S. *Migration and Industrial Development in Tennessee.* A report to the Industrial Development and Migration Subcommittee of the Tennessee Legislative Council, October, 1958. (Mimeographed.)

Industrial Committee of 100 of the Chamber of Commerce. Chattanooga, July, 1959. (Mimeographed.)

Johnson, D. Gale. "Some Effects of Region, Community Size, Color and Occupation on Family and Individual Income." Conference on Research in Income and Wealth, National Bureau of Economic Research, *Studies in Income and Wealth,* XV (1952), 49-60.

Lefeber, Louis. *Policies of State and Local Governments to Promote Local Industrialization in the South of the United States.* Center for International Studies, Massachusetts Institute of Technology, Italy Project, D155-38. Cambridge, Mass., December 29, 1955. (Mimeographed.)

Lepawsky, Albert. *State Planning and Economic Development in the South.* N.P.A. Committee of the South, Report No. 4. Washington: National Planning Association, 1949.

Local Government Services and Industrial Development in the Southeast. Joint Statement by: University of Alabama, Bureau of Public Administration; University of Florida, Public Administration Clearing Service; University of Georgia, Bureau of Public Administration; University of Kentucky, Bureau of Government Research; University of Mississippi, Bureau of Public Administration; University of North Carolina, Institute for Research in Social Science; University of Tennessee, Bureau of Public Administration in cooperation with the Tennessee State Planning Commission; Tennessee Valley Authority, Division of Regional Studies. University, Alabama: Bureau of Public Administration, University of Alabama, 1952.

McCarren, Kenneth J. "Luring Industry through Tax Exemption," *Tax Exemptions.* Symposium conducted by the Tax Policy League, December 28-30, 1938. New York: Tax Policy League, 1939.

McElveen, J. V. "Changes in the Structure of Farming of the South." A paper presented to the annual meeting of the Association of Southern Agricultural Workers, Little Rock, Arkansas, February 3-5, 1958.

McLaughlin, Glenn E., and Robock, Stefan. *Why Industry Moves South.*

Report No. 3, National Planning Association. Washington: Committee of the South, N.P.A., June, 1949.

Mississippi Agricultural and Industrial Board. *Mississippi's BAWI Plan.* (Pamphlet.)

Moore, Arthur. *Underemployment in American Agriculture.* Planning Pamphlets No. 77. Washington: National Planning Association, 1952.

Morris, James A. "A Reappraisal of Regional Wage Differentials." A paper read before the meeting of the Southern Economic Association, Jacksonville, Florida, November 20, 1959.

Quittmeyer, C. L. *Summary Report on Appalachian Questionnaire,* Charlottesville, Va., October, 1959. Berea, Ky.: Berea College, 1959.

Redman, Albert E. *Study on Special Inducements to Influence Plant Location.* Ohio Chamber of Commerce—American Industrial Development Council. Washington, April 1, 1952. (Mimeographed.)

Starnes, George T., Wilkins, William M., and Wissman, Paul P. *The Labor Force of Two Rural Industrial Plants.* Charlottesville, Va.: Bureau of Population and Economic Research of the University of Virginia, 1951.

Sutherland, J. G., and Bishop, C. E. *Possibilities for Increasing Production and Incomes on Small Commercial Farms, Southern Piedmont Area, North Carolina.* North Carolina Agricultural Experiment Station Technical Bulletin No. 117, Raleigh, 1955.

The Impact of Industry in a Southern Rural County. The Bureau of Population and Economic Research of the University of Virginia, 1956.

UNPUBLISHED MATERIALS

Discussion, Gordon Tullock, University of South Carolina.

Discussion, J. M. Buchanan, University of Virginia.

Information furnished by Mississippi Agricultural and Industrial Board.

Letter, Georgia Department of Commerce Official.

Letter, North Carolina Department of Conservation and Development Official.

Letter, Official of the Alabama State Planning and Industrial Development Board.

Letter, Ronald M. Reifler of Fantus Factory Locating Service.

Personal Interviews and Correspondence.

Index

www.ingramcontent.com/pod-product-compliance
Lightning Source LLC
Chambersburg PA
CBHW020344270326
41926CB00007B/305